LANGUAGE, MUSIC AND THE SIGN

The four graces representing the Arts observing Nature. Painting holds a
pencil in her hand and gazes directly at Nature; Poetry looks towards
Nature but also appears self-absorbed; Music carries a lyre, looks away from
Nature, and her face is entirely hidden from us. (Reproduced from Daniel
Webb, *Miscellanies* (London, 1802).)

Language, music and the sign

A study in aesthetics, poetics and poetic practice from Collins to Coleridge

KEVIN BARRY

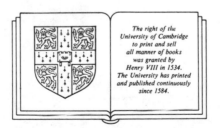

The right of the
University of Cambridge
to print and sell
all manner of books
was granted by
Henry VIII in 1534.
The University has printed
and published continuously
since 1584.

CAMBRIDGE UNIVERSITY PRESS

Cambridge

New York   New Rochelle   Melbourne   Sydney

Published by the Press Syndicate of the University of Cambridge
The Pitt Building, Trumpington Street, Cambridge CB2 1RP
32 East 57th Street, New York, NY 10022, USA
10 Stamford Road, Oakleigh, Melbourne 3166, Australia

© Cambridge University Press 1987

First published 1987

Printed in Great Britain at
the University Press, Cambridge

British Library cataloguing in publication data
Barry, Kevin
Language, music and the sign: a study in
aesthetics, poetics and poetic practice from
Collins to Coleridge.
1. English poetry – 18th century –
History and criticism
I. Title
821.5′09   PR551

Library of congress cataloguing in publication data
Barry, Kevin, 1950–
Language, music, and the sign.
Bibliography.
Includes index.
1. Music and literature.   2. Music – 18th century –
Philosophy and aesthetics.   3. Music – 19th century –
Philosophy and aesthetics.   4. Poetry.   I. Title.
ML3849.B28   1987   780′.08   87-8078

ISBN 0 521 34175 2

TO MY
FATHER AND MOTHER

CONTENTS

vii

4   SAMUEL TAYLOR COLERIDGE

ILLUSTRATIONS

'The Four Graces', from Webb's *Miscellanies*. Reproduced by kind permission of the British Library.   *frontispiece*

Plate 1: (i) title-page from Robert Dodsley (ed.), *A Collection of Poems* (London, 1748); (ii) title-page from William Collins, *Odes on Several Descriptive and Allegoric Subjects* (London, 1747); (iii) title-page from Thomas Gray, *Poems* (Dublin, 1768); (iv) frontispiece from *The Works in Verse and Prose of William Shenstone*, Vol. 1 (London, 1765); (v) frontispiece from *The Works in Verse and Prose of William Shenstone*, Vol. 2 (London, 1765). Reproduced by kind permission of Cambridge University Library.   *pages 4–5*

Plate 2: portrait of Ann Donne Cowper (1703–37), by D. Heins, c.1723 (oil on copper). Reproduced by kind permission of Cambridge University Library.   *page 79*

ACKNOWLEDGEMENTS

I am greatly indebted to Richard Luckett for his extraordinary assistance and support; indebted also to Seamus Deane, Denis Donoghue, Jennifer Fitzgerald, John Barrell, James Mays, Rosemary Bechler, Tom Dunne, Dermot Moran, James Day, Allon White and Richard Kearney for their encouragement, intelligence and advice. I am grateful to the Master and Fellows of Gonville and Caius College, Cambridge, for their generous support of my work through a Gonville Research Studentship and through their frequent hospitality. Thanks are due also to my colleagues in the Department of English at St Patrick's College, Maynooth, and to the College itself for maintaining a policy of sabbatical leave that is invaluable to those who work there. The staff at the Cambridge University Library, at the British Library, at Archbishop Marsh's Library, at the Library of the Royal College of Music, of Trinity College and of University College, Dublin, have never let me down. Kevin Taylor and Hilary Gaskin have been scrupulous and precise in guiding the typescript into print. Finally, the largest debt is to Louise, Naoise, Anna, Cillian and Ruth who have always given much more than patience.

Cambridge, November 1986   KEVIN BARRY

ABBREVIATIONS

ELH	*English Literary History*
JAAC	*Journal of Aesthetics and Art Criticism*
JHI	*Journal of the History of Ideas*
JWCI	*Journal of the Warburg and Courtauld Institutes*
MP	*Modern Philology*
MQ	*Musical Quarterly*
NLH	*New Literary History*
PRMA	*Proceedings of the Royal Musical Association*
UTQ	*University of Toronto Quarterly*

OTHER WORKS

BL (Shawcross)	*Biographia Literaria,* edited by John Shawcross, 2 vols (Oxford, 1907)
CC	*The Collected Works of Samuel Taylor Coleridge,* edited by Kathleen Coburn and Bart Winer, 16 vols (London and Princeton, N.J. 1969–)
CL	*The Collected Letters of Samuel Taylor Coleridge,* edited by E. L. Griggs, 6 vols (Oxford, 1956–1971)
CN	*The Notebooks of Samuel Taylor Coleridge,* edited by Kathleen Coburn (New York, Princeton, N.J. and London, 1957–)
CPW	*The Complete Poetical Works of Samuel Taylor Coleridge,* edited by E. H. Coleridge, 2 vols (London, 1912)
Collins	William Collins, *The Works,* edited by Richard Wendorf and Charles Ryskamp (Oxford, 1979)
Cowper	*The Letters and Prose Writings of William Cowper,* edited by James King and Charles Ryskamp, 3 vols (Oxford, 1979)
Encyclopédie	*Encyclopédie, ou dictionnaire raisonné des*

	sciences, des arts et des métiers, 17 vols (Paris, 1751–1765)
Goldsmith	*The Collected Works of Oliver Goldsmith*, edited by Arthur Friedman, 5 vols (Oxford, 1966)
Grove, 1980	*The New Grove Dictionary of Music and Musicians*, edited by Stanley Sadie, 20 vols (London, 1980)
Hazlitt	*The Complete Works of William Hazlitt*, edited by P. P. Howe, 20 vols (London and Toronto, 1930)
MC	*Coleridge's Miscellaneous Criticism*, edited by T. M. Raysor (London and Cambridge, Mass., 1936)
PL	*The Philosophical Lectures*, edited by Kathleen Coburn (London, 1949)
Prelude (1959)	William Wordsworth, *The Prelude or Growth of a Poet's Mind*, edited by Ernest De Selincourt, 2nd edition revised by H. Darbishire (Oxford, 1959)
Prelude (1977)	William Wordsworth, *The Prelude, 1798–1799*, edited by Stephen Parrish (New York and Sussex, 1977)
SC	*Coleridge's Shakespearean Criticism*, edited by T. M. Raysor, 2 vols (London, 1930)
Stewart	Dugald Stewart, *Collected Works*, edited by Sir William Hamilton, 10 vols plus 1 supplementary vol. (Edinburgh, 1854)
Supplément	*Supplément à l'encyclopédie ou dictionnaire raisonné des sciences, des arts et des métiers*, 4 vols (Amsterdam, 1776–1777)
The Spectator	Joseph Addison, *The Spectator*, edited by D. F. Bond, 5 vols (Oxford, 1965)
TT	*Specimens of the Table Talk of the late Samuel Taylor Coleridge*, 2 vols (London, 1835)
W Prose	*The Prose Works of William Wordsworth*, edited by W.J.B. Owen and Jane Worthington Snyser, 3 vols (Oxford, 1974)

INTRODUCTION

Music and the sign in the eighteenth century

A study of ideas about music during the eighteenth century is an enquiry into one part of eighteenth-century theories about signs in general. Theories about the sign have not been widely discussed in intellectual histories of this period. Few have given space to the history of what John Locke called σημειωτική, or *the Doctrine of Signs*. For Locke signs are, in general, marks which stand for ideas of things: that is 'their proper and immediate Signification'.[1] It is not obvious what place music, or indeed any mode of language other than simple names, might occupy within such a theory of the sign.

Stephen K. Land's history of the movement after Locke, *From Signs to Propositions: The Concept of Form in Eighteenth Century Semantic Theory* (London, 1974), shows us how writers on literary aesthetics, such as John Dryden, Edmund Burke and Hugh Blair, contribute to a re-interpretation of ideas about signs both in linguistics and in philosophy. The elements of literature and especially of poetry provoke doubts about the Lockean model, precisely because the literary use of words as signs appears to exceed the functions of naming and representing.

If language is simply a collection of signs each of which has exactly the meaning it derives from its referent why is a verbal description effectually different from its object, why are different verbal descriptions of the same object qualitatively different from one another, and why are we affected differently by words and pictures? These practical, rhetorical problems, which cannot be raised within the terms of Lockean semantics, make an important contribution to 18th century linguistics.[2]

As much as literary aesthetics contributed to that more general epistemology, so also did ways of thinking about signs affect discussions of literature. We can take the hint from Land that words and pictures are for an aesthetics of literature key elements in a representational theory of writing. During the eighteenth century, at least until the final discourses of Sir Joshua Reynolds, painting stands as the type of the 'full' sign, and holds first place

1

in any theory of representation. Indeed, studies of literature by such scholars as Jean Hagstrum, Walter Hipple and John Barrell have explored the variety of ways in which the painters and the poets entered into a complex agreement in their 'imitations' of the sublime, of the beautiful, of the picturesque, and of the natural and social landscape.[3]

Much attention has been given to the interaction between concepts of the pictorial and of the poetic. Little attention has been given to the ways in which eighteenth-century thinking also includes another interaction: that between a concept of language and a concept of the 'empty' sign. Such an interaction presupposes ideas about the inadequacies of representation. It looks to music, rather than to painting, in order to describe an alternative and conflicting model of interpretation and of value.[4]

There has been relatively little historical study of the ways in which ideas about music and language interact in eighteenth-century poetic theory and practice.[5] There has been no full study of this interaction which analyses its function both in the writing *about* poetry and also in the writing *of* poetry. It is the purpose of this book to provide an historical study of the place of concepts of music in eighteenth-century poetic theory and practice. I examine first the complex subversion of a representational theory of the sign by ideas about music. Second, I consider the interaction of this non-representational theory of the sign with poetic theory and practice from William Collins to Samuel Taylor Coleridge.

Nowhere do I suggest that poets during the eighteenth century adopt some back-dated version of the *ut musica poesis* of Symbolist aesthetics. No significance is given to that cliché. For the process of ideas about music has a quite different perspective. Wherever these ideas emerge in discussions about the origins of language, about linguistic structure, about poetry, or about passional speech, they tend towards a theory of response and of interpretation as relatively uncertain and free. It is this activity of response as opposed to notions of description or specific naming, which ideas about music and about 'empty' signs are used to analyse.

Also there is little stress on concepts of music being developed in such a way as to provide a model of the relationship between author and text, of expressiveness or intentionality. Instead, the analogy with music is used to define and to articulate the relationship between signs and response, between words and interpretation. The response of the listener to the 'empty' signs of music becomes a model of the response of the reader to the text.

Music becomes, in relation to poetry, an analogy by which there can be a movement from a principle of representation to a principle of interpretation. Given that a piece of instrumental music must appear, according to Lockean principles, to be empty of signification, its enjoyment is evidence of the necessity for an aesthetic complex enough to include the pleasures of uncertainty in interpretation and of some free subjectivity in response. Although in 1751 D'Alembert, in the 'Discours préliminaire' to the *Encyclopédie*, writes that 'Any piece of music that does not portray something is only noise',[6] and although Rousseau in his impatient article on the sonata argues that merely instrumental music can signify nothing,[7] the texture of music continued to enchant and to win attention. In 1789 an editor of Aristotle's *Poetics* finds it relevant to describe how music leaves the listener 'to the free *choice* of such ideas as are, *to him*, most adapted to react upon and heighten the emotion which occasioned them'.[8] This kind of response to music is paralleled in language-use by at least one practice which radically questions the Lockean principle of representation: the practice of metaphor. One writer on linguistics in the eighteenth century, James 'Hermes' Harris, attributes the reader's unusual pleasure in this figure to his having 'to discover something *for himself*'.[9] From 1793 to 1810 Dugald Stewart elaborates this interpretative model, specifically in relation to metaphor and to indeterminate meanings in discourse.

Ideas about music support ideas about language which give attention to the process of interpretation. It is these indeterminate processes which are central anxieties for both Wordsworth and Coleridge in the first prefaces they address to their readers: Coleridge's Preface to his *Poems on Various Subjects* (1796) and Wordsworth's Preface to *Lyrical Ballads* (1800 and 1802). The preface of 1796 puzzles over the problem that poems are 'written at different times and prompted by very different feelings', but they are 'read at one time and under the influence of one set of feelings'.[10] The preface of 1802 unfolds the paradox that poetry should be so made as to 'divest language, in a certain degree of its reality, and thus to throw a sort of half-consciousness of unsubstantial existence over the whole composition'.[11]

It is therefore surprising that eighteenth-century writings

A

COLLECTION

OF

POEMS

IN THREE VOLUMES.

BY

SEVERAL HANDS.

LONDON: Printed by J. HUGHS,
For R. DODSLEY, at Tully's-Head in Pall-Mall.
M.DCCXLVIII.

ODES

ON SEVERAL

Descriptive and *Allegoric*

SUBJECTS.

By WILLIAM COLLINS.

——Ειπη

Ευρητιεπης αναγτιϑαι
Προϛφορος εν Μοιταϊ Διφρω·
Τολμα δε και αμφιλαφης Δυναμις
Εϛποιϑο.——   Πιδαρ. Ολυμπ. Θ.

LONDON:
Printed for A. MILLAR, in the *Strand.*
M.DCC.XLVII.
(Price One Shilling.)

POEMS

BY

Mʀ· GRAY.

DUBLIN:
PRINTED BY WILLIAM SLEATER
IN CASTLE-STREET,
1768.

Plate 1: (i) title-page from Robert Dodsley
(ed.), *A Collection of Poems* (London,
1748); (ii) title-page from William Collins,
*Odes on Several Descriptive and Allegoric
Subjects* (London, 1747); (iii) title-page
from Thomas Gray, *Poems* (Dublin,
1768); (iv) frontispiece from *The Works
in Verse and Prose of William Shenstone*,
Vol. 1 (London, 1765); (v) frontispiece
from *The Works in Verse and Prose of
William Shenstone*, Vol. 2 (London, 1765).

which link poetry with music have not been more thoroughly
studied. The period offers many relevant titles: Hildebrand
Jacob, *Of the Sister Arts* (1734), James Harris, *Three Treatises* . . .
The Second concerning Music and Poetry (1744); James Beattie, *An
Essay on Poetry and Music as they Affect the Mind* (written 1762);
Daniel Webb, *Observations on the Correspondence between Poetry
and Music* (1769); Thomas Twining, *Aristotle's Treatise on Poetry,
Translated: with Notes on the Translation, and on the Original; and
two Dissertations, on Poetical, and Musical, Imitation* (1789).
Works by Jean-Jacques Rousseau and Michel-Paul Guy de
Chabanon can also be added. Such works do not include the even
more numerous discussions of music in writing on the arts in
general, on taste, on language, on signs, and on representation.
The published work of, for example, Alexander Gerard, Adam
Smith, James Usher, Sir William Jones, Dugald Stewart, and the
unpublished papers of such different writers as Thomas Twining
and Samuel Taylor Coleridge, are also of especial importance.

In poems also we find images of music. It has been observed
that amongst emblematists of the late seventeenth century it is
painting which most commonly appears as the sister-art of poetry.
A glance at the emblems prefacing the work of mid-eighteenth
century poets gives us an immediate contrast. Several of the early
editions of James Thomson's *The Seasons*, of William Collins's
Odes, of Thomas Gray's *Poems*, as well as of Dodsley's many
Miscellanies, are illustrated with emblems of various sorts and all
of them identify poetry with music. In some instances the poems
may be prefaced by an illustration of a song-bird. More
usually the picture represents musical instruments (harps, lyres,
flutes, and the odd trumpet) to emphasise a convention often
repeated in the poems: that the arts of poetry and music define
each other.[12]

The general theory of signs in the eighteenth century can best be
introduced by considering Joseph Addison's posthumous *Dia-
logue on the Usefulness of Ancient Medals* (1726). Addison's
purpose is to ridicule and to dismiss the notion that the sign on the
medal or coin is an hieratic hieroglyph which might reveal an
ancient mystery. He will cancel any Hermetic conventions. In the
place of demands for esoteric explanations Addison argues that
the emblems are clear and rationally-based metonymies which are

to be read as conventional representations. This argument, according to E. H. Gombrich, establishes Addison's essay as 'a turning point in the conception of symbolism'.[13]

With a similar purpose but in a more extravagant and prolix manner, William Warburton provides a history of the development of script from picture-writing and hieroglyphics to the phonetic marks of the alphabet. Warburton's history of signs forms one part of his *The Divine Legation of Moses* (1738), and his concept of the sign agrees with Addison's insofar as both prescribe an original and determinate relationship between signifier and signified. Warburton's argument is complex (more complex even than that of Vico to whom he is often erroneously compared) and the principles offered in the *Legation* constitute a relatively flexible theory of representation. For Warburton there are three kinds of writing: picture-writing, hieroglyphics and the alphabet. These correspond to three kinds of discourse: the language of action, the language of fable, and catachresis (although this last is called 'metaphor' or 'similitude in little' by Warburton).[14] History, then, is the principle of economy by which each of these forms replaces its predecessor and by which the world can be represented in a more abbreviated and efficient manner. It is Warburton's argument that the early prophetic books of the Bible, for example, can be rationally and exactly interpreted if one uses the historically appropriate convention of discourse. The use of such an historical method of decoding will remove any fanatical belief in 'supernatural Visions':

> The judicious Reader therefore cannot but observe that the reasonable, the true Defence of the *Prophetic Writings*, is what we here offer: Where we shew, that *Information by Action* was, at this Time, and amongst those People, a *very common and familiar Mode of Conversation* . . . And the *Fanaticism* of an Action being only supported by this Principle, – *that the delighting in unusual Actions and foreign Modes of Speech is an Indication of that Turn of Mind*; when it is shown that those in Question are idiomatic and familiar, the Suspicion must drop of Course. To illustrate this last Observation by a domestic Instance: When the *Sacred Writers* talk of being *born after the Spirit*, of being *fed with the sincere Milk of the Word*, of *putting their Tears into a Bottle* . . . they speak the common, yet proper and pertinent Phraseology of their Country; and not the least Imputation of *Fanaticism* can stick upon those original Expressions.[15]

All figural discourse can therefore be decided to be simply representational according to the convention of usage and idiom contemporary with it. Any mixture of these conventions is regarded as no less than the symptom of a mania. The key to interpreting 'the sincere Milk of the Word' is a recognition that 'this Method of *expressing* the Thoughts by ACTION perfectly coincides with that of *recording* them by PICTURE'. As history economises on its forms of representation there develops the fable and the hieroglyph and, after that, catachresis and the alphabet. One sign comes to stand for many things but a convention of representation remains constant. 'Thus we see the *common Foundation* of all these various Modes of *Writing* and *Speaking*, was a *Picture* or *Image*, presented to the Imagination thro' the Eyes or Ears.'[16]

The French translation of this portion of the *Legation* appeared separately under the title, *Essai sur les hiéroglyphes*. Its influence on the notion of '*le langage d'action*' in Condillac's *Essai sur l'origine des connaissances humaines* (1746) and, subsequently, on Diderot's *Lettre sur les sourds-et-muets* (1751) has been well documented.[17] Condillac argues, as had Warburton, that '*le langage d'action*' is '*une vraie peinture*'.[18] For Condillac there is a great value in this mode of signification because it simultaneously holds together unanalysed states of mind and feeling. Diderot further extends this notion of the central value of gestural/pictorial action by transposing the mode of the hieroglyph to include all imaginative representation.[19] Synthetic and simultaneous clusters of images, the material of poetry, form '*un tissue d'hieroglyphes*'; they avoid the discursive and, therefore, represent more accurately states of mind and feeling which are, by their nature, experienced all at once.[20] Because states of mind and feeling exist 'as a whole and all at once' their appropriate correlatives are paintings. Lieselotte Dieckmann has described how Diderot, if only for reasons of completeness, comes to extend this idea of the hieroglyph beyond painting to include music also. However, we can notice here that in this instance of music alone the principle of representation becomes quite destabilised:

Its hieroglyph is so light and so fleeting; it is so easy to lose or misinterpret it, that the most beautiful symphony would not have any great effect if the infallible and sudden pleasure of the pure and simple sensation were not infinitely above that of frequently equivocal expression.[21]

Within any principle of picturing or representing ideas and feelings music proposes a risk of indeterminacy, of loss, of misinterpretation. The epistemological status of signs in music can only be radically unstable within a general theory of signs which attributes meaning to reference. In discovering when and how such a general theory of signs turns away from itself, it has become common to recognise Rousseau's *Essai sur l'origine des langues* (1764) as a central text. For our purposes here it is worth noting that Rousseau's essay, according to its full title, also 'treats of Melody and Musical Imitation'.[22]

Disagreement about this text between Jacques Derrida and Paul de Man has been about whether 'Rousseau remains faithful to a tradition that is unaffected by his thought.' It is Derrida's argument that Rousseau

stays convinced that the essence of art is imitation (*mimesis*) . . . It is *expressive*. It 'paints' the passions. The metaphor that transforms song into painting can force the inwardness of its power into the outwardness of space only under the aegis of the concept of imitation, shared alike by music and painting. Whatever their differences, music and painting both are duplications, representations.[23]

Rousseau's ideas both of music and of painting therefore support, according to Derrida, a 'metaphysics of presence': both, that is, support an assumption which persists in Rousseau that signs are substitutes for timeless realities, transcendent entities which it is the purpose of language merely to name. Such a perspective cannot notice the emphasis, however unwilling, on the uncertainty of any interpretative response to music which we have cited in Diderot and which we can observe also in Rousseau's famous repetition of the cliché: '*Sonate, que me veux-tu?*'[24] Paul de Man's reading of Rousseau does, on the other hand, allow some room for this hesitant question.

De Man's argument is that Rousseau alters conventional eighteenth-century models. Rousseau asserts

the priority of music over painting (and, within music, of melody over harmony) in terms of a value-system which is structural rather than substantial: music is called superior to painting despite and even because of its lack of substance.[25]

According to de Man the *Essai* asserts and happily persuades that music can imitate nothing: 'Sleep, the quiet of the night, solitude and even silence can enter into the picture that music paints.' The pictorial terms used by Rousseau do not lead back to conventional notions of imitation, but instead they point forward to the meditations of *La Nouvelle Héloise*:

tel est le néant des choses humaines qu'hors l'Être existant par lui-même, il n'y a rien de beau que ce qui n'est pas.[26]

In defence of his argument de Man might well have added here Rousseau's definition of the peculiarities of musical imitation as it is found in his *Dictionnaire de musique* (1767).

> Let all nature be in a slumber, he that contemplates it, sleeps not; and the art of the musician consists in substituting, in the place of the insensible image of the object, that of the movements which his presence excites in the heart of the contemplator. He will not only agitate the sea, animate the flame of a conflagration, make rivulets flow, the rain fall, and torrents swell, but he will paint the horrors of a boundless desert, calm the tempest, render the air tranquil and serene, and spread over the orchestra, a new and pleasing freshness. He will not directly represent things, but excite in the soul the same movement which we feel in seeing them.[27]

Rousseau's general theory of language looks back to Condillac and, perforce, to Warburton. He at once conserves and revises their idea of signs. For Rousseau all language is first of all figurative, but its figural mode is again that of catachresis. He repeats Condillac's notorious example of the primitive savage who, out of fear, first names a man a 'giant'. However, Rousseau revises Condillac by admitting another mode of signs: those of music, which do not represent objects but which give rise to feeling by virtue of the absence of a correlative object.

In a precise way this looks forward to Wordsworth's Preface to *Lyrical Ballads*. Wordsworth accepts that the first language of passion is figural speech. Like Warburton he argues that this extraordinary language of primitive poetry 'was really spoken by men'.[28] It was at some later date that this linguistic convention became 'a motley masquerade of tricks, quaintnesses, hieroglyphics, and enigmas'.[29] Like Rousseau, however, Wordsworth revises that poetics of figural imitation and defines the poet, as Rousseau had defined the musician, as one who is 'affected more than other men by absent things as if they were present'.[30] More than this, Wordsworth also revises Rousseau. For Rousseau's musician had made present 'in the soul the same movement which we feel' from absent objects when they appear. Wordsworth's poet, on the other hand, has 'an ability of conjuring up in himself passions, which are indeed far from being the same as those produced by real events'.[31]

An indirect mode of signs, as in music, is constituted first by their relative emptiness, and second by their intention towards a response which is relatively uncertain. Rousseau hesitates between the first, which is a representational principle, and the second, which is a principle of interpretive process. The contradictions that follow from this hesitation in the *Essai* provide the evidences upon which Derrida and de Man state their contrary readings. Their agreement with each other is one of value. Their disagreement is largely about Rousseau's blindness or insight before the glare of that value.[32]

Writers in the idiom of modernity, shared by Derrida and de Man, make us familiar with a consciousness

which does not result from the absence of something, but consists of the presence of a nothingness. Poetic language names this void with ever-renewed understanding and, like Rousseau's longing, it never tires of naming it again. This persistent naming is what we call literature. In the same manner that the poetic lyric originates in moments of tranquillity, in the absence of actual emotions to create the illusion of recollection, the work of fiction invents fictional subjects to create the illusion of the reality of others . . . Here the human self has experienced the void within itself and the invented fiction, far from filling the void, asserts itself as pure nothingness, *our* nothingness stated and restated by a subject that is the agent of its own instability.[33]

Any search in the eighteenth century which is directed to find this consciousness would do better to look aside from Rousseau towards others who provide a more radical description of the empty signs of discourse. One such writer, James Usher, a 'minor' commentator on aesthetic and philosophic questions, tells us 'that music is related to poetry' because poets and musicians

have a confused idea, without ability to arrive at it. But although they know it not they are sensible when they approach the unknown object, that seems at the same time to appear and hide from the imagination.[34]

Another description, equally paradoxical, by Michel-Paul Guy de Chabanon, tells us how

Les Matelots . . . sont gais au moment où ils chantent tristement. Ainsi, la Musique pour eux n'est pas un langage d'expression: ce n'est pas un Art qui imite, ni qui cherche même à imiter.[35]

Finally Adam Smith tells us that instrumental music 'presents an object so agreeable, so great, so various, and so interesting, that alone, and without suggesting any other object, either by imitation or otherwise, it can occupy, and as it were fill up, completely the whole capacity of the mind'.[36] The empty sign, the texture and structure of music, directs attention towards the process of response. But this emphasis on response has consequences for the 'author'. Like Chabanon's sailors or like Usher's musician and poet, the 'author' can now be relatively free of an environment which otherwise he must appear to imitate, inescapably. The poet, by analogy with the musician, can play with the presence of nothingness or with the fiction of absence, can sing from within an imprisoning cage or, in Wordsworth's phrase, be 'chiefly distinguished from other men by a greater promptness to think and feel without immediate external excitement'.[37]

Once the necessity of art is no longer placed in a representation or imitation of its circumstance, its relative freedom gives rise to other questions than those placed in the eighteenth century by Derrida and de Man. For example, it can be asked: what produces and gives form to the relatively autonomous structures that proliferate in music and in the other arts? What are their methods? Is not the perception of their complex relationships like that in other intellectual discourses? It can be asked also: what do these different structures tell us about the societies which produce specific instances of some but not of others? What different social meanings do they imply, or do they by being relatively free imply no such thing?

Music, precisely because it appears to be outside the principle of mimesis and to imitate nothing, can bring under analysis these questions which otherwise may not be asked at all. These questions indicate the strengths of working with a notion of 'empty' signs. The signs of music appear, with some note of surprise in the eighteenth century, to be much emptier than words. Writing about his always to be written poem, 'Soother of Absence', Coleridge asks: 'O that I had the Language of Music . . . Words halt over & over again!'[38] Also, reflecting the pictorial model exploited from Addison to Erasmus Darwin, Coleridge looks back to a moment when words were less impeded: before 'poetry forgot its essence in those forms which were only hieroglyphic of it'.[39]

Three concepts of language dominate the study of poetics in the late eighteenth century. First, there is the Lockean concept of words as the arbitrary names for ideas of things. In its rationalist version this accounts for the notion which we have already described, that all figural language is a mode of catachresis. That is the use of one term economically to designate a number of ideas for which proper terms do not exist: 'the leg of the table', 'the sincere milk of the Word', 'the mouth of the river'. This concept of language gives rise not only to Warburton's grammatology but also at the end of the century to John Horne Tooke's etymological principle. For Horne Tooke 'all words are originally and essentially names for perceptions . . . all parts of speech are merely diversified functions of the primal noun'.[40] For Erasmus Darwin the 'numerous abbreviations' of these original names 'so well illustrated by Mr Horne Tooke in his *Diversions of Purley*, make[s] up the general theory of language'.[41]

Second, there is the quite different concept that structure has priority over words or names. Fundamental language structures are looked for in such works as James 'Hermes' Harris's universal grammar of 1751, and in Lord Monboddo's and Sir William Jones's comparative investigations, of the 1770s and 1780s, into Sanscrit and other languages 'sprung from some common source'.[42] The idea of structure promotes that of context. George Campbell's *Philosophy of Rhetoric* (1776) argues that 'words and names themselves, by customary vicinity, contract in the fancy a relation additional to that which they derive purely from being symbols of related things. Further, this tendency is strengthened by the structure of language.'[43] Like I. A. Richards in a work of the same title (which is, ironically, directed against eighteenth-century rhetoricians) Campbell adopts a 'context theory of meaning'. Both Richards and Campbell understand rhetoric as a 'study of misunderstanding and its remedies'.[44] Leibnitz's ideal of a language comparable in its structure to a systematic calculus is undermined by the actual structures of language in discourse.[45] The indeterminate and connective process of interpreting both different kinds and different moments of discourse becomes of the first importance.

Between 1795 and 1810 Dugald Stewart continues Campbell's work:

Our words, when examined separately, are often as completely insignificant as the letters of which they are composed; deriving their meaning solely from the connection, or relation, in which they stand to others.[46]

Stewart resists, therefore, any notion that words are (according to the more accepted idiom) pictures of ideas of things.[47] The concept of language as a structure or set of contexts is used to oppose the concept of language as an aggregate of names. That concept is clearly the cornerstone of the tradition in the theory of signs and of rhetoric which supports what Paul Ricoeur calls 'the tyranny of the word in the theory of meaning'.[48] This theory had been based always on 'the correlation between word and idea'.[49] The result of such a concept of language for a theory of metaphor is its restriction to a model of necessary substitution, of efficient transference, of catachresis.

The second concept, that of structure and of context, is part of a quite different tradition which, as it resists the first, emphasises the vague, imprecise, polysemic nature of signs.[50] In this tradition the consequence for a theory of metaphor is the introduction of a model of the relatively free play of language and, therefore, of an active interpretative process. '*Lively* expression is that which expresses existence as *alive*.'[51]

A third concept of language which has dominated the study of late eighteenth-century poetics is that which centres on the idea of the symbol. The use of the term 'symbol' has conventionally defined its provenance by an opposition with that of 'allegory'. Angus Fletcher in his study of *Allegory: The Theory of a Symbolic Mode* (New York, 1964) provides the best analysis of 'this unhappy controversy'. Allegory had been for Goethe 'where the particular serves only as an example of the general': the convention, that is, of the hieroglyph. The symbol, however, had been 'where the particular represents the more general, not as a dream or a shadow, but as a living momentary revelation of the Inscrutable'.[52] Fletcher acutely comments on the evaluative principle which both contrasts good ('symbolic') poetry with bad ('allegoric') poetry and also leads to the more recent phenomenon by which the term 'myth' inherits all the values previously inscribed in the term 'symbol'.[53]

Coleridge's authority stands behind that habit as it continues in literary criticism. 'An allegory,' he writes, 'is but a translation of abstract notions into a picture-language, which is itself nothing but an abstraction from objects of sense.'[54] Catachresis and the hieroglyph once again! Whereas the symbol is characterised by 'the translucence of the eternal through and in the temporal', and is itself 'a living part in that unity of which it is the representative' Strictly speaking, as Fletcher shows us, Coleridge's definition of the symbolic is in fact a definition of synecdoche.[55]

It appears to me that Fletcher's work has, silently, directed the re-reading of early Romantic poetics with which we are now so familiar among American post-structuralists. In place of the consensus, expressed for example by Wimsatt, Abrams and Wasserman, that the symbol presumes a 'fundamental unity that encompasses both mind and object', we have a new consensus which replaces figures of unmediated vision, of organic unity and of creative life, with a figure of 'the sign of mortality at the origin of language'.[56] Such a condition of language which always 'speaks of something that is gone' is defined, not as symbolic, but as allegoric. This is not the allegorical sign which, in Coleridge's and Goethe's sense of it, acts as a picture-language or hieroglyph. It is instead a sign constituted by absence and by loss, by renunciation and by error.

Whereas the symbol postulates the possibility of an identity or identification, allegory designates primarily a distance in relation to its own origin, and renouncing the nostalgia and the desire to coincide, it establishes its language in the void of this temporal difference. In so doing it prevents the self from an illusory identification with the non-self which is now fully, though painfully, recognised as a non-self. It is this painful knowledge that we perceive at the moments when early romantic literature finds its true voice.[57]

This mode of signs indicates, according to one recent study of Wordsworth's poetry and his idea of language, 'not only the process of learning to do without but also that of recognising that one has always been doing without'.[58] More than any other trope the figure of the lamp, in preference to that of the mirror held up to nature, has confirmed through the work of M. H. Abrams the earlier consensus about an illuminating and creative romantic symbol. By turning this trope against itself Jonathan Culler has argued for the newer consensus by pointing to the ways in which 'lamps are only another version of mirrors and belong to the same system of specularity and representation'.[59]

With similar destructive effect it is asserted by Paul de Man that in the instance of Coleridge's celebrated definition of the symbol in *The Statesman's Manual*, although we start 'from the assumed superiority of the symbol in terms of organic sub-stantiality, we end up with a description of figural language as translucence'.[60] At the very moment of its inception, therefore, the idea of the symbol is defined in terms (of emptiness and fullness at once) which betray its conceptual inadequacy. According to this re-reading the idea of the symbol returns awkwardly to an Adamist version of the idea of the name. The third concept of language, that of the symbol, offers no way out of the conflict between the first and second concepts, that of names and that of structure. It follows then that eighteenth-century poetics is likely to look beyond the signs of language in order to understand language. This can be done only by turning to another concept, that of 'empty' signs, the signs of music.

In this there is to be found an alternative to the pictorial, specular analogies of lamps and mirrors and pictures. The specular analogy with painting, on the one hand, and the aural analogy with music, on the other, indicate opposed ideas about language and poetics. It will be clear that in the argument which follows, except in the instance of William Cowper, I do not enquire in any detail into the main descriptive and representational mode of poetry in the period between Collins and Coleridge. That mode implies a comparison between language and specularity. Instead, my argument privileges an alternative poetic mode which follows from comparisons between language and music. Such a poetic mode may be only one aspect, even an infrequent aspect within a poet's writing. Nevertheless, it is certain that this poetic mode is historically important and new, even in those instances where it is not representative of a poet's work taken as a whole.

The chief anxiety which early Romantic poetics inherits from discussions about signs and about language is an anxiety shared by Descartes, Locke, Berkeley, Hume and Dugald Stewart. It is the anxiety about the probable priority of words over thoughts. 'Words', writes Wordsworth, 'are too awful an instrument for good and evil to be trifled with: they hold above all other external powers a dominion over thoughts.'[61]

The notion of the empty sign of music, however, proposes a model by which that anxiety is reduced through an emphasis on the interpretative process as an unstable but decisive source of meaning. Such a concept of signs tends to produce a theory of metaphor which is, perhaps, closest to that recently described by the philosopher Donald Davidson. Davidson argues for a theory of metaphor which emphasises, on the one hand, an intention (what 'its author wishes to convey'), and on the other hand, an interpretation (what can be derived from the author's literal statement). The literal statement, according to conventions of context and use, presents itself to be interpreted not as itself but as metaphor. 'The central mistake against which I shall be inveighing,' writes Davidson, 'is the idea that metaphor has, in addition to its literal sense or meaning, another sense or meaning.'[62] The model he presents, therefore, stresses the emptiness of the signs when taken literally. In the face of this emptiness which a metaphoric mode produces 'the act of interpretation is itself a work of imagination . . . There are no instructions for devising metaphors; there is no manual for determining what a metaphor "means" or "says"; there is no test for metaphor that does not call for taste.'[63]

Such a definition can only return us to Wordsworth's strategic refusal to defend his theory of poetry because to do so 'it would be necessary to give a full account of the present state of the public taste in this country . . . which, again, could not be determined, without pointing out in what manner language and the human mind act and re-act on each other'.[64] Davidson's contemporary version of metaphor and reading as a play between 'empty' signs and imaginative response also returns us to Coleridge's 'reading' of the music of the Abyssinian maid:

> on her dulcimer she played
> Singing of Mount Abora.
> Could I revive within me
> Her symphony and song,
> To such a deep delight 'twould win me,
> That with music loud and long
> I would build that dome in air,
> That sunny dome! those caves of ice!
> And all who heard should see them there.

This interpretative structure of 'empty' signs and response in 'Kubla Khan' is one which is repeated in numerous poems of the period. In such poems there is a recurrent figure of language as a kind of music that is heard as if it were the more intense insofar as it is the more empty. We can give as instances: Wordsworth's 'The Solitary Reaper', many poems about nightingales or cuckoos ('No bird but an invisible thing, / A voice, a mystery'), poems about the inarticulate or vacuous speech of a child, of a vagrant woman or of a solitary old man (whose 'voice to me was like a stream / Scarce heard; nor word from word could I divide'). Poems, finally, in which a central word of the text is without a referent: *Abora* in 'Kubla Khan' is the name of no mountain; 'Was it for *this* . . . For *this* . . . Was it for *this* . . . ?' in the opening lines of the 1798/1799 *Prelude* indicates that which has no antecedent. *Abora* and *this*, the 'music' of the Abyssinian maid and of the solitary reaper, are instances of 'empty' signs.[65]

According to Edmund Burke in *A Philosophical Enquiry into the Origin of our Ideas of the Sublime and Beautiful* (1757) the 'common effect' of words is not their 'raising of ideas of Things'. This flat rebuttal of John Locke implies a poetics that exploits anti-representational ideas of language. It appears to be a poetics of the sublime, of mountain glory, of fear. It can be argued that the consequence of such a poetics is to place the reader or listener under a compulsion to attend to the text with nothing less than awe, reverence, a stunned assent. There is, however, an alternative consequence for such a poetics: the decision that such a mode of language gives the reader of the poem an opportunity to respond individually and actively. It can appear – and to the earlier Romantics it *does* appear – that such a mode of language allows its readers to perceive the active and imaginative *power* of their own minds.

Music and its audience in the eighteenth century

There has been some consequence to the decision that music was of little importance to eighteenth-century epistemology and aesthetics. John Hollander has not been alone in considering that an imaginative, thoughtful or speculative interest in music ends at about 1700. That date saw the 'Untuning of the Sky'.[66] Hollander has further argued that the eighteenth and the early nineteenth centuries show an interest not in the sound of music but in the music of sound: birds, waterfalls, echoing cliffs.

Neither the concert-hall in which the virtuosi performed, nor the bourgeois drawing room in which the daughter of the household would display her accomplishments on the ever more widely received pianoforte, could qualify for the auditory attention of the Romantic Imagination in England.[67]

This view has been supported from the quite different perspective of musicology. R. R. Subotnik, in a recent article on a semiology of music, concludes that

instrumental music began to receive more serious theoretical attention during the eighteenth century, but on the whole the explosion of great instrumental writing that occurred in this period had little impact on contemporary aesthetic theory. Vocal music still enjoyed superior status; and indeed, music itself, on account of its inadequate ability to represent the outside world, was generally considered the lowest of the arts.[68]

To contradict these statements and to remove the assumption that eighteenth-century discussions of music are hostile, meagre and unimportant, I will argue that there is considerable, if uneven, critical and speculative response to new developments especially in instrumental music.

As early as 1958 Stanley Sadie drew attention to the developed standards of audiences, which made it possible that 'concert life in eighteenth-century England as a whole had a variety and vitality to which it would be hard to find a parallel'.[69] In the provinces, not only in the market towns and industrial centres but also in small villages, concerts after the 1740s included both the late Baroque or 'ancient' styles (Corelli, Geminiani, Handel, Avison) and also the *galant* and Mannheim, or 'modern', styles (J. C. Bach, Abel, Stamitz, Richter, Haydn). East Anglia, where Thomas Twining lived, had an extraordinarily busy concert life. So too did Chichester and Oxford, where William Collins spent most of his life away from London. So too did Bristol.

Charles Avison complained of the 'innumerable foreign Overtures . . . this Torrent of Confused Sounds',[70] but he could not hold the tide back. Many British composers, notably the Earl Kelly, adopted the 'modern' styles and the audiences welcomed recent Italian and especially German compositions.[71] The eighteenth-century concert room and bourgeois household included audiences that admired more than virtuosities and daughters. As early as 1955 H. C. Robbins Landon indicated from newspaper reviews of Haydn's London concerts the acute recognition of music that had developed in England. Certainly Britain produced during the eighteenth century a number of minor but interesting and not unimportant symphonists. Also, the cities and towns produced a broad and enlightened audience which responded enthusiastically to modern Continental composers.[72] Edinburgh welcomed the Mannheim style. London, after the successes of C. F. Abel, J. C. Bach and Peter Salomon, welcomed Haydn. The *Morning Chronicle*, in particular, with its reviews of the Salomon/Haydn concerts, shows evidence of the responsiveness evoked by the new classical symphonies. German music prospered in spite of its reputation for opacity and difficulty. Giardini in London was less successful than Salieri in Vienna at enforcing the claims of Italian music: his efforts were answered by the opinion that Italian music was not original or progressive enough for London audiences.[73] Edinburgh, in the person of George Thomson, and London, in the person of William Shield, show instances of an extraordinarily rapid acceptance of Beethoven.

London in the eighteenth century was distinguished by a proliferation of concert rooms, music clubs and performances in the pleasure gardens. Twenty-six gardens provided musical entertainments for a broad section of the London public throughout this period, the highest number being in operation between 1770 and 1800. Marylebone (c.1659–1778), Vauxhall (1661–1859) and Ranelagh (1743–1803) provided overtures, concertos, symphonies, songs and excerpts from the operas. The concerto was the most popular form. Composers included Corelli, Handel, J. C. Bach, the Mannheim symphonists, Pleyel, Arne, the Earl Kelly, Arnold and other British composers. In the years after 1783 Haydn was the most popular composer in the garden programmes, which, by then, were fully advertised and listed. The gardens hosted many tastes. Charles Burney, the young Mozart and Pleyel all performed at Ranelagh. Handel was still popular in the 1780s, with the great festival in his honour at Westminster Abbey in 1784. Gluck was revived in programmes of the 1790s.[74] In 1742 the large rotunda had been built at Ranelagh; in the 1750s Vauxhall acquired its indoor 'umbrella' and its outdoor 'moorish–gothic' temple. Admission was not expensive. Henry Fielding commented that the gardens were 'by reason of their price . . . not entirely appropriated to the people of fashion'. Birmingham, Newcastle, Bath, Tunbridge Wells and Scarborough each had a garden, and Norwich had three. John Lampe came to Edinburgh from Dublin's musical life in 1750 and began open-air concerts in Heriot's gardens. By 1800 the gardens were in general decline.[75]

The concert rooms provided for the middling classes: Thomas Hickford's Rooms were fashionable and spacious; the Hanover Square Rooms provided elegance and could accommodate an audience of up to 800; at the King's Theatre, during the 1790s, Haydn could relish earning four times his annual Esterhaza salary at a single concert.[76] The Hanover Square rooms had been built to house the Bach/Abel concerts in 1776 after their popularity outgrew the space available at Carlisle House. These concerts introduced the contemporary Continental symphonists, Bach and Abel themselves, Richter, Stamitz, Mozart and Haydn. They introduced also the pianoforte as a chief instrument in concertos. They ceased only after Bach's death in 1782. In 1783 a number of musicians continued this 'modernist' policy and inaugurated the Professional Concerts from which, in 1784, Peter Salomon broke away. From 1791 to 1795, in response to the composer's already established popularity, Salomon hosted Haydn in London. The attendance at Haydn's concerts was always enormous: even for the final season demand exceeded the number of tickets available.[77] Salomon's success was enough to ruin the Professional Concerts, at which the main attraction had been Haydn's less sparkling pupil, Pleyel.

The response to Haydn's London music is well documented and it tells us a great deal about how people enjoyed and admired music and musical performances. The Salomon symphonies, as the London compositions are now called, can be seen as a culmination of developments in instrumental music during the eighteenth century. Therefore, programmes and newspaper reviews of Haydn's 'opera concerts' refer quite indiscriminately to his symphonies as concerti or as overtures. This accords both with developments in other musical forms and with the overlapping characteristics which the interchangeable terms reflect.[78] The twelve London or 'Salomon' symphonies, Nos. 93–104, are described as follows by Robbins Landon:

the composer often returns to devices he had abandoned years ago, such as the *concerto grosso* technique of *concertino* and *ripieno* found in the second movement of Nos. 93 and 96, or the concerto-like violin solos in Nos. 95, 97, 98 and 103. These devices from the symphonies of the seventeen-sixties are not, however, simply borrowed and used in their old settings, but clothed in Haydn's most modern instrumental and harmonic garb. Thus the 'Salomon' symphonies sum up and synthesise all he had done in the field, and at the same time look forward into the future, to the orchestral works of Beethoven and Schubert, of Mendelssohn and Schumann.[79]

More recently Robbins Landon has indicated that, not only this element of synthesis in these compositions, but also the manner of their performances, place the London concerts at the centre of developments during the Classical period. Salomon's hospitality toward emigré musicians included his welcome in 1794 for the great Italian violinist, Viotti, who was in flight from the Paris 'terror'. Viotti's playing revolutionised not only the way in which the violin was constructed but also orchestral technique. 'The modern orchestra was born when Viotti came to London and joined forces with Salomon.'[80] It is to this combination of compositional and performance innovations that London audiences responded.

A contrast between the popular response and the academic response to Haydn was made by Charles Burney: 'We are not certain that our present musical doctors and graduates are *quite up* to Haydn yet: but the public are . . . unanimous in applauding.'[81] The reviewer in the *Morning Chronicle* is of Burney's and the audience's modernist spirit.[82] Of Symphony No. 99 the reviewer writes:

It abounds with ideas, as new in music as they are grand and impressive; it rouses and affects every emotion of the soul . . . the effect of the wind instruments in the second movement was enchanting . . . but indeed the pleasure of the whole was continual.[83]

Of Symphony No. 101 (the 'Clock') he writes:

the character that pervaded the whole composition was heartfelt joy . . . Nothing can be more original than the subject of the first movement; and having found a happy subject, no man knows like HAYDN how to produce incessant variety, without once departing from it.[84]

Of Symphony No. 100 (the 'Military') he writes: 'the hellish roar of war increase[s] to a climax of horrid sublimity'. Of the final Symphony No. 104 he writes:

for fullness, richness, and majesty, in all its parts, it is thought by some of the best judges to surpass all his other compositions. A Gentleman, eminent for his musical knowledge, taste and sound criticism, declared this to be his opinion, That, for fifty years to come Musical Composers would be little better than imitators of Haydn; and would do little more than pour water on his leaves. We hope the prophecy may prove false; but probability seems to confirm the prediction.[85]

The appreciation shown here for large instrumental forms goes along with an admiration for Salomon's accurate and powerful orchestra, and, especially, for Viotti. This violinist, according to the *Morning Chronicle*, 'awakens emotion, gives a soul to sound, and leads the passions captive'; and later, 'he indeed possesses not only sweetness, vigour, and every variety that the bow and the finger seem capable of affording, but he adds the grand ingredient, soul, without which music is either insipidity, trick, or noise'.[86]

In the face of this kind of appreciation it is a false conceit for John Hollander and others to place as the limit to eighteenth-century musical life the performances of virtuosi and bourgeois daughters, and to assume that music is held to be the lowest in status among the arts. Indeed this is, as Charles Burney noticed, an academic conceit.

It should not surprise us, therefore, that poets and writers are to be found among the enthusiastic audiences for contemporary music. William Collins was 'passionately fond of music' and enjoyed with a 'raptured ear' the gardens of Vauxhall and Ranelagh as well as domestic performances. Of Collins's two surviving letters, one is to his friend John Gilbert Cooper (1723–69), author of *The Power of Harmony*, a Shaftesburian poem in two books of which the first is about 'The Harmony of Music, Poetry, and the Imitative Arts'. The other letter is to William Hayes, professor of music at Oxford, and in this Collins discusses a setting for one of his poems and another proposed poem about music. Both letters refer to contemporary musicians and singers.[87] Thomas Gray brought back from his Continental travels contemporary, especially Italian, music. Thomas Twining tells us how, as a Cambridge student, he was enabled by Gray's 'enthusiastic love of expressive and passionate music' to move from an appreciation of 'ancient' to one of 'modern' music.[88]

At the Crown and Anchor, a tavern which had hosted many music societies since the Philharmonic Society first began there in the 1730s and which was visited by Haydn in 1791, there was held an evening of music in 1775. The music included settings by Jonathan Battishill (1738–1801), conductor at Covent Garden, and the poems included work by Shakespeare, Milton, Pope and Collins.[89] 'To such readers as are interested in the knowledge of low manners,' wrote the 'musical knight' Sir John Hawkins,

it may be some gratification to mention that there were concerts of this kind at the following places, the Blacksmith's Arms on Lambeth Hill, behind St. Paul's; the Cock and Lion in St. Michael's Alley, Cornhill; the Coachmaker's Arms in Windmill-Street, Piccadilly; at sundry alehouses in Spitalfields, frequented by journeymen weavers; and at Lambeth Wells, and the Unicorn at Hoxton. The keepers of these houses were generally men that loved music.[90]

William Blake composed, adapted and sang melodies for his songs.[91] Samuel Taylor Coleridge was familiar enough with such contemporary performers as the Linley brothers to suggest collaboration with them. Coleridge's liking for Mozart and Beethoven, for Palestrina and Purcell, his preference for these over Rossini, places him in the convention of popular taste and also places him close to one of Haydn's most enlightened colleagues in England, William Shield.[92]

Shield came from Durham; he had been a one-time boat-builder's apprentice and afterwards a student of Charles Avison. A successful composer of operas and melodramas, Shield met and befriended Haydn in 1791 and, some years later, Viotti. Haydn admired Shield's often complex music, and Shield's subsequent approach to composition was decisively formed by Haydn. After the Salomon concerts Shield helped found in 1813 the London Philharmonic Society, which championed the music of Beethoven. Shield's taste in music is best illustrated by his publications at the turn of the century, in which he includes often rare examples of music from J. S. Bach, from an otherwise unknown piece by Mozart, and from a Beethoven sonata. Shield was a lifelong friend of Thomas Holcroft. Holcroft introduced Shield to the Godwin circle, and Shield introduced Holcroft to Haydn. Holcroft published a poem (its first appearance was, as we might expect, in the *Morning Chronicle*) addressed to Haydn, a poem which appears to respond in particular to Symphony No. 100 (the 'Military') and to the French war:

> the distracted ear, in racking gloom
> Suspects the wreck of worlds, and gen'ral doom;
> Then HAYDN stands, collecting Nature's tears,
> And consonance sublime amid confusion hears.[93]

Edinburgh had in George Thomson a proficient similar to London's William Shield. In the same year as Shield helped found the London Philharmonic Society, Thomson wrote to Beethoven admiring the first Razoumovsky Quartet. David Johnson in his *Music and Society in Lowland Scotland in the Eighteenth Century* writes:

This was only five years after the quartet had been published; and when we consider the lukewarm reception that it met with at its first performance in Vienna, we see that Thomson's musical taste was advanced for his time.[94]

Edinburgh's 'modernist' attitude towards the development of classical music moved at a fairly similar pace to that of London. Just as the Bach/Abel concerts of the 1770s and their successors developed London opinion, so too the Edinburgh Musical Society provided broadly similar programmes. The Earl Kelly dominated music in Edinburgh during its most vital period from 1760 to 1780. A student of Stamitz at Mannheim from 1753 to 1756 and afterwards a friend and correspondent of Abel, his compositions and performance first introduced the 'modern' style and made it popular in Scotland.[95] His contemporary, Edward Topham, writes of the years 1774 and 1775 in Edinburgh:

> The degree of attachment which is shewn to Music in general in this Country exceeds belief. It is not only the principal entertainment, but the constant topic of every conversation; and it is necessary not only to be a lover of it, but to be possessed of a knowledge of the science, to make yourself agreeable to society.
>
> In vain may a man of letters, whose want of natural faculties has prevented him from understanding an art, from which he could derive no pleasure, endeavour to introduce other matters of discourse, however entertaining in their nature: everything must give place to music. Music alone engrosses every idea.[96]

Some men of letters made good their loss. Out of this situation James Beattie gives us *An Essay on Poetry and Music as they affect the Mind* (1776), and Adam Smith his essay (1795) separating music from 'the Imitative Arts'.[97] Beattie's is one of the most specific and Smith's one of the most comprehensive discussions of instrumental music in the eighteenth century. It is by the too little known Edinburgh writer Thomas Robertson, in his *Inquiry into the Fine Arts* (1784), that the Earl Kelly's music is most admired. Over-enthusiastic about his principle that music, because it is unmediated and abstract, can alone reproduce the spirit of its time and place, Robertson discovers an index of the '*fervidum ingenium* of his country', Scotland, in the musical style which Kelly had imported from Mannheim.[98] To that extent, no less among men of letters than among the Scottish and English symphonists who imitated Stamitz, Abel and Haydn,[99] contemporary instrumental music was accepted. It could become a part of more general topics of thought.

1

WILLIAM COLLINS

Anti-pictorialism: Harris, Hartley and Burke

William Collins's poem, the 'Ode to Evening', emerges through a series of drafts and revisions to take its place among Collins's other poems about the fate of poetry in his *Odes on Several Descriptive and Allegoric Subjects* (1747). There is agreement among writers as different as W. K. Wimsatt, Martin Price and Geoffrey Hartman that the 'Ode to Evening' is an important and obscure poem; indeed, that it is important because it is obscure. We are told that Collins's poem, 'By addressing in epiphanic terms a subject intrinsically nonepiphanic', opens up the possibility of the greater Romantic ode.[1] The impossibility of an epiphany in Collins's poem is what constitutes its obscure manner and style. More than any other contemporary poem to which the terms of literary pictorialism have been applied, this ode, therefore, seems to elude the conventions of the sister-arts of poetry and painting as they have been described by Jean Hagstrum. Hagstrum includes Collins among the eighteenth-century neoclassical and visionary poets for whom, if we are to read them correctly, 'more than seeing is required. We must see pictorially.' It is part of Hagstrum's argument that 'The pictorial in a verbal medium necessarily involves the reduction of motion to stasis or something suggesting such a reduction.'[2] Also the eighteenth-century poet is said to specify a meaning 'by using publicly accepted iconic detail' in order to elicit the 'reality of nature and normative human experience'. The pictorial is, therefore, a world of established values and its conventions are said to be those of the descriptive-and-allegoric which we find, for example, in Collins. To read this poetry well is to agree that 'The creation of precise visual responses to poetry is of course the business of all of us.'[3]

The advantage of Hagstrum's method is the way in which it discovers affiliations between certain eighteenth-century poems and certain critical interests which a number of the poets shared in recent and contemporary painting. Poetic conventions are seen to overlap with certain principles in contemporary taste and aesthetics. The painting of Claude Gelée (Lorrain), of Salvator Rosa and of Nicolas Poussin contributes material and formal elements to the representation of landscape and mythical subjects in the work of James Thomson and of other descriptive poets. Hagstrum has recognised the presence of a strong anti-pictorialism in eighteenth-century theory, if not in eighteenth-century practice. The key text is Edmund Burke's *A Philosophical Enquiry into the Origin of our Ideas of the Sublime and Beautiful* (1757). The presence, however, of such a text at the very centre of the period under discussion has not been allowed to disturb the consensus that has settled around the pictorialist view.[4]

The uncertain fate of anti-pictorialism in eighteenth-century poetic theory and practice has not been analysed. Burke, if only in this, has appeared isolated. Nevertheless, Oliver Goldsmith in a review of Burke's *Enquiry* points out how poets should respond to some of the consequences of sublimity:

To heighten this terror, obscurity, in general seems necessary . . . Thus in Pagan worship, the idol is generally placed in the most obscure part of the temple . . . Wherefore it is one thing to make an idea clear, and another to make it affecting to the imagination. Nay, so far is clearness of imagery from being absolutely necessary to influence the passions, that they may be considerably operated on, as in music, without presenting any image at all. Painting never makes such strong impressions on the mind as description, yet painting must be allowed to represent objects more distinctly than any descriptions can do; and even in painting, a judicious obscurity, in some things contributes to the proper effect of the picture . . . Clearness . . . is, in some measure, an enemy of all enthusiasm whatsoever.[5]

Burke had been, as we shall see, chiefly interested in the obscurity of language.

However, Goldsmith's comments show how those considerations of the obscurity of language can become a matter of poetic theory. Goldsmith's repetition of a comment by Burke about music – that it works by presenting no ideas at all to the imagination – shows the way in which relatively uncommon thoughts about language and poetry could be developed through the use of more common thoughts about music. The anti-pictorialism of Goldsmith's review, in particular his comments on painting itself, leaves Hagstrum's arguments in some confusion. Descriptions in language, according to Goldsmith's assumptions, are more energetic insofar as they are to a degree unlike painting. Language in poetry can give to an image 'motion and succession too'; like music, it does not evoke clear and distinct ideas.[6]

Before the end of the period, marked by James Thomson, William Collins, Thomas Gray and Christopher Smart, there is not any thorough discussion which compares poetry and music. There is, however, a conventional assumption, apparent in Goldsmith's comments, that an analogy between the two arts can be developed in order to say something about words in poetry. James Thomson's poem about the Aeolian harp and his figure of Pope as a druidic bard playing a powerful and inspiring music in *The Castle of Indolence*; Thomas Gray's consistently maintained figure for poetry as music in the 'The Progress of Poesy' and in 'The Bard'; Christopher Smart's explicit denigrations of painting and his preference for music throughout *Jubilate Agno*; these figures all precede Daniel Webb's *Observations on the Correspondence between Poetry and Music* (1769). Webb's book is of interest not least because it organises notional statements which had preceded it. The earlier, looser theorising is at work most forcefully in the drafts and fragments of William Collins. In the absence of any discursive poetics written by Collins himself, these drafts and fragments proved the best context for reading the 'Ode to Evening'.

The poetry of William Collins needs to be related briefly to a number of other works. These include, in particular, James Harris's *Three Treatises. The First Concerning Art. The Second Concerning Music, Painting and Poetry. The Third Concerning Happiness* (1744), a work which Collins constructively misread and for which he showed great enthusiasm. Also we must look to Burke's *Enquiry* (1757), which was published in the same year as Gray's Pindaric odes. Collins was perhaps insane and had less than two years to live when the *Enquiry* appeared. He was at the height of his powers as a poet and most acutely developing his aesthetic when he read Harris's *Three Treatises*.

James Harris, who was to publish in 1751 his more famous work *Hermes: or, a Philosophical Inquiry Concerning Language and Universal Grammar*, would have been known to Collins in the 1740s as an active patron of musical life in Salisbury. The second of the *Three Treatises* remains as a constant point of reference in almost all eighteenth-century discussions of music. The 'Ode to

Evening' and its fragmentary drafts clarify the important relationship between Harris's *Three Treatises* and Burke's *Enquiry*, and in
their turn these two works help to explain the mode in which
Collins's poem is written. For what Harris says about music in
1744, Burke says about words in 1757. Both writers argue for an
alternative to the Lockean identification of words, ideas and
mental pictures.

Harris's purpose is to discuss 'Music considered not as an
Imitation, but as deriving its Efficacy from *another* Source'.[7] His
example is Handel, in particular Handel's sacred music. The
'genuine Charm' and magnificence of music appears to Harris to
be

A Power, which consists not in Imitations, and the raising *Ideas*; but in the
raising *Affections*, to which Ideas may correspond.[8]

On the other hand, in the fifth section of the *Enquiry*, Burke
proposes to discuss words in general and also words in poetry.
Words, writes Burke, 'seem to me to affect us in a manner very
different from that in which we are affected by natural objects, or
by painting or architecture'. His intention is to contradict the
'common notion . . . that they affect the mind by raising in it ideas
of those things for which custom has appointed them to stand'.[9] In
order to do this Burke follows Hartley's discussion of language in
the *Observations on Man* (1749). Both writers divide language into
groups of words which are increasingly less concrete and more
abstract. The first group includes names/'pictures' such as 'nurse'
or 'walk' or 'castle'; the second group includes category terms
such as 'square' or 'red'; the third includes abstract terms such as
'gratitude' or 'mercy'. Hartley includes a fourth group of words
'Such as have neither Ideas nor Definitions', for example 'the',
'of', 'to'.[10]

Burke is most interested in the third group of 'Compounded
abstract' words, because ultimately the *Enquiry* will assert that all
language is in this mode. 'The common effect' of words, he writes,
is 'not by raising ideas of Things'. Burke's rhetorical figure of how
language works is the blind poet Thomas Blacklock and the blind
mathematician Nicholas Saunderson. These instances are used to
assert that there is no credit to be given to clear conceptions
painted on the mind. For words to work,

three effects arise in the mind of the hearer. The first is the *sound*; the second the
picture, or representation of the thing signified by the sound; the third is, the

affection of the soul produced by one or both of the foregoing. *Compounded abstract* words, of which we have been speaking, (honour, justice, liberty, and the like,) produce the first and the last of these effects, but not the second. *Simple abstracts,* are used to signify some one simple idea without much adverting to others which may chance to attend it, as blue, green, hot, cold, and the like; these are capable of affecting all three of the purposes of words; as the *aggregate* words, man, castle, horse, *etc.* are in a yet higher degree. But I am of opinion, that the most general effect even of these words, does not arise from their forming pictures of the several things they would represent in the imagination;[11]

The similarity between Harris's concept of music and Burke's concept of language is an obvious one. Both bypass fixed and specific ideas/pictures and construct an indirect, associative and relatively uncertain link between the sounds and the effects words produce. The signifier is released from the specificity of a pictorial signified. The agreement between Burke and Harris is probably established through Hartley. By placing 'The Doctrine of Sounds' at the centre of a theory of association Hartley is led to a consideration of music:

The Pleasures of Music are composed, as has already been observed, partly of the original, corporeal Pleasures of Sound, and partly of associated ones. When these Pleasures are arrived at tolerable Perfection, and the several compounding Parts cemented sufficiently by Association, they are transferred back again upon a great Variety of Objects and Ideas, and diffuse Joy, Good-Will, Anger, Compassion, Sorrow, Melancholy, *etc.* upon the various Scenes and Events of Life; and so on reciprocally without perceptible Limits.[12]

It is, therefore, only a prefiguring of Burke's examples of blind poets and mathematicians when Hartley asserts that in this way,

the Ear becomes, like the Eye, a Method of Perception suited to the Wants of spiritual Being. And indeed when we compare the Imperfections of such as have never heard, with those of Persons that have never seen, it appears, that the Ear is of much more Importance to us, considered as spiritual Beings, than the Eye. This is chiefly owing to the great Use and Necessity of Words . . .[13]

In the following analysis of Collins's 'Ode to Evening' we can derive some confidence from the way in which Harris, Hartley, Goldsmith and Burke so easily interpolate ideas about music into their discussions of language and poetry.

Changing ideas of expression: Charles Avison

Discussions of music in England in the mid-eighteenth century undermine the idea of imitation.[14] By doing so they turn against the Baroque aesthetic which had described music as the 'Art of

Painting the Passions'.[15] The analogy with painting had been used in order to ensure that Aristotle's dictum about music being an imitation of the internal could be adapted to a Cartesian psychology which defines the internal as a set of discrete and constitutive passions. The aesthetic of the *Affektenlehre*, 'according to which music can portray passions, affections or sentiments', appears to be an 'essentially Cartesian theory . . . based upon the assumption that emotions are definite in character, concrete in form, and separable in the mind and in fact'.[16] Manfred Bukofzer and Bertrand Bronson have described how this rationalist aesthetic seeks the objectification of the emotional life. Bronson indeed finds the pictorial analogy irresistible: 'it is a major effort' of this music, he writes, 'to get the passions out where men can look at them'.[17] Consequently, the literary parallels for this procedure are personification, emblems, and a publicly acknowledged iconography: that is, the elements of literature which most readily lend themselves to a doctrine of *ut pictura poesis*.

The other analogy for music within this aesthetic is that of rhetoric, where rhetoric is considered as a flamboyant kind of oratorical speech. The musical sounds are designed to have specific effects upon the imagination and feelings. A recent study of Bernard Lamy (1640–1715), whose *L'Art de Parler* (1675) includes one of the chief formulations of this aesthetic of music, concludes that he 'provides a rational approach of bringing musical techniques within the mechanistic principles of the new science'.[18] Music can then acquire the directive force and specific range celebrated in Dryden's *Alexander's Feast* (1697), which is the fullest statement in England of this Baroque aesthetic. Discussing Handel's setting for this ode, Bernard Bronson writes:

The prevailing tonality is D major, and the spirit of it, over all, is one of confidence and power and thrust. The choice of key is of course by no means haphazard. This particular tonality is selected not because Handel has thought of some musical themes that promise to lie comfortably in the key of D major, but because the dominant mood of Dryden's Ode *means* D major.[19]

To propose that there is an established code of this kind is also to propose that it is elaborate, learned and always potentially complex. It presupposes a recognition of its system and a public aware of its signification. This model of intelligibility in music is quite separate from the associationist and indeterminate models of interpretation, based as they are on a psychology of experience.

The elaborate Baroque inheritance is, perhaps for the first time, radically undermined by Addison's opinions about music in *The Spectator* No. 29:

A man of an ordinary Ear is a Judge whether a Passion is express'd in proper Sounds, and whether the Melody of those Sounds be more or less pleasing.[20]

This is a statement of great importance, for it cancels at one democratic stroke the systematic rhetoric of the Baroque, and it cancels also the whole conception of musical allegory which culminates in J. S. Bach. Manfred Bukofzer finds

five different allegories simultaneously appearing in a single cantata by Bach not one of which would be perceptible to the untutored listener at a performance.[21]

Addison's common man at the concert room or pleasure garden would be deaf to these representational complexities and to their intellectual precision.

Lamy, Marpurg, Scheibe and Mattheson, in the spirit of Cartesian psychology which proposes that music by the 'use of figures' imitates distinct emotions, conclude that music is an expression of passion. *Expression* in this sense is the consequence of a systematic *imitation* of specific internal states of feeling. It is clear that these two terms no longer support each other in so mutual a way when, in 1766, John Gregory comments that 'the most common blunder in composers, who aim at expression, is their mistaking imitation for it'. For Gregory, a friend of Beattie and Akenside, and professor of medicine at Edinburgh, as well as being an enthusiast for that city's musical life, this comment is part of his confused and divided loyalties for, on the one hand, the Handelian tradition, and on the other, the new Mannheim style.[22]

By opposing expression to imitation Gregory points us toward the fact that throughout the first half of the eighteenth century there is a massive and subtly realised change in the meaning of the word 'expression'. Among all his eclectic and confused materials (the primitivism of John 'Estimate' Brown, of Rousseau and of Hugh Blair on the simplicity of an original melodic music lies side by side with appreciations of 'a Complex Concerto' and of 'the contrivance and ingenuity of the composer') Gregory discovers only two writers whom he can confidently support: James Harris and Charles Avison.[23] The word 'expression' formally enters theories of music in Britain in 1752 with Charles Avison's *Essay on Musical Expression*. Although himself a conservative composer Avison follows the argument of James Harris and dismisses ideas of musical imitation.

Immediately he finds himself at the centre of controversy. It is here that critical interest lay. John Jortin, in a *Letter* published with Avison's *Essay*, argues that modern musical language is 'the most true and exact and liable to the fewest defects, obscurities and ambiguities' of all languages.[24] And William Hayes pinpoints the dispute by attacking Avison on the issue that 'without *Imitation* there cannot possibly be any such Thing as true musical Expression'.[25] It has been suggested that these contradictions are resolved by Thomas Twining when, in 1789, he concludes that those who 'speak of Music as imitation . . . appear to have solely, or chiefly, in view, its power over the *affections*. By *imitation* they mean, in short, what *we* commonly distinguish from imitation, and oppose to it, under the general term of *expression*.'[26] It has been acknowledged that this change in terminology reflects a shift in aesthetic theory, but it has not been made clear that there is a mid-eighteenth-century idea of music which is quite distinct from that of the Baroque *Affektenlehre*.[27]

The main differences between the mid-eighteenth-century view and the previous Baroque terminology arise from changes in the apparent specificity of the passions and the moods, and therefore changes in the kind of response appropriate when we listen to music. One no longer finds discussions about specific rhetorical effects and precise allegorical representations. Avison does indeed look for the meaning of music in an audience's responses to it, but the relationship between the listener and the music is now a delicate and relatively vague one. Avison gives as his authority for writing the *Essay* 'a Taste cultivated by frequent hearing of Music'. He speaks of the pleasure of music as one which derives from a 'much more refined Nature than the external senses', and concludes that 'The Energy and Grace of *Musical Expression* is of too delicate a Nature to be fixed by Word's because the peculiar joys of music are 'Beyond the Power of Words to express'.[28]

Avison allows something to previous theories of music insofar as he gives space to the earlier Baroque idea of an exact musical vocabulary. But he has no time for the related idea that music dominates its audience, and the very innovation of Avison's idiom which *contrasts* music with language admits that music is not reducible to systems of rhetoric and allegory. The removal of a controlling principle of imitation gives a radical importance to Avison's decision about the relative value of instrumental as opposed to vocal music. Others, including James Harris, had supported a view that the job of music was to support and to 'aggravate' the words of a piece. According to a contributor to *The Spectator* it was considered necessary that music have a specific 'Passion or Sentiment to express, or else . . . afford an Entertainment very little above the Rattles of Children'.[29] When Charles Avison comes to reply to William Hayes he refuses this literal-minded notion of expression and declares that he has 'always thought, that the Passions might be very powerfully expressed, as well by Instrumental Music, as by Vocal'.[30] Any questions about the needs of signification could, therefore, be a much less determinate affair.

William Collins's 'The Passions'

Again it seems to be Joseph Addison who looks forward to the terms this discussion exploits. Sounds, he wrote in 1712,

have no Ideas annexed to them . . . Yet it is certain, there may be, confused, imperfect Notions of this Nature raised in the Imagination by an Artificial Composition of Notes . . . melancholy Scenes . . . pleasing Dreams of Groves and Elysiums.[31]

A strong instance of the contrast between a set of systematic principles and a less determinate aesthetic appears at the mid-eighteenth century in William Collins's ode, 'The Passions'. We can contrast this poem with that upon which Collins most depends, John Dryden's *Alexander's Feast*. Collins's poem is placed at the end of his *Odes on Several Descriptive and Allegoric Subjects*, and its first and final stanzas regret the loss of poetic inspiration in contemporary society by analogy with the loss of an original art of music. This figure of a primitive, simple, enchanting, but now quite lost art of music is used also by James Thomson, by the young William Blake and by Thomas Gray in order to describe the contemporary fate of poetry. The idealisation of a lost art of music ought not to conceal the fact that, although the poets speak of music as a primitive and lost art, they do so largely in terms of a *contemporary* aesthetic. Collins's 'The Passions' superimposes a cultural nostalgia, which is about the fate of poetry in an age of one-dimensional reason, upon a contemporary idea of music. This idea of music is used to indicate a way in which poetry can recover its lost energies and powers. Exactly the same analogy between music and poetry is used in Gray's thematically similar poem, 'The Progress of Poesy'. The contemporary idea of music is treated especially in the middle stanzas, lines 17–94, of Collins's poem. It is also these stanzas which recall and revise Dryden's *Alexander's Feast*.

The most important difference between these two poems is that whereas *Alexander's Feast* describes the domination of the listener (Alexander) by the musician (Timotheus), in Collins's 'The Passions' there is no audience. There are only solo players, the passions themselves, each of which listens to its own music. Each one by an 'expressive impulse' plays and listens to its individual and changeable music as if it were a kind of self-consciousness. In Dryden's poem a single musician ranges disinterestedly through a set of specific emotions which impel Alexander into a set of specific actions. The force of Timotheus's music and (in a slightly different sense) of Dryden's ode is the gathering of detail into climactic strokes of Joy, Pity, Love and Revenge. Saint Cecilia's music is its spiritual equivalent: in terms of specific power hers is equal to his.

> He raised a Mortal to the Skies;
> She drew an Angel down.[32]

The movement of Collins's poem is less theatrical. There is a more various range of emotions presented and Collins displays each of them with far less specificity than does Dryden. Collins's method is generally diffusive, and his poem is designed to draw in, rather than to strike out at, the reader.

The passions represented in Collins's poem are more various both in number and in complexity. Fear, Anger, Despair, Hope, Revenge, Pity, Jealousy, Melancholy, Cheerfulness and Joy (with the addition of others mentioned incidentally) indicate by mere numbers a diffusion of impetus. Also Hope, Melancholy and Joy are made especially various in themselves:

> But Thou, O *Hope*, with Eyes so fair,
> What was thy delightful Measure?

Still it whisper'd promis'd Pleasure,
   And bade the lovely Scenes at distance hail!
Still would Her Touch the Strain prolong,
   And from the Rocks, the Woods, the Vale,
She call'd on Echo still thro' all the Song;
   And, where Her Sweetest Theme She chose,
   A soft responsive Voice was heard at ev'ry Close,
And *Hope* enchanted smil'd, and wav'd Her golden Hair. . . . .

With eyes up-rais'd, as one inspir'd,
Pale *Melancholy* sat retir'd,
And from her wild sequester'd Seat,
In Notes by Distance made more sweet,
Pour'd thro' the mellow *Horn* her pensive Soul:
   And dashing soft from Rocks around,
   Bubbling runnels join'd the Sound;
Thro' Glades and Glooms the mingled Measure stole,
Or o'er some haunted Stream with fond Delay,
   Round an holy Calm diffusing,
   Love of Peace and lonely Musing,
   In hollow Murmurs died away. . . . .

Last came *Joy's* Ecstatic Trial,
He with viny Crown advancing,
   First to the lively Pipe his Hand address'd,
But soon he saw the brisk awak'ning Viol,
   Whose sweet entrancing Voice he lov'd the best.
   They would have thought who heard the Strain,
   They saw in Tempe's Vale her native Maids,
   Amidst the festal sounding Shades,
To some unwearied Minstrel dancing,
   While as his flying Fingers kiss'd the Strings,
   LOVE fram'd with *Mirth*, a gay fantastic Round,
   Loose were Her Tresses seen, her Zone unbound,
   And HE amidst his frolic Play,
   As if he would the charming Air repay,
   Shook thousand Odours from his dewy Wings.[33]

Collins is here elaborating upon Addison's principle, which presents music as suggestive of 'confused, imperfect notions'.[34] Also an assortment of contemporary writers on music, such as John Lampe (1740) and William Turner (*c.* 1750), comment on how music ought to be judged by its variegated 'Delicacy in the *Expression*'. The 'nerves' and 'delicate feelings' are again the interest of a commentator in the *Critical Review* (1760), and after Avison's influence is widely diffused Benjamin Stillingfleet (1771) parallels the movements of music with the 'inflections of feeling'.[35]

These terms are in strong opposition to what we find in Shenstone's *Elegies* which were published later than Collins's odes. Elegy VI is 'To a lady on the language of birds', and the poem determines that the birds have something to say and that what they say can be stated intelligibly in the full signs of words: ''tis no Italian song / No senseless ditty'. Consequently the bird is given by Shenstone a formal speech and acts as the mouthpiece for an equation of music with the 'voice of virtue and of love'.[36] This is a sort of parody of the Baroque aesthetic insofar as it follows its principle of comparing music with speech, but robs the aesthetic of all its energy and complexity. Shenstone's poem also contrasts with the principles of Collins's 'The Passions'. Collins is not persuaded that there is any settled public signification for Joy, Melancholy or Hope. The ode elaborates a range of signification through delicate and varied images of music and sound, through complex and vague personification, and through the rapidity and assonantal density of the verse.

One might put it another way and say that with Collins the abstract words, Hope and Joy (the compounded abstracts to which in Burke's *Enquiry* no ideas are fixed), elaborate a pattern of associations. Musical expression is the model of that associative pattern: 'They would have thought, who heard . . .' It is this trope and its 'mingled Measure' that Coleridge seizes upon for 'Kubla Khan'. The signification is completed only in the response of the listener or reader. Neither music nor the poem is thought to be self-contained.

David Hume and Daniel Webb on impressions

Daniel Webb's *Observations on the Correspondence between Poetry and Music* (1769) describes music as 'an art of impression' and argues that 'pleasure . . . springs from a succession of impressions'.[37] According to Webb the influence of music on the passions does not 'arise from associating certain ideas with certain sounds'. He dismisses the 'forced imitations' of Handel and Purcell. Musical sounds 'excite similar vibrations' to those of certain feelings, but Webb does not allow that this amounts to an association of *ideas*. The music does not amount to anything so specific and complete: however transported we are when listening to music, argues Webb, 'In these moments, it must be confessed, we have no determinate idea of any agreement or imitation; and the reason of this is, that we have no fixed idea of the passion to which this agreement is to be referred.'[38] The most important additional term used by Webb is that of *impression*, which complements the terms of *sound* and *idea* used by Harris, Burke and Avison. The term *impression* is from now on used widely in constructing an aesthetic for music. Its source is Books 1 and 2 of David Hume's *A Treatise of Human Nature*, 'Of the Understanding' and 'Of the Passions', which were published in 1739 four or five years before Collins began composing his odes.

For our purpose it is in two especially important ways that Hume offers a different epistemology to that of John Locke. For Locke the association of ideas is a type of unreasonableness. Because associations are grounded in chance or in custom they cannot approach the 'Office and Excellency of our reason' which traces 'a natural Correspondence and Connection' of one idea with another.[39] The certainty of reason is assured by, and indeed it depends upon, the clarity and distinctness of ideas. This distinctness and clarity is a consequence of Locke's presumption about the adequate connection between sensations and ideas.

That connection is presumed to be immediate. When the mind looks in upon itself it finds that 'the Perception, which actually accompanies and is annexed to any impression on the Body, made by an external Object, being distinct from all other Modifications of *thinking*, furnishes the mind with a distinct *Idea* which we call *Sensation*; which is, as it were, the actual entrance of any *Idea* into the Understanding by the Senses'.[40] These sensations/ideas may be thought about in many ways, ranging from recollection to ecstasy, but neither they nor their 'natural connections' can be essentially modified.

It is Hume's assertion, at the very outset of his *Treatise*, that he will 'restore the word, idea, to its original sense, from which Mr *Locke* had perverted it, in making it stand for all our perceptions'.[41] Therefore, between sensations and ideas he constitutes a new term to describe 'merely the perceptions themselves; for which there is no particular name either in the *English* or any other language, that I know of'. These then are *impressions*. Impressions are immediate and acute. Consequently, what Locke had called ideas appear to lose their clarity and to be no more than 'the faint images of these in thinking and reasoning'. There is an

interaction between impressions and ideas. The force and
vivacity of impressions can direct them towards ideas and, in
their turn, ideas can direct themselves back towards impressions.
Impressions are momentary. Ideas are constant. Nevertheless,
ideas can re-evoke momentary impressions, and, in this fashion,
impressions can be given some persistence within the self. 'All
impressions are internal and perishing existences,' writes
Hume,[42] but the *Treatise* gives them a relative presence.

These impressions are far less stable and far less precise than
ideas, and their instability allows Hume to defend the legitimacy
of the association of ideas. In the first place, 'the imagination is not
restrained to the same order and form with the original impressions'. Given the fact that 'all our ideas are copy'd from our
impressions, and that there are not any two impressions which are
perfectly inseparable', it is therefore a legitimate *'liberty of the
imagination to transpose and change its ideas'*.[43] This associative
principle 'commonly prevails' and this faculty of the imagination
allows individual experience, with its random and momentary
impressions, to appear intelligible. In this way, 'among other
things, languages so nearly correspond to each other'.[44]

This attention to the pre-meaning of impressions and to the
process through which these empty signifiers become intelligible
is important to discussions about music. We find an indication of
how this is so by noticing James Harris's regret that '*Music*, when
alone, can only raise *Affections*, which soon *languish* and *decay*, if
not maintained and fed by the nutritive Images of Poetry.'[45] This
regret allows Harris to propose that instead of the usual situation,
in which music is accompanied by words which immediately
compensate for a lack of signification, the reading of the poet's
verse should be preceded by music.

A Poet, *thus assisted*, finds not an Audience in a Temper, averse to the Genius of
his Poem, or perhaps at best under a cool Indifference; but by the Preludes, the
Symphonies, and *concurrent Operation* of the Music in all its Parts, rouzed into
those very Affections, which he would most desire.[46]

In this situation the audience do not merely 'embrace with
Pleasure the Ideas of the Poet, when exhibited; but, in a manner,
even *anticipate* them in their several Imaginations'.[47] The important recognition here is that of a form of pre-meaning which
interposes between the sensation of the sound and the ideas the
poet imitates. It is this same intermediary form of the signifier that
Hume names 'impressions'.

Daniel Webb adopts Hume's terms and extends his argument, as it can apply to music, beyond the negatively stated aesthetic of Harris and Avison. Webb's definition of the pleasure of music as 'a succession of impressions' allows him to emphasise music as movement and to analyse its 'dramatic spirit'. It is the movement of the music which directs the 'imagination to conceive something more than is executed': this

> motion which just rises above the measure of simplicity, if happily designed, commits as it were to our fancy the completion of the idea and prompts us to the exertion of our finest feelings.[48]

After the imagination has 'hurried through . . . impressions' she 'wonders at the splendor of her own creating': 'It is curious to observe what a chain runs through our feelings.'[49] These possibilities arise in music because it takes time. The mind pursues a pattern which, afterwards, it can re-trace. The arts differ from each other insofar as they represent that pattern as more or less uncertain and indeterminate:

> it is the province of music to catch the movements of passion as they spring from the soul; painting waits until they rise into action, or determine in character; but poetry, as she possesses the advantages of both . . . her imitations embrace at once the movement and the effect.[50]

This aesthetic gives to the primitivist history of the arts its most apt epistemology. Music is related to the earliest passional speech in which 'words followed the motion of . . . sensations'. Painting is related to a later kind of speech in which words are used by 'compact' and 'ill correspond with the vivacity of our sensations'. Given these values and given his entrancement with the processes of music in imagination and feeling, it is not surprising that Webb would like poetry to return to a primitive form of articulation and energy in which music would be its 'elder sister, the tutoress'.[51]

For Webb, therefore, music is a process which continues in a relatively immediate form the internal process of sensibility. It is, as he says, 'a mode of conveying and enforcing sentiment'.[52] The idea, therefore, of poetic imagery, the 'language of passion', can be seen to derive from these correspondences between poetry and music.[53] Webb's definition of poetic imagery is, as we shall soon see become more apparent, extraordinarily close to the statements about imagery declared and practised in the drafts and revisions of William Collins.

> While we are [writes Webb] under the united influence of the natural motion of the passion, and the artificial motion of the verse, we lost sight of the imitation in

the simplicity of the union and the energy of the effect . . . the image must correspond with the motive; consequently it should be bold, concise and decisive that the fancy may not seem to dwell on her own operations.[54]

This fine and subtle argument replaces the idea of a relationship between images and imitation with the idea of a relationship, both mediated and complex, between the play of the signifier and its effects upon a reader: 'we lose sight of the imitation'. As in Collins's 'The Passions' the mode of music/language derives from an 'expressive impulse', in Webb's phrase from 'motive'. This mode of writing is characterised by a poetry of motion, energy and flexibility. It is quite opposed to the pictorialist ideals of 'the reduction of motion to stasis' and of 'publicly accepted iconic detail' which Hagstrum proposes. James Harris makes this contrast in the treatise to which we will see William Collins so indebted. 'Every Art,' writes Harris in words filched from Aristotle, 'will be accomplished and ended in a WORK or ENERGY': the 'Perfection of Statuary' typifies art as a work; the 'Perfection of a Musician (which is only known, while he continues playing)' typifies art as an energy.[55] This instability of music as event, as momentary occasion, as something already vanishing, the meaning of which is too hesitant for words or for images or for ideas, is the notion of music which William Collins assumes in his desire for a poetic mode of language which can indicate a crisis of instability and of hesitation: the moment of Evening.

Poetry and music: the 'Ode to Evening'

Pictorialists have been quick to notice Collins's *Verses . . . to Sir Thomas Hanmer*, in which the poet consistently maintains the analogy between painting and poetry and in which there are many echoes of comparable Augustan poems addressed to famous painters, such as Dryden's 'To Sir Godfrey Kneller' and Pope's 'Epistle to Mr. Jervas'.[56] Collins's poem was written and published in 1743. However, between 1744 and the publication of the *Odes* in 1746, Collins revised these assumptions. The drafts and fragments of Collins's work during this period were found among the Warton papers some thirty years ago and were first published in 1956. This work-in-progress constitutes a testing-ground for conventional ideas about language and their apparent inadequacy to Collins's new poetic.

The 'Ode to Evening' derives from one of these fragments in particular: 'Ye genii who, in secret state'. In these lines we see Collins explicitly dismiss the pictorialist analogy from the area of poetics in which it had most strongly established itself, the area of landscape description. Collins adopts a sense of landscape which requires him to find an alternative to the pictorialist mode of language. The fragment's first twenty-four lines are confident, establishing a contrast between urban society and the retirement of the pastoral poet. It is after these lines, in the description of the rural pastoral scene, that the fragment loses its confidence and remains incomplete:

Some times, when Morning o'er [the] Plain
    Her radiant Mantle throws
I'll mark the Clouds where sweet Lorrain
    His orient Colours chose

Or when the Sun to Noon tide climbs
    I'll hide me from his view
By such green Plats and chearfull Limes
    As   Rysdael drew

Then on some Heath, all wild and bare
    With more delight I'll stand
Than He who sees with wond'ring air
    The Works of Rosa's hand:

There where some Rocks deep Cavern gapes
    Or in some tawny dell
I'll seem to see the Wizzard Shapes
    That from his Pencill fell

But when Soft Evning o'er the Plain
    Her gleamy Mantle throws
I'll mark the Clouds whence sweet Lorraine
    His   Colours chose

Or from the Vale I'll lift my sight
    To some
Where e'er the Sun withdraws his light
    The dying Lustre falls

Such   will I keep
    Till
The modest Moon again shall Peep
    Above some Eastern Hill

All Tints that ever Picture us'd
    Are lifeless, dull and mean
To paint her dewy Light diffus'd

What Art can paint the modest ray
  So sober, chaste and cool
As round yon Cliffs it seems to play
  Or skirts yon glimmering Pool?

The tender gleam her Orb affords
  No Poet can declare
Altho' he chuse the softest words
  That e'er were sigh'd in air.[57]

These stanzas are of extraordinary importance not only to the
'Ode to Evening' but also to eighteenth-century poetics in
general. For we shall see from similar material in other poets that
Collins's anxiety is typical of an anxiety about language that can
be found also elsewhere during this period. The painters, Claude
Gelée (Lorrain), Jacob van Ruisdael and Salvator Rosa, along with
Nicolas Poussin, are the seventeenth-century painters of landscape whose influence dominates the categories of taste and
aesthetics in England after James Thomson's *The Seasons*. Collins
finds them inadequate to his purpose not in the sense that he
might favour some other pictorial style over those which these
painters represent; his critique in this fragment extends to all
painters and to all painting. Indeed it extends to all arts that
'paint', that is to all arts which take their principles from
pictorialism. Perhaps the most effective dismissal of the pictorial
occurs in the structure of the last line of the fragment. The 'play'
of evening light provokes a use of language which is in this line
densely assonantal: the threefold repetition of a single sound
('That *e'er were* sigh'd in *air*') precludes the signifier from all
conventions of representation. It would appear that by this use of
echolalia Collins, no less than James Thomson and Samuel Taylor
Coleridge in their poems on the Aeolian harp, than Coleridge
again in 'Kubla Khan', and than John Keats in stanza 6 of the
Nightingale ode, is elaborating on a pun by which 'air' alludes
also to melody.[58] Both in practice and in theme, therefore,
Collins's fragmentary lines about evening direct us away from the
failure of painting to the possibilities of music.

Two aspects of language are the focus of Collins's distrust.
First, there is the problem of words-as-pictures insofar as this idea
of language is defeated by the instability, uncertainty and
temporality of dusk. Second, there is a related problem of words-
as-abstractions which could establish the moment of dusk in

terms of such qualities as sobriety, gentleness and chastity. The end of the fragment reduces both these descriptive-and-allegoric elements of language to a play upon the sound and music, the acoustic materials, of words. This is the connective link between the fragment and the 'Ode to Evening'. It is in this idiom of self-reference that the 'Ode to Evening' begins:

> If aught of Oaten Stop, or Pastoral Song,
> May hope, chaste *Eve*, to soothe thy modest Ear,
> Like thy own solemn Springs,
> They Springs, and dying Gales . . . .
>
> Now Air is hush'd . . .[59]

The poem presents itself as a reciprocation of sounds. Painting and the pictorial are not mentioned. One of the effects of Collins's new idiom is to produce an idea of the poem as an occasion or event in which poet and evening play some kind of duet. The puns on music now become persistent:

> Now teach me, *Maid* compos'd,
> To breathe some soften'd Strain,
> Whose Numbers stealing thro' thy darkening Vale,
> May not unseemly with its Stillness suit,[60]

In place of a fiction that the poet represents in verse the clouds which Claude Lorrain had represented on canvas, the poem gives us the fiction that the poet's words blend and disappear into the sounds, the atmosphere, the 'air' of evening. The analogy of the visual, with its guarantee of distance, is replaced by that of the ear.

Collins's anxiety about interrupting whatever is described, by the act of writing about it, is an anxiety shared by others. James Thomson had declared in *The Seasons* that there are 'Hues on hues Expression cannot paint, / The Breath of Nature and her endless Bloom'. Both poets look forward to Wordsworth's phrase about an 'eye-music of slow-waving boughs'. Also Mark Akenside puzzles out the difficulty of replacing the analogy of seeing with that of hearing by exploiting a mythical machine which could, harmlessly, do the job for him:

> As Memnon's marble harp, renown'd of old
> By fabling Nilus, to the quivering touch
> Of Titan's ray, with each repulsive string
> Consenting, sounded thro' the warbling air
> Unbidden strains; ev'n so did nature's hand

> To certain species of external things,
> Attune the finer organs of the mind:
> So the glad impulse of congenial pow'rs,
> Or of sweet sound, or fair-proportion'd form,
> The grace of motion, or the bloom of light,
> Thrills thro' imagination's tender frame,
> From nerve to nerve: all naked and alive
> They catch the spreading rays: till now the soul
> At length discloses every tuneful spring,
> To that harmonious movement from without
> Responsive. Then the inexpressive strain
> Diffuses its enchantment: fancy dreams[61]

The mechanism of this machine elaborates upon Addison's comments about how we respond to music: 'fancy dreams'. Also Akenside's version of the machine appropriates it for the mid-century aesthetic of music and poetry. Akenside published these lines in the first edition of *The Pleasures of Imagination* in 1744. Not only do they look back to James Thomson's anxiety about language and natural description, but they look also forward to Collins's writings between 1744 and 1746. It is not surprising, perhaps, that they anticipate the introduction into England of a machine which also elaborates on Memnon's harp: Père Louis Castel's 'Colour Organ'.

This was a curious and popular contraption which was exhibited in France in 1735 and in London in 1757. Claims on its behalf included how it allowed the deaf to 'see the music of the ears' and the blind to 'hear the music of the eyes'. Like Memnon's harp this machine externalises a post-Newtonian version of compatible ratios of pleasure between the different senses. Of course it could also serve the pleasure of those who can both see and hear: for they can now 'enjoy music and colors better by enjoying them both at the same time'.[62] A question immediately presents itself: given the anticipations of Collins and Akenside, which sense would be chosen to aspire to the condition of the other? With Memnon's harp and in the fragmentary draft for the 'Ode to Evening' the eye is replaced by the uncertainties of the ear. But with Castel's machine things could work either way, and commentators could take their choice.

Count Algarotti, a writer on opera and the reform of opera, enthusiastically welcomed the machine, because at last the 'transient pleasures of the ear will be fixed in the eye'. Algarotti elsewhere shows in his comments on the Pindaric odes of Thomas Gray that his sole criterion of good poetry is pictorial vividness.[63] In contrast with him we can give the example of Christopher Smart. *Jubilate Agno* states even more strongly the revisionary terms of Collins. Smart's characteristic interest in all the extravagances of his day appears to have made him familiar with the publication – *An Explanation of the Ocular Harpsichord Upon Shew to the Public* (1757), with a postscript by Robert Smith (1762) – which coincided with the exhibitions of Castel's machine. Smart elaborates on how

> . . . . the warp and woof of flowers are
>   worked by perpetual moving spirits.
> For flowers are good for both the living
>   and the dead.
> For there is a language of flowers.
> For there is a sound reasoning upon all flowers.
> For elegant phrases are nothing but flowers.
> For flowers are peculiarly the poetry of Christ . . . .
>
> For flowers are musical in ocular harmony.[64]

Smart's lines are, in a strong sense, a parody of Robert Smith's concept of seeing and hearing. Smith (1689–1768), a teacher of mathematics and professor of astronomy at Cambridge, was best known for his work on *Opticks* (1738) and *Harmonics* (1749). These books respond to Newton's speculation that,

the seven Colours, red, orange, yellow, green, blue, indigo, violet, in order . . . are to one another as the Cube Roots of the Squares of the eight lengths of a Chord, which sound the Notes in an eighth, *sol, la, fa, sol, la, mi, fa, sol.*

Also in his Fourteenth Query Newton raises the possibility that the 'Vibrations propagated through the Fibres of the optick Nerves' might correspond to the 'Vibrations of the Air'.[65] In a similar vein John Locke tells the story of a man born blind who 'saw' the colour red by comparing it with the sound of a trumpet.[66] In this same tradition of doubtful illuminations Robert Smith writes about the ocular harpsichord or 'colour organ'. Also he attempts to construct musical instruments of mathematical precision (referred to by Thomas Twining as 'perfect monsters'), and in his *Harmonics* Smith is happy to risk the speculation that 'there is reason to suspect that the *Theory of vibrations* here given will not prove useless in promoting the philosophy of other things besides musical sounds'.[67]

Smart's disagreement is not with Newton's and Smith's principle of analogy but with their assumption about what constitutes the visible world. Smart's aesthetic presupposes a plenitude and a set of transformations in nature which is far more extensive and varied than what is available in a discrete prismatic sequence:

> For Newton's notion of colours is
>   *alogos* unphilosophical.
> For the colours are spiritual.
> For WHITE is the first and the best.
> For there are many intermediate colours.
>   before you come to SILVER
> For the next colour is a lively GREY . . . .
>
> For Red is of sundry sorts till it
> deepens to BLACK
> For black blooms and it is PURPLE.
> For purple works off to BROWN which is
> of ten thousand acceptable shades.
> For the next is PALE God be gracious to William Whitehead.
> For pale works out to White again.[68]

Smart locates his disagreement especially in those colours which, while they do not appear in the Newtonian spectrum, do constitute (white, silver, grey and pale) the 'dewy light' which challenges Collins. The interest in the uncertainty of half-light, of evening, is not limited to these two poets. Nor are they unusual in relating it to music. An anonymous 'Ode to Aeolus's Harp' associates the process of that instrument and of its 'silversounds' with a moment 'at eve' when fancy sees in the wind

> silken pinions stream,
> While on the quiv'ring trees soft breezes sigh,
> And through the leaves disclose the moon's pale beam.[69]

That figure of breezes/leaves/beam naturalises the figure of Memnon's harp and the ocular harpsichord. Also Coleridge's lines on the Aeolian harp, which analyse these figures, have their setting at twilight under the 'star of eve'.[70]

The uncertainty of light can be a figure which calls into question the stability of seeing. This, in turn, calls into question the stability of ideas and words. Smart extends his critique of the *Opticks* to a parody of a theory of taxonomy ('there is a language of flowers') and also of a theory of colour-notation ('Brown which is of ten thousand acceptable shades'). As far as this goes, it is not outside a convention in contemporary scientific discussion. A certain Dr William Porterfield, in *A Treatise on the Eye, the Manner and the Phaenomena of Vision* (1759), supports the accepted notion that 'Colours are sensations produced in our Mind . . . the modifications of the Mind itself.' Further, he notices that these modifications are many and varied to the extent that they exceed language:

> The Reason why Colours, and our other Sensations, cannot be explained by Words, is because Words are only arbitrary Signs of Ideas already perceived.[71]

Jubilate Agno experiments with this problem. It is accurate of Geoffrey Hartman to argue that 'In Smart the very *medium* of representation – visionary language itself – has become questionable',[72] but it is also an insufficient account of Smart's project. For Smart proceeds beyond *Jubilate Agno* to his *Hymns and Spiritual Songs*, in which any mode of representation and of vision is replaced by something else.

> Pull up the bell-flow'r of the spring,
> And let the budding greenwood ring
>   With many a chearful song;
> All blessing on the human race,
> From CHRIST, evangelist of grace,
>   To whom these strains belong.
>
> To whom belong the tribe that vie
> In what is musick to the eye,
>   Whose voice is 'stoop to pray' –
> While many colour'd tints attire
> His fav'rites, like the golden wire,
>   The beams on wind flow'rs play.[73]

There is an extraordinary mode of language at work in these lines, which establishes and subverts categories in a play of the signifier with turns and returns upon puns and upon asyntactic parallels. This mode of poetry depends upon Smart's rejection of the pictorial in *Jubilate Agno*:

> For Painting is a species of idolatry,
>   tho' not so gross as statuary.
> For it is not good to look with [y]earning
>   upon any dead work.
> For by so doing something is lost in the
>   spirit and given from life to death.[74]

The rejection of pictorialism from Collins to Smart, therefore, works through the contrast between art as a work and art as an energy. Harris, and the poets after him, consider music alone to be an 'energy'. According to this figure they present the fiction that their poem, by its materials of breath and sound, participates in the nature it celebrates. The poem does not establish a distance between who sees and what is seen. Instead the poem presents the fiction that it has itself a part to play among the sounds and silences of half-light.

This fiction collapses a whole convention of intelligibility. That convention is one which specifies a certain distance between what is imitated and the medium of imitation. Upon that distance depends meaning, representation, clarity. A mirror or a *camera obscura* requires such a distance. So also does the eye. These are the very figures of intelligibility after John Locke. In *The Light of Nature Pursued* (1768) Abraham Tucker writes:

Idea is the same with respect to things in general as image with respect to objects of vision . . . After all that has been said, I think we may look upon the passivity of the understanding as fully established.[75]

The act of seeing is the central analogy for the Lockean operations of ideas and of words. The act of hearing is therefore peripheral but also subversive to this passive way of knowing.

To quote Abraham Tucker again is to notice how the act of hearing, by eliminating the distance between subject and object, endangers intelligibility:

It is remarkable that although both visible and sonorous bodies act equally by mediums, one of light and the other of air, vibrating upon our organs, yet in the former case we reckon the body the object, but in the latter the sound of the air. I suppose because we can more readily and frequently distinguish the place, figure, and other qualities, of bodies we see than of those affecting our other senses.[76]

The difference between seeing and hearing, whereby one does and the other does not designate a co-ordinating perspective and objectivity, affects the status of the subject. For the perceiving subject who *sees* is situated and placed within a set of clarities and distinctions, but the perceiving subject who *hears* is displaced within a set of obscurities. This point is made with reference to sight alone by Richard Price, in his *Review of the Principal Questions and Difficulties in Morals* (1758):

As bodily sight discovers to us *visible* objects; so does the understanding (the eye of the mind, and infinitely more penetrating) discover to us intelligible objects.[77]

This analogy between intelligibility and the sense of sight is confirmed later in the century by Joseph Priestley and Erasmus Darwin. It is, as we will notice later, resisted by Dugald Stewart and (largely in Stewart's terms) by Coleridge.[78]

The necessity of distance for the intelligible is most fully stated in the 1760s by John Gregory, in his *A Comparative View of the State and Faculties of Man with those of the Animal World* (1766). Gregory praises James Thomson and derides Edward Young. Young's *Night Thoughts* are obscure, dark and offensive, whereas 'Thomson, in that beautiful descriptive poem, the Seasons, pleases by the justness of his painting'. Gregory appears not to know of Collins's verse, but his judgement of it might be guessed from the following:

Whatsoever is the object of Imagination and Taste can only be seen to advantage at a certain distance, and in a particular light. If brought too near the eye, the beauty which charmed before, may appear faded, and often distorted. It is therefore the business of judgment to ascertain this point of view, to exhibit the object to the Mind in that position which gives it most pleasure, and to prevent the Mind viewing it in any other. This is generally very much in our own power.[79]

This convention, both preventive and repressive, of visuality, distance and intelligibility is broken by Collins's 'Ode to Evening'. It is broken by his strategy of replacing the figure of the poet as painter with that of the poet as musician: by doing this Collins cancels the distance between the perceiving subject and the objects he describes.

> If ought of Oaten Stop, or Pastoral Song,
> May hope, chaste *Eve*, to soothe thy modest Ear,
>   Like thy own solemn Springs,
>   Thy Springs, and dying Gales,
> O *Nymph* reserv'd, while now the bright-hair'd Sun
> Sits in yon western Tent, whose cloudy Skirts,
>   With Brede ethereal wove,
>   O'erhang his wavy Bed:
> Now Air is hush'd, save where the weak-ey'd Bat,
> With short shrill Shriek flits by on leathern Wing,
>   Or where the Beetle winds
>   His small but sullen Horn,
> As oft he rises 'midst the twilight Path,
> Against the Pilgrim born in heedless Hum:
>   Now teach me, *Maid* compos'd,
>   To breathe some soften'd Strain,

> Whose Numbers stealing thro' thy darkening Vale
> May not unseemly with its Stillness suit,

The poem subsequently follows a wholly temporal sequence: 'For when . . . But then . . . While . . . While . . . While . . .' And it concludes,

> So long, sure-found beneath the Sylvan Shed,
> Shall *Fancy, Friendship, Science*, rose-lip'd *Health*,
> Thy gentlest Influence own,
> And hymn thy fav'rite Name!

The landscape of the poem is, therefore, the landscape of a moment and of an uncertainty of presence. The poem's structure includes both the temporal accretions and the evanescence of what it describes. Moreover, in the section of the poem (lines 21–40), in which the poet is represented not as a singer but as an observer of a Thomsonian/Salvator Rosa landscape, Collins again refuses the stasis of the pictorial. The '*last* cool gleam' of reflected light; the presence of the perceiving subject reducing scene to contingency; the hearing of the 'simple bell'; perhaps most important, the revisions of 1748 which diffuse the single image of the ruin into a number of manifestations without perspective and each one less substantial than another; all these are features that mark time's changefulness and also the participation of the poem in that moment which constitutes it.

The poem writes itself over in the conventional poetic figures for music. These are generally Spenserian and Miltonic as is usual with all of Collins's figures: the 'oaten stop' being the archaic pipe, and the 'softened strain' its melody. Within itself the poem is presented as a piece of music. It is in the context of that fiction that it makes its 'descriptive' statements. There has been, from Alan D. McKillop to Geoffrey Hartman, a consensus among readers of the poem that these 'descriptions' are entirely elusive and uncertain.[80] Indeed the poem 'concludes' with the refusal of its main statement: Evening's precise *name*. This refusal of the name is the empty and enigmatic sign around which the poem perpetually and irresolutely revolves. It is in its own terms a 'hymn', which is the very type of both the recurrent and the tentative.

The poem refuses determinate finality in its mode of imagery, in its syntax and in its withholding the favourite name of Eve. It is worth recalling Edmund Blunden's reading of the poem which finds that, successively, evening is 'a country-girl, a Fairy Queen, a priestess, a goddess, a ghost in the sky'. McKillop makes the sensitive point that more accurately 'these roles can be read into the poem'.[81] Evening is characterised by both physical/descriptive and abstract/allegoric elements. The physical elements, as we have seen, are diffused in an uncertain, extensive and temporal variety, in a landscape without perspective, in a context always densely 'literary' and allusive. The abstract elements also constitute a further (and, it would appear, deliberate) break with the pictorial. In this instance the break is with the pictorial convention of personification. For this purpose Collins uses specifically Milton and, incongruously, James Harris.

The 'Ode to Evening' precisely recalls Milton's description of Eve:

> Grace was in all her Steps, Heav'n in her Eye,
> In every Gesture Dignity and Love;

Collins's memory of these lines would have been renewed by their appearance in James Harris's *Three Treatises* which Collins was reading during the writing of the drafts and revisions of the 'Ode to Evening'. Harris expresses his doubts about Milton's lines because he finds them inadequately pictorial:

we have an Image *not* of that Eve, which Milton conceived, but of *such* an Eve *only*, as every one, *by his own proper Genius*, is able to represent, from reflecting on those Ideas, which he has annexed to those several *Sounds*. . . when we view Eve as painted by an *able Painter*, we labour under no such Difficulty.[82]

It is apparent that Collins ignores these strictures on non-pictorial personification. Also he draws a more radically anti-mimetic conclusion than does Harris about the relative value of the sister-arts.

Harris had allowed that music derives 'its Efficacy from another source' than imitation. Therefore he had prescinded from a final comparison of the value of the different arts.[83] Collins decisively favours music, however, and he misreads the *Treatises* insofar as he credits Harris, the Salisbury patron of music, with the same opinion. In his 'Lines Addressed to James Harris', written immediately after the publication of the *Treatises*, Collins addresses music in terms not dissimilar to those he uses in his invocation of evening:

> O teach me Thou, if my unpolish'd lays
> Are all too rude to speak thy gentle praise
> O teach me softer sounds of sweeter kind

Then let the Muse and Picture Each contend
This plan her Tale, and that her Colours blend
With me, tho' both their kindred charms combine
No Pow'r can emulate or equal thine! . . . .

O I will listen as thy [Harris's] lips impart
Why all my soul obeys her pow'rful Art
Why at her bidding or by strange surprise
Or wak'd by fond degrees my passions rise
How well-form'd Reed's my sure Attention gain
And what the Lyre's well-measur'd strings contain.[84]

We know that Harris neither attached this relative value to music, nor, beyond agreeing that it is not a mode of imitation, did he actually explain why and how the vagueness of music's effects earns the praises he and Collins give it. Quite simply, Harris could not answer Collins's questions; although he did enough to raise them in the first place. If Harris did not approve of Milton's vague use of words, at least he approved of the vagueness of music. Edmund Burke's approval of the vagueness of words and his emphasis on the general importance of the associative response to the mere *sounds* of language might, if such had been available to him, have helped Collins more. In such a case he might not have needed the analogy with music at all.

In a celebrated and definitive essay Northrop Frye has described the 'Age of Sensibility' as a period in which poets exploit 'unpredictable assonances, alliterations and echolalia'. Frye characterises the poetry of this period as a poetry of process. In that poetic process, he argues, 'there is a primary stage in which words are linked by sound rather than sense'. Frye notices, in particular, the extraordinarily assonantal and alliterative lines with which the 'Ode to Evening' begins.[85] The poetic which underlies these practices is, we have seen, best understood in its exploitation of a notion of the empty sign of music.

The 'Ode to Evening' is, therefore, a decisive instance of the use of ideas of language, music and poetry in the mid-eighteenth century. It is itself more fully understood in that context of thought and it is itself a part of that thought. Avison's discussion of musical expression being too delicate and energetic for words; Akenside's use of the figure of Memnon's harp to represent a transformation from seeing to hearing; Smart's exploitation of the colour organ and of a twilight prism of what Collins calls 'paly' light; the reaction against Gregory's and Tucker's conventional decisions about visual distance and intelligibility; Harris's statement that music does not imitate ideas; Burke's similar insistence that neither do words; Webb's use of 'impressions' in order to indicate the empty sign; all these are either completed or anticipated by the unspoken 'fav'rite Name' of the 'Maid composed'.

2

WILLIAM BLAKE AND WILLIAM COWPER

James Usher: 'the impression of this obscure presence'

the question is no longer concerning the existence of a thing distinct from *Spirit* and *idea*, from perceiving and being perceived; but whether there are not certain Ideas, of I know not what sort, in the mind of God, which are so many marks or notes that direct Him how to produce sensations in our minds in a constant and regular method – much after the same manner as a musician is directed by the notes of music to produce that harmonious strain and composition of sound which is called a tune, though they who hear the music do not perceive the notes, and may be entirely ignorant of them.

The Principles of Human Knowledge, no. 71 (1710)

absolute external entity, is still concealed. For though it be the fiction of our own brain, we have made it inaccessible to our Faculties.

Preface to *Three Dialogues* (1713)

These sentences from George Berkeley are a suitable introduction to the most important ideas about music in the later part of the eighteenth century. It can be argued that the 'immaterialism' of Berkeley has little importance for those philosophers who appear to dominate in Britain during this period – such as Hume, Condillac and Reid. The analogy between a piece of music, which is written with notes or marks but which is heard as a tune, and the absolute ideas, which are written elsewhere and otherwise but appear as sensation to the mind, would be noted more usually for its appearance in a Coleridge poem than for its appearance in philosophical discourse. However, there is a trace of that analogy to be found in writings on the aesthetics of music and also on language and the arts.

Berkeley's figure includes a number of features: first, it notices the discontinuity between the musical notation, on the one hand, and its production and reception, on the other. Second, it notices an ignorance which that discontinuity produces: an ignorance which in no way impairs the enjoyment and understanding of the listener. For subsequent writers it will require no great mental

56

leap to add the suggestion that the enjoyment of listening to music might actually *depend upon* this discontinuity, this incomplete perception, this ignorance which Berkeley emphasises. It can also become apparent that what happens in listening to music, the transformation of incomplete perceptual data into knowledge, may extend also to other areas of human perception and meaning such as, for example, language.

In later chapters we will find such an idea of music applied to the more general study of perception and of language, in the writings of, among others, Lord Monboddo, Dugald Stewart and Samuel Taylor Coleridge. In this chapter we are first of all interested in an earlier and far more obscure writer, James Usher, who develops the idea that music and the pleasure of music depend upon such a discontinuity and ignorance as Berkeley had indicated.

James Usher (1720–72) was, a generation after Berkeley, educated in the city of his birth at Trinity College Dublin. His life was not a conventional one. He became a convert to Catholicism, moved to England and, according to rumour, became a Catholic priest. In London he opened a school with the philologist and acquaintance of Samuel Johnson, John Walker (1732–1807). John Walker's writings on elocution, which include pronouncing dictionaries, his Oxford lectures on the *Elements of Elocution* (1781), and his *The Melody of Speaking Delineated; or, Elocution taught like Music* (1787), place him among minor popular writers on educational topics, such as Thomas Sheridan and Joshua Steele. Coleridge was familiar with Walker's rhyming *Dictionary of the English Language* (1775), and there will be reason later on for us to notice the possibility that Walker's musical notation for poetic metre, with its emphasis on the relative unimportance of the number of syllables in a line, provided Coleridge with a description of his method in writing *Christabel*.[1]

The writings of James Usher have a more intrinsic interest. Usher remains virtually unknown, in spite of the fact that his *Clio, or a Discourse on Taste* (1767) was re-edited a number of times up to its final annotated edition of 1803, again reprinted in 1809. The first edition of the *Discourse*, and especially its second edition 'with large additions' (1769), has been given honourable mention by Samuel H. Monk in his writing on the sublime, but Monk's conclusion is that Usher's *Discourse* is 'unclassifiable' in its time.[2]

Usher's writings are of especial interest because he discusses the issues of taste and of the arts in the context of an explicit interest in contemporary philosophy. Indeed his first and last works, *A New System of Philosophy* (1764) and *An Introduction to the Theory of the Human Mind* (1771), have little direct reference to the arts at all. His purpose in this work is to define some mediation between Cartesian innate ideas and the Lockean philosophy of experience. His solution is to emphasise 'instinctive' capabilities of the mind, capacities or energies which include among their more obvious symptoms laughter, gesture, and eventually all the arts.[3]

An emphasis on instinctive capacities and, indeed, the very title of his final work clearly relate Usher's work to that of Thomas Reid and, in particular, to Reid's *Inquiry into the Human Mind* (1764). However, they are otherwise quite different. Usher has less interest in the basics of 'common sense' philosophy, the immediate knowledge of the material world. The 'common sense' philosophy of Reid and of his followers, George Campbell, Dugald Stewart and Thomas Brown, always offers a revision of empiricism. Usher will have nothing at all to do with it. Although, like the Scottish school, Usher does wish to question the clarity of ideas and their distinctness, and in this way to challenge the passivity of the mind supposed by Locke and the uniformity of thought supposed by Descartes, Usher's conclusions annihilate sensible ideas altogether.

Usher confronts both Locke and Descartes when he seeks to defend the existence of some general principle of taste. At first his argument appears unpromising. He attributes to Locke the contemporary emphasis on association and custom as explanations for the diversity of taste. Usher, instead, decides that these varieties of taste are differentiations of an original divine idea which is still discoverable in man's religious sense. God, he argues, in polytheism and in Christianity 'makes his presence known by an awe that does not attend on sensible objects'.[4] The religious sense can take many different forms, and no set of ideas is innately and uniformly present to the mind. On the other hand, custom is not as diverse as experience, working alone and without the religious sense, might cause it to be. Usher fights on both fronts at once. Therefore, his purpose is to describe that 'instinct' of the mind which responds to something of which it has neither an appropriate idea nor a complete experience.

It is at this point that the manner of Usher's writing becomes extraordinary. He does not separate his secular aesthetic from the religious or sublime. 'Enthusiasm' towards nature and 'religious passion' are not only one 'inseparable appendage of the mind', but as a single instinct of the mind they constitute the essential human activity of desire. For this they have as their object a kind of *negative* of the concept of experience after Locke:

> The object of this religious passion is no idea, it is unknown; therefore the passion itself is obscure, and wants a name; but its effects are very remarkable, for they form the peculiar character of human nature. Curiosity and hope carry with them the plainest symptoms of a passion that wanders and is astray for its object . . . The truth is, the impression of this obscure presence, however it be felt, is beyond the verge of the philosophy of the ideas of sense. The disciples of this philosophy cannot upon their principles admit that an object which neither the memory can treasure up, nor the imagination form, has been present to the mind. They are not able to conceive that an object has been there which was not represented by a sensible idea, and which makes itself felt only by its influence.[5]

This obscure object of desire, traced by the 'orphan mind', is reduced in 'Mr Locke's ludicrous explication of it' to mere self-interest. It is in fact, argues Usher, the characteristic and highest power of humanity.[6]

In 1766 Alexander Gerard had edited a collection of *Essais sur le goût* by Voltaire, D'Alembert and Montesquieu. Usher appears to develop one part of Montesquieu's essay in which the French author, dividing pleasure into that which comes from the soul, that which comes from custom, and that which comes from the soul's unity with the body, argues that no original and simple pleasure exists outside a social context. The soul itself would know its pleasure – 'But at present we love almost always only that which we do not know.'[7]

The problem for such an extended argument as Usher's, which moves outside the principles of empiricism, is to provide a correlative figure for this obscurity toward which the mind wanders. It is not sufficient for him to bring on some quasi-Platonic notion of pre-existence because that seems able to explain lunacy as much as it explains anticipations of a future state. Instead, Usher looks to the products of 'enlightened' culture, to the arts. It is for this reason that his philosophy includes an aesthetics. The arts, by their fictive character, declare that 'the confused ideas of the mind are still infinitely superior to, and beyond the reach of all description'.[8] When discussing painting and sculpture and in his early discussion of poetry, however, Usher can do no more than point to their recurrent epic content, the machinery of gods and heroes, and the degree of inspiration these indicate. The arts as a whole do not easily provide him with a correlative for that indeterminate and unknown object which the mind seeks. In general the arts do no more than give evidence in support of the notion that the mind enjoys autonomy from 'the near objects that charm it' into the closed circle of Locke's empiricism.[9]

It is only in deliberate confusions, such as in that of a landscaped garden or of the Gothic sublime, that art can 'create in the imagination affecting ideas that do not appear'. However, 'distinct picturing' and determinate form and manner finally intrude upon all these media.[10] Sublimity, therefore, is only an aspect of the visual or plastic arts. It is only *by association* with the sublime that gardens and buildings include indeterminacy and infinitude. In none of these arts is the mind directly and continuously presented with an object constituted as much by its absence as by its presence. And only such an object, according to Usher's theory of mind, can be a correlative for desire and for thought.

Previous works on the sublime had not been so exclusive. John Baillie, for example, in *An Essay on the Sublime* (1747), argues that 'whatever the *Essence* of the *Soul* may be, it is the *Reflection* arising from *Sensations* only which makes her acquainted with Herself, and know her *Faculties*'. The material world, at least of sights and prospects, is given no such place by Usher. For Baillie association is the principle governing the sublime. A building is sublime, for example, because of its associations with wealth and power. Only music, in which he has little interest, appears to Baillie to be sublime without any priority of association.[11]

It is precisely for this reason, which does not detain Baillie, that Usher gives music so much attention both in his writings on aesthetics and also those on philosophy. In the first edition of the *Discourse on Taste* he had written that with music, 'we are at a loss when we would discover the powers by which it invests and captivates the soul, or the reasons why the tastes of men should be so various on this head'.[12] Four years later, when he comes to write about music in his *Introduction to the Theory of the Human Mind*, Usher is less 'at a loss' with these questions than any other writer before Coleridge.

In the early work of 1767 Usher first of all discusses the conventional relation of music to the passions. By its 'clearest flashes of light breaking through the deepest obscurity' music not only enchants our feelings, but also 'it awakens some passions which we perceive not, in ordinary life'. Then, in an extraordinary passage, he inserts a concept of music into the terms of rationalism and empiricism in such a way as to subvert their very assumptions.

> The most elevated sensation of music arises from a confused perception of ideal or visionary beauty and rapture, which is sufficiently perceivable to fire the imagination, but not clear enough to become an object of knowledge. This shadowy beauty the mind attempts, with a languishing curiosity, to collect into a distinct object of view and comprehension; but it sinks and escapes, like the dissolving ideas of a delightful dream, that are neither within the reach of memory, nor yet totally fled. The charms of music then, though real and affecting, seem yet too confused and fluid to be collected into a distinct idea.[13]

This description of the relationship between music and the nature of perception is the one that Usher uses in his later philosophical work. Its extra importance there is that Usher places it at the centre of a theory of mind. Being so placed music is inevitably grouped together with poetry, and, in Usher's attempt at a coherent aesthetic, both are contrasted with the visual arts. In the *Introduction to the Theory of the Human Mind* in 1771 Usher equates music and poetry because both include that principle of knowledge and enigma which the mind desires. Usher had earlier raised the hypothesis that Milton, Shakespeare and Dryden might have had the same genius for music as for literature. He had decided that at the highest point of poetic thought the ideas and the music of the words would be lost in each other. He had further emphasised this equivalence of the two media in the enlarged edition of the *Discourse on Taste*.[14] Finally stated, therefore, as an aesthetic which forms a part of his speculations on the mind, Usher writes of an extreme and obscure idealism:

> We comprehend by instinct, without the assistance of reason, that music is related to poetry. The principal object of both, is something beyond conception rapturous and elevating; when we would fix our view upon it, we find that it lies

yet below our horizon, and only appears in a dawn whose splendor surprizes us; accordingly, there is a perfection, a *plus ultra* still behind, beyond expression and attainment in both, of which great poets and great musicians have a confused idea, without ability ever to arrive at it. But although they know it not, they are sensible when they approach the unknown object, that seems at the same time to appear and hide from the imagination.[15]

It must be noticed that Usher does not repeat Alexander Pope's line about a 'grace beyond the reach of art'.

Instead, he defines extensively the obscure but 'principal object' of poetry and music. This is most easily to be discovered in the empty signs that make up the material of music. It can be found in poetry, but it is unrealisable in the visual arts except by extraneous association. A Longinian in his tastes, Usher places within perception but quite outside the comprehension of the mind something vague enough to compare both with Berkeley's inaccessible 'absolute external entity' and with Kant's 'thing-in-itself'. Whatever it is, Usher is hypnotised by it. He is in love with whatever recedes from his knowledge of it, and for this reason music enchants his thought. He is entranced by enigma, and although, by equating it with God's hidden presence, he provides an ontology to rescue enigma from emptiness, the emphasis throughout his writing is upon the experience of the indeterminate simply as itself.

Usher's description of music and poetry as models of a venture by the mind to grasp that which both initiates and eludes its power, and also his description of music as perceivable by the mind but too unstable to be grasped as knowledge or as idea – both these descriptions indicate a notion of music which looks forward to and which can facilitate the relationship between reader and text which becomes one part of Romantic poetics. It is precisely this anticipation, which only an aesthetics of music develops, that we shall be explaining in later chapters. It is clear that for the idea of music to become a useful one in defining a poetics the principles we find in Usher must be extended to include also an idea of language.

There is much else that we will discover in the work of subsequent writers which is missing from Usher's description of music. Not least is his lack of practical attention to actual music. Without this he must also ignore how music is constructed, man-made. His notion of music is of its simplest form, and it remains a notion which is limited to the medium of music and to its epistemology. Nevertheless, Usher is more explicit and more interesting than any of his contemporaries in his use of such an idea of music in order to analyse the inadequacies of the empiricist concept of the idea. Also, by describing music as an object not merely of feeling but also of thought, by elaborating on it as an 'image' which conceals significance at the very moment that it might appear, by finding in it a negative idea which is its own absence and which delights us by replying to the mind's desire for what is known indistinctly, Usher's work is the first aesthetics of music to place it in a useful relation to philosophy and to poetics.

To men of the Enlightenment the kind of sensibility to music which Usher celebrates usually appears both too delicious to refuse and too private to publish. It is a sensibility most often committed to a writer's unpublished reflections and letters. Diderot's *Rameau's Nephew* remained unpublished until Goethe edited it in the first decade of the nineteenth century. We have to wait until the same decade for a veritable flood of memoirs of a musical life.[16] The whole world of musical sensibility through which that great friend to the French Enlightenment, Thomas Twining, meanders in his private papers and letters is committed to little more than a footnote in his published work.[17]

It has been a mistake to see in these small beginnings no more than what anticipates, say, Beckford's *Dreams, Waking Thoughts and Incidents* (1783) or De Quincey's reminiscences and dream-fugues. Those works, so full of 'musical memory', are not the only or the most important culmination of this effusive and usually private subjectivity. During the eighteenth century music and poetry are usually discussed in terms of an epistemology. Therefore, the emphasis on music promotes (i) a new idea of the relationship between the work of art and its auditor or reader; and (ii) a new idea of the work of art as an effect of the individual or social state of mind coincident with it.

James Usher, despite all his love of obscurity, is important for developing these issues. His elaboration of the relationship between the empty signs of the music and the desires of the mind clearly develops the first; in his writings he considers also the second. In his early work on the standards of taste he had decided, not unconventionally, that only the leisured classes could decide what the standard should be. The business of hard work concealed from most men those privileged glimpses into transcendence available only to the few with few employments. This is a view Usher comes to reject. He chooses instead an opposite view that 'the sense of the untutored part of mankind is the true standard, and can never be wrong'.[18] This more democratic aesthetic is stated in a discussion of how music has been corrupted in higher forms of civilisation from an original simplicity into a Rococo excess and triviality.

It is not surprising that this bit of primitivism should prompt a rejection of the privileged standards of taste. For a consideration of the social relation of music leads Usher to dismiss the more conventional model of standards maintained within a classical canon, and leads him to replace this with another model by which a particular art is a necessary production of a certain kind of society. Christians, writes Usher,

ought by all the rules of theory, to excel the heathens in music, whose religious ideas are so superiorly passionate and noble. It is certain, that Christianity naturally familiarizes us to the great, the affecting, and the plaintive passions that form the epic part of harmony; and it may be asserted with some degree of confidence, that wherever the taste of music is revived, it will assist in awaking the other powers of genius, and impressing the mind with a sublime habit of thinking. In statuary and painting, Christians have no prospect of equalling the heathens. Passion and pride are the very soul of painting.[19]

I would not claim that this model of the arts' relation to society is completely novel for its day. The early eighteenth-century 'progress poem' narrates the translation of the arts from one society to another according to the migrations of the spirit of liberty which they require.[20] Writers such as Goldsmith and Smart do indeed attribute different arts to different stages of social decay or virtue. However, Usher's statement about the links between Christianity and music is remarkable in asserting that his argument is true 'by all the rules of theory'. Indeed his reversal of the conventional standards of taste makes the question no longer one of standards at all, but instead a question of the relations between one kind of art and a certain form of thinking.

The late eighteenth-century replacement of the notion of the social propriety of art with the notion of the necessary social responsibility of art is, therefore, likely to be facilitated by the idea that music can be simply expressive of a dominant form of thought. Music, it can be argued, because it does not imitate

Nature in either its generalised or its particular forms, and because its medium of mere sound and empty signs cannot represent either the world 'out there' or (given its variety) a constant nature of man, is alone among the arts expressive. Such an argument is one part of Coleridge's interest in music. It offers immediately the occasion of a 'synthetic' social history of art. Other writers towards the end of the eighteenth century develop the point. 'The music of a nation, in it's [sic] most imperfect form, and favourite tunes,' writes Herder in 1785, 'displays the internal character of the people . . . more truly and profoundly, than the most copious description of external contingencies.'[21] In the previous year and in the same spirit Thomas Robertson had written: 'How vain, then, an abstract comparison of Ancient and Modern music . . . Modern music is highly suited to modern times.'[22]

Such an idea of music as part of a new critical principle must be introduced to balance the more popular notion of 'harmonious madness', the Romantic wallowing in the subjectivity of music, that has been the object of much research.[23] At the moment when eighteenth-century epistemology noticed that the signs of music evade the categories of distinctness and clarity of ideas, it became possible (i) to locate the significance of music in its composition, in its structure or source; and (ii) to locate the significance of music in its emptiness, in its absence of meaning, and therefore in the act of listening, in the energy of mind which its emptiness provokes.

Autonomous song: Chabanon and Blake

The choice between, on the one hand, describing the pleasure of music to be the index of an obscure desire, and, on the other, describing it to be mere sensation, independent of the subjective and the social, divides Usher from an important French contemporary, Michel-Paul Guy de Chabanon. Chabanon's *Observations sur la musique* appeared in the same year, 1769, as the enlarged edition of Usher's *Discourse*. Usher's notion of music claims to annihilate the philosophies of the ideas of sense; so also does Chabanon's. The important difference introduced by Chabanon, however, is his notion that the empty or evasive signs of music are *not* obscure. They are a clear and precise sensation. Whatever obscurity is attributed to the musical sign is only a figment of old habits of representation which it had claimed to annihilate. In fact, music is autonomous: it neither imitates nor expresses anything other than itself.

The transition to this idea is most apparent in discussions about music in France. The arguments used on either side in the *querelle des bouffons* in order to defend either French or Italian music against one another; the variety of statements about music in the *Encyclopédie* and in its *Supplément*; the theoretical questions raised about music and speech by Rousseau, and also the contribution made by his *Dictionnaire de musique* (1767); all of these allowed the conventional French Baroque notion that music is a specific representation of feelings and ideas to be called into question.[24]

In 1785 Chabanon claimed that the *querelle* had been a result of a confusion about the status and character of melody. At the same moment he places at the centre of his claim the assertion that each sound in music is insignificant in itself and can be related, whether melodically or harmonically, only to another sound. With eighty-five years of hindsight he decides that the *querelle* had been not so much a contest between different kinds of national opera, as it had been a feature in an epistemological argument.[25] In order to understand that epistemology and in order to notice its difference from that in Britain, I will consider, therefore, not the *querelle* itself but the more general changes in the description of music that accompany and survive it. Most important to us will be the changes in the descriptions of music between the first volumes of the *Encyclopédie* (1751–65) and the *Supplément* (1777), Rousseau's non-polemical writings, and the contributions of Chastellux and of Chabanon.

The classification of the arts in France is also initially decided according to the terms of imitation. Upon the grid of the mimetic each of the arts is placed in a hierarchy comparable to that which had been described by Charles Batteux.[26] In the 'Discours Préliminaire' to the *Encyclopédie* we are told that music 'tient le dernier rang dans l'ordre d'imitation'. Music is, therefore, compared to a kind of discourse of language that would be judged according to the effects it might produce.[27] The achievement of those effects is summed up in the term 'expression'.

D'Alembert, the author of the 'Discours Préliminaire', appears to share with Rousseau and with most of the other contributors on music an impatience with instrumental music. Their use of the word 'expression' contrasts with its understanding in Britain after Avison. The definition of 'expression' in the *Encyclopédie* always circles around the idea of imitation. All art is expression 'parcequ'on n'imite point sans exprimer'. However, expression itself depends upon imitation and 'un concerto, une sonate doivent peindre quelque chose, ou ne sont que du bruit'.[28]

The principle of imitation ought not to be considered, however, a simple and uniform idea among the encyclopedists. The artificial character of imitation, its conventional and formal presuppositions, are well illustrated by Grimm in his article on 'Poème Lyrique . . .':

Tout art d'imitation est fondé sur un mensonge: ce mensonge est un espece d'hypothese établie & admise en vertu d'une convention tacite . . .[29]

This can, for Grimm, be contrasted with the character of music, which is a universal, vague and immediate mode of language; in this way music is more like the lyric poem, which ought to be at once simple, graceful and disordered.

Grimm and Rousseau mutually supported one another during the *querelle*.[30] Both championed the Italian opera and, indeed, Grimm takes the opportunity to do so again in the article on lyric poetry. The *querelle des bouffons* has been called a dispute between supporters of the French Baroque and those of the Italian Rococo. Contrasts between the two styles included comments on 'la richesse, la chaleur et la variété' of the Italians and on the 'indigence . . . froideur . . . monotonie' of the French.[31] Grimm and Rousseau agreed with, among others, Diderot and D'Alembert in supporting the emotion, morality of sentiment, and the vocal melodies of *opera buffa*, and in attacking the frigidity, rationalism and instrumental harmonies of *opera seria*. However, there is an important disagreement in the use of the term 'imitation'. For Grimm it denotes an artificial and conventional system of illusory perception, while for Rousseau it is, both in music and in language, the primitive and original act of meaning.

In the *Essay on the Origin of Languages which treats of Melody and Musical Imitation* Rousseau contrasts a figurative/ hieroglyphic mode of language with an arbitrary/alphabetic mode which has historically replaced it. 'The illusory image presented by passion is the first to appear, and the language that corresponds to it was also the first invented.'[32] In the chapter 'On Script' Rousseau asserts that the conventional alphabetic mode of language has become prolix, dull and cold. What Grimm had defined as a lie established by silent compact may be recalled in the illusory nature of the original image given by passion, but the conventional basis of Grimm's 'imitation' can be applied only to the later alphabetic stage of language in Rousseau. In its early and original form language is tied to that which it represents. Not only in its dictional figures 'but even in its mechanical part it would have to correspond to its initial object'.[33]

In the chapters on 'The Origin of Music & its Relations', 'On Melody', 'On Harmony', and on 'How Music has degenerated' (that is, the chapters which immediately follow the assertion of the corruption of language and which immediately precede the final chapter on the 'Relationship of Language to Government') Rousseau equates the syntactical and phonological aspects of language with music, and he attributes the degeneration of both music and language to the separation of their semantic and formal elements. The description of that separation is a social criticism. For Rousseau the symptom of the degeneration of language is 'commercial' alphabetic script, which rather analyses than represents the movements of speech. The symptom of the degeneration of music is 'aristocratic' modern harmony, which analyses its own complexity rather than represents what speech and music originally did represent, the *mouvemens de l'âme*. The re-uniting of music and speech, therefore, is a recovery within society of its origins in freedom and sentiment. For Rousseau, as it is stated in this essay, the recovery is twofold: the public rhetoric of oratory, which is the language of liberty; and the more private rhetoric of vocal melody, which is the language of feeling.[34]

It is in this moral and social history that Rousseau locates his idea of music. Music ought to be melodic, representing and including the character of speech. Only in this way can music again recover its lost original object. Melody alone, as he defines it in the *Dictionnaire de musique* (1767), can 'excite in the soul the same movement which we feel' in experience of nature and passion. Harmony and purely instrumental music are degenerate and relatively incompetent.

Let all nature be in a slumber, he that contemplates it, sleeps not; and the art of the musician consists in substituting, in the place of the insensible image of the object, that of the movements which his presence excites in the heart of the contemplator.[35]

For Rousseau, the author of the homage to Gluck and the composer of the opera *Le Devin du Village*, the musician is an Orpheus dreaming of the recovery of a lost innocence and, with backward glance, substituting for an irrevocable loss the emotions of the music itself. Although Rousseau insists on the fullness and mimetic character of music there is ironically a recognition of its emptiness.

The pleasure of melody and music, is a pleasure of interest and sentiment which speaks to the heart . . . music ought then necessarily to sing for the touching, the pleasing, and sustaining the interest and attention.[36]

Given the implicit irony of Rousseau's position it is not surprising that we find various gestures of disagreement with him. For example, the articles in the *Encyclopédie* on instruments and instrumentation, which are by Diderot, provide evidence of some patience with non-vocal music.[37] The *Supplément* includes contributions by Marmontel in which it is argued that no one principle, not even that of imitation, can account for all of the arts. Poetry, painting and sculpture may, according to Marmontel, have nature as their object and imitation as their method, but this is not true of architecture or of music.[38]

A further disagreement with Rousseau is expressed by his sometime ally, Chastellux. The point at issue for Chastellux is whether music or language predominates in the expression of emotion. The emotions of opera appear to Chastellux to require *l'incohérence*, a rupture of sense, a defiance of grammar. This energy of emotion and its vagueness is, however inexpressible in words, directly expressible in music. By assuming the correspondence of music with irrational emotion, Chastellux decides that musical elements ought to determine the form of a vocal melody. To the extent that he agrees that song must represent *mouvemens de l'âme* he is at one with Rousseau. But Chastellux's *Essai sur l'union de la poésie & de la musique* (1765) also argues that the difference between poetry and music is that music is closer to feeling. According to Rousseau music imitates *la parole*. According to Chastellux it does not.[39] This disagreement is enormously important, for it is only by separating music from speech that the relation between music and feeling, between music and thought, can become indeterminate, empty or abstract.

Chabanon chooses the emphasis of Chastellux. The epistemology of music which Chabanon develops is more analytic and
more extensive than anything produced during the *querelle* or in
the *Encyclopédie*. In his *Observations sur la musique* (1764) and in
the fuller revised version of that work, *De la Musique Considérée
en elle-même et dans ses rapports avec la parole, les langues, la poésie
et le théâtre* (1785), Chabanon directly introduces us to the idea of
music within a more general theory of signs and of their
interpretation.

The limitation of painting, argues Chabanon, is its precision of
imitation. Music, by contrast, operates with almost imperceptible
analogies and is not restricted in its signification.

Musique purement instrumentale laisse leur esprit en suspens & dans
l'inquiétude sur la signification de ce qu'ils entendent.[40]

Instrumental music is also the most primitive form of signs, being
prior to language itself. As such it is a mode of signifying at once
both natural and universal. Verbal language and the idea of
beauty may show ethnic and national variations. But 'Le Huron
chante comme le Laboureur de Vaugirard!'[41]

This is not as naive a statement as may first appear. Chabanon
writes of music as a practice of extreme abstraction. From this
comes its uncertainty of signification, and from this also comes its
universal effectiveness. Chabanon is threading a course between
Rousseau's notion of an irrevocable bond of signifier and signified
in original speech, and Grimm's argument that all imitation is
illusory and conventional. An excellent example of this approach
is found in Chabanon's analysis of Gluck's strategy when
presenting operatically the wrath of Achilles.

N'en doutez-pas; ou de réflexion, ou de génie, voici comme il a raissoné. 'J'ai à
peindre la fureur de l'homme le plus violent: ces mots seuls, *la colère d'Achille*,
annoncent une passion extraordinaire & terrible. Comment élever le chant
jusqu'à cette situation? La colère est un sentiment qui ne chante pas: produisons
un effet de symphonie & d'ensemble, imposant, effrayant, s'il est possible.
L'illusion de ces effets sera réversible sur mon héros; & les Spectateurs qui
entendra le bruit de tout l'Orchestre, croira que ses cent voix sont la voix
d'Achille.'[42]

It is not only that Chabanon defends an abstract relationship
between music and its signifieds. He also whittles away the idea
that there is any representational correspondence between music
and other 'objects' at all. Music is compared to dancing ('le

rhythme musical rendu sensible aux yeux') and also to architecture (the beauty of both is not 'ce qui conforme à la nature').[43]
Indeed, music and dance

ne disent à l'esprit rien de positif. Leur effet est une sensation, & par conséquent
a quelque chose de vague. Il faut un travail de l'esprit pour attacher à cette
sensation une situation & des mots analogues; & c'est cette dernière opération
qui fait de la Danse & de la Musique deux Arts imitatifs.[44]

To impose on these arts this representational mode is to misread
them. There is a choice available whether to interpret their signs
as imitation or not. At no point does Chabanon imply that to
interpret the signs as imitations of something else is desirable. The
implication, in fact, runs the other way. Our senses 'sont juges
sans la médiation de l'esprit'.[45] If music is translated as if it were
an imitative action this can only be done by replacing it with a
relatively more specific and, therefore, less affective mode such as
that of language. More important, more scandalous, such translation is not necessary insofar as Chabanon can provide positive
terms with which to describe the 'vague' satisfaction of music.
That is to say, music will not need a more determinate signification if it can be shown to give to the mind a quite different
precision from what is given by the representational function of
language.

D'où provient cette différence? De ce que les tours & les mots ne sont que les
signes conventionnels des choses: ces mots, ces tours ayant des synonymes, des
équivalens, se laissent remplacer par eux: mais les sons en Musique ne sont pas
les signes qui expriment le chant; ils sont le chant même . . . Il suit delà qu'en
Musique on ne peut jamais exprimer obscurément sa pensée. On chante, on note
les sons que l'on a dans sa tête: ces sons ne sont pas l'expression de la chose; ils
sont la chose même.[46]

It is, therefore, not by virtue of its indeterminacy when
considered as a mode of representation, but by virtue of its clarity
when considered as a mode of performance, that music differs
from language. By cancelling the metaphysics of image and origin
upon which mimesis depends, Chabanon establishes the priority
of music among the arts.

It is after all only the imposition of a representational mode of
interpretation which makes music appear obscure. This is of
course what James Usher had done in order to provide evidence
for his notion of an object of desire which is always absent from
our knowledge of it. Chabanon has no use for that kind of

obscurity; the only model of interpretation he allows is that of performance. Unlike words, sounds are

nuls par eux-même & sans signification, ils n'en acquièrent que par les inflexions qu'on leur donne, par le contraste qu'on y met.[47]

Music is clear because it works as a system of differences, a system of relationships which it constructs and by which it is constructed.

Throughout the *Observations* we notice a set of polarities:

music	language
the empty or abstract sign	the imitative or expressive sign
sensation	intelligence
the non-signifying	the representational
the precise	the imprecise
undetermined interpretation	specific interpretation

The apparent contradiction, between language being at once more specific and less precise, can be explained in terms of Chabanon's assumption that imitation and expression are necessities from which we desire to be free.[48] Consequently, he argues against Rousseau who identifies both of these as the one instinct which produces language and music. According to Chabanon song does not have its origin in a figurative and picturesque discourse;[49] nor is musical expression an imitation of inarticulate cries.[50] Our instinct is not for a representational mode (*signes conventionnels des choses*) in which interpretation can only act as a terminus. Language in practice works in that way. Music does not.[51] Music is, therefore, thought to be free so long as its interpretation remains at the level of sensation and performance, and avoids the level of either imitation or expression.

The freedom in music can be found in a more direct way than by analysing Gluck. It is, in fact, common:

Les Matelots . . . sont gais au moment où ils chantent tristement. Ainsi, la Musique pour eux n'est pas un langage d'expression: ce n'est pas un Art qui imite, ni qui cherche même à imiter.[52]

Music, therefore, need not stand in place of *parole*, or *choses*, or *mouvemens de l'âme*. It is determined by no source. It refers neither to what is without nor what is within. It subsists in relation only to itself in the sense that its performance is at once production and reception. The sailors sing for the pleasure of listening. The music is unnecessary. It exists in a space between imitation and expression. So long as it is outside their limits it is free and precise. Hence, 'ses sensations voluptueuses & ses jouissances immédiates'.[53]

Chabanon found these notions difficult to maintain. The revised and augmented version of the *Observations* which appeared in 1785, *De la Musique Considérée en elle-même et dans ses rapports avec la parole, les langues, la poésie et le théâtre*, is described by its author as 'plus modérés'. While it does not retract the leading idea the revised text appears to subdue it by placing it in the wider context of the 'origins' of music and its relation with language. Two main consequences follow from these changes: first, there is the argument that music is independent of the society which produces it; second, there are more specific points made about affinities between poetry and music.[54]

Both of these consequences reflect the delight and sense of freedom in the *Observations* back upon the anxieties of Chabanon's earlier writing, *Sur le Sort de la poésie en ce siècle philosophe* (1764). That work is comparable, in its cultural pessimism about the fate of poetry, to Thomas Warton's history of English poetry, or to William Collins's and Thomas Gray's allegories of the present-day collapse of the poetic imagination. Collins, in his 'Ode on the Poetical Character', and Gray, in 'The Progress of Poesy' and 'The Bard', outline a mythical version of the history of music in order to describe what is thought to be the actual history of poetry. Similarly Chabanon uses a notion of the epistemology of music, instead of its mythical history, in order to rescue poetry from its apparent fate.

Music provides Chabanon with a figure of how art may be independent of the spirit of its age, and may flourish within rationalism or whatever else opposes it. Because it is indeterminate in its meaning and resists interpretation, and because it is not determined by its origin, which it neither imitates nor expresses, music is not inhibited by what surrounds it. Chabanon allows that all the other arts may be symptoms of the customs and of the moral and political character of a people. Indeed, he supplies examples from England to Angola to reinforce that argument.

mais la Musique, qui ne peint ni les hommes, ni les choses, ni les situations, n'a pas les mêmes dépendances . . . le caractère de chant le plus familier à une Nation, n'est pas un indice certain de son caractère & de son genie.[55]

In the same way as the sailors who sing sad songs when they are happy, so also a people, 'sombre & profond dans le caractère de ses pensées, pourroit être vif & léger dans celui de sa mélodie'.[56]

To argue that music has a casual or a negative relation to the society which produces it allows the inference that music does have at least one significance for mind and feeling. The empty signs leave a space which makes music free and undetermined. Music can therefore be an index of the autonomy of mind and feeling over and beyond whatever context would restrict them.

It is in this way that music can become a figure for imaginative power, relatively indifferent to the moment of its composition, in a poem by the young William Blake:

Song

How sweet I roamed from field to field
    And tasted all the summer's pride,
Till I the prince of love beheld,
    Who in the sunny beams did glide.

He showed me lilies for my hair,
    And blushing roses for my brow;
He led me through his garden fair,
    Where all his golden pleasures grow.

With sweet May dews my wings were wet,
    And Phoebus fired my vocal rage.
He caught me in his silken net,
    And shut me in his golden cage.

He loves to sit and hear me sing,
    Then, laughing, sports and plays with me –
Then stretches out my golden wing,
    And mocks my loss of liberty.[57]

This lyric from *Poetical Sketches* is one of a number that are both entitled 'Song' and are about song. The singer/bird can, of course, sing only a wordless song. If only for that reason the poem is able to avoid any suggestion that the 'song' expresses the singer's dereliction. The ambiguous phrase, 'vocal rage', is used in the happier part of the poem's narrative. Subsequently, there is the recognition that the song is enjoyed in spite of, or on account of, the singer's imprisonment. The poem and its figure of birdsong are immediately allegorical. The poem signifies the absence of that which its figure presents: song as self-expression. Its irony states a discontinuity between the occasion, the song, and the response to

the song. Unhappiness becomes delightful. The reader's response
to the poem (that is, to the 'Song') becomes ambivalent. For does
not the reader also love 'to sit and hear' the song of the desolate
singer? May not the singing bird also enjoy its own song? Indeed,
given the indeterminacy of music and the uncertainty of its
interpretation, may not the gaoler, the reader and the singer weep
at a music occasioned by happiness, enjoy a music occasioned by
misery?[58]

Precisely these ironies are put to work by Blake in the
'Introduction' to *Songs of Innocence*. Throughout that poem the
pastoral 'I' enacts a carefully marked sequence of transitions from
instrumental music to singing, and then to writing. The response
of the child in the poem is not given as continuous with the
apparent happiness of the music which 'he wept to hear'. An
anxiety, similar to that in 'How sweet I roamed', emerges in this
lyric also insofar as the child's interpretation of the music and the
song displaces the apparent simplicity of its innocence. Again we
can speak of the allegorical ironies of the poem insofar as the
music of the pipe and the song of the lamb signify to the child
(and, therefore, to the reader also) the absence of which they are
the figure.

None of the music that Blake is said to have composed has
survived, but we do have descriptions of his use of music by those
who knew him. John Thomas Smith visited Blake's friends, the
Mathews family, as early as 1784. There

I first met William Blake, the artist, to whom she (Mrs. Mathews) and Mr.
Flaxman had been truly kind. There I have often heard him read and sing several
of his poems. He was listened to by the company with profound silence, and
allowed by most of the visitors to possess original and extraordinary merit.[59]

Many years later Blake 'still sang, in a voice tremulous with age,
sometimes old ballads, sometimes his own songs to melodies of his
own'.[60] As if to confirm his childish allegory of the imprisoned
bird who nevertheless sings delightfully we have the following
account, documented and relished by Blake's Victorian
biographer:

'On the day of his death', writes Smith, who had his account from the widow, 'he
composed and uttered songs to his Maker, so sweetly to the ear of his Catherine
that, when she stood near him, he, looking upon her most affectionately, said,
"My beloved! they are *not mine*. No! they are *not* mine!" He told her they would
not be parted; he should always be about her to take care of her.' . . . he lay

chaunting Songs to Melodies, both the inspiration of the moment, but no longer, as of old, to be noted down.[61]

Again, during Blake's years of mature composition it is recorded how

In sketching designs, engraving Plates, writing songs, and composing music, he employed his time, with his wife sitting at his side, encouraging him in all his undertakings. As he drew the figure he meditated the song which was to accompany it, and the music to which the verse was to be sung, was the offspring too of the same moment.[62]

I think we learn some of the reasons for this juxtaposition of music and the written text if we place the ideas of music found in Usher and in Chabanon beside Blake's intention to resist the 'stubborn structure' of a public language. Music is then a model of a way in which such a language can be mediated and displaced in poetry.[63] The discontinuity between occasion, text and interpretation, which is allowed for by the idea of the clear, empty and evasive signs of music, also withholds a poetic text from becoming stubborn and fixed. In *The Marriage of Heaven and Hell* Blake gives a history of the way in which the allegories of the poets had been reified into 'forms of worship':

Till a system was formed, which some took advantage of and enslaved the vulgar by attempting to realise or abstract the mental deities from their objects. Thus began priesthood . . . Thus men forgot that all deities reside in the human breast.[64]

Such a priesthood anticipates the idea of the book, the idea of a determined and single work of interpretation, which we find in *The First Book of Urizen.*

> Lo, I unfold my darkness and on
> This rock place with strong hand the Book
> Of eternal brass, written in my solitude.

> 'Laws of peace, of love, of unity,
> Of pity, compassion, forgiveness.
> Let each chuse one habitation,
> His ancient infinite mansion,
> One command, one joy, one desire,
> One curse, one weight, one measure,
> One King, one God, one Law.'[65]

Music can counteract the singularity of Urizen. The account that is handed down to us of Blake's composing melodies to which his lyrics might be sung is evidence of the practical intention behind the figure of 'song' in 'How sweet I roamed' and in the 'Introduction' to *Songs of Innocence*. His book has then the clarity and freedom of a performance-text. This, of course, is not the only way in which Blake's texts are explicitly open to uncertainty of interpretation. In contrast with the book of Urizen, Blake's engraven texts require the constant and opposite actions of the reader's eyes to recognise in a multiple gaze both the pictorial image and also the abstract alphabetic signs.[66]

It is by virtue of these indeterminacies in his mode of composition that Blake instances the imagination as relatively independent of the 'stubborn structure' within which (as if within a silken net or golden cage) it sings. As with Chabanon the song does not express its source or singer. As with James Usher music and the arts become the figure for how the mind can remain free of 'the near objects that charm it'.

In the address to the reader at the beginning of *Jerusalem* Blake again brings together the concept of music and that of the engraven text. He is announcing the return to print of his 'giant forms . . . & fairies'. Also he is explaining the kind of free verse in which the poem is to be composed, and its contrast with the monotony and bondage of iambic blank verse: 'I therefore have produced a variety in every line, both of cadences & number of syllables.'[67] It is the relationship between this music of the verse and the pictorial engravings which Blake describes in the prefatory verses of *Jerusalem*. The sequence is again, as before, first the ear and second the eye. The idea of writing as at once both music and engraving is given the status of a prophetic or performative utterance.[68]

> Reader, *lover* of books *lover* of heaven,
> And of that God from whom *all books are given*,
> Who in mysterious Sinai's awful cave
> To man the wondrous art of writing gave.
> Again he speaks in thunder and in fire –
> Thunder of thought, & flames of fierce desire.
> Even from the depths of Hell his voice I hear,
> Within the unfathomed caverns of my ear.
> Therefore I print; nor vain my types shall be;
> Heaven, Earth & Hell henceforth shall live in harmony.[69]

Defined in this way the poetic imagination has an autonomous power even within the restrictions it suffers. The derelict singer sings. Usher and Chabanon had in their writings allowed for such a relative indifference of music to the conditions from which it emerges.

The anxiety of portraiture: Cowper and Reynolds

It is useful to contrast the idea of the undetermined significance of music, as it is dramatised in the poetry of William Blake, with the determined significance of painting, as it is dramatised in the poetry of William Cowper. Cowper composed in 1790 a poem 'On the Receipt of My Mother's Picture out of Norfolk: The Gift of my Cousin Ann Bodham'. More than any other poem this will illustrate, in contrast with Blake's use of the figure of music, a use of the opposite figure for art: realistic portraiture.

This poem on his mother and on the painting which is her image was written by Cowper in his sixtieth year. His mother had died when he was six. During the interval his writing had recurrently traced to her death the first occasion of his depressiveness, his anxiety and his pessimism.[70] The poem on her portrait is the most complex and the most extended response to that sense of loss; a sense of a loss for which the portrait is both the index and the icon.

I will attach such importance to transitions and repetitions throughout the detail of this poem that it will be helpful to reproduce it here in full.

ON THE RECEIPT OF MY MOTHER'S PICTURE OUT OF
NORFOLK
The Gift of my Cousin Ann Bodham

Oh that those lips had language! Life has pass'd
With me but roughly since I heard thee last.
Those lips are thine – thy own sweet smiles I see,
The same that oft in childhood solaced me;
Voice only fails, else, how distinct they say,
'Grieve not, my child, chase all thy fears away!'
The meek intelligence of those dear eyes
(Blest be the art that can immortalize,
The art that baffles time's tyrannic claim
To quench it) here shines on me still the same.   (10)
    Faithful remembrancer of one so dear,
Oh welcome guest, though unexpected, here!
Who bidd'st me honour with an artless song,

Plate 2: portrait of Ann Donne Cowper (1703–37),
by D. Heins, c.1723 (oil on copper)

Affectionate, a mother lost so long,
I will obey, not willingly alone,
But gladly, as the precept were her own;
And, while that face renews my filial grief,
Fancy shall weave a charm for my relief —
Shall steep me in Elysian reverie,
A momentary dream, that thou art she.   (20)
   My mother! when I learn'd that thou wast dead,
Say, wast thou conscious of the tears I shed?
Hover'd thy spirit o'er thy sorrowing son,
Wretch even then, life's journey just begun?
Perhaps thou gav'st me, though unseen, a kiss;
Perhaps a tear, if souls can weep in bliss —
Ah that maternal smile! it answers — Yes.
I heard the bell toll'd on thy burial day,
I saw the hearse that bore thee slow away,
And, turning from my nurs'ry window, drew   (30)
A long, long sigh, and wept a last adieu!
But was it such? — It was. — Where thou art gone
Adieus and farewells are a sound unknown.
May I but meet thee on that peaceful shore,
The parting sound shall pass my lips no more!
Thy maidens griev'd themselves at my concern,
Oft gave me promise of a quick return.
What ardently I wish'd, I long believ'd,
And, disappointed still, was still deceiv'd;
By disappointment every day beguil'd,   (40)
Dupe of *to-morrow* even from a child.
Thus many a sad to-morrow came and went,
Till, all my stock of infant sorrow spent,
I learn'd at last submission to my lot;
But, though I less deplor'd thee, ne'er forgot.
   Where once we dwelt our name is heard no more,
Children not thine have trod my nurs'ry floor;
And where the gard'ner Robin, day by day,
Drew me to school along the public way,
Delighted with my bauble coach, and wrapt   (50)
In scarlet mantle warm, and velvet capt,
'Tis now become a history little known,
That once we call'd the past'ral house our own.
Short-liv'd possession! but the record fair
That mem'ry keeps of all thy kindness there,
Still outlives many a storm that has effac'd
A thousand other themes less deeply trac'd.
Thy nightly visits to my chamber made,
That thou might'st know me safe and warmly laid;
Thy morning bounties ere I left my home,   (60)
The biscuit, or confectionary plum;

The fragrant waters on my cheeks bestow'd
By thy own hand, till fresh they shone and glow'd;
All this, and more endeavouring still than all,
Thy constant flow of love, that knew no fall,
Ne'er roughen'd by those cataracts and brakes
That humour interpos'd too often makes;
All this still legible in mem'ry's page,
And still to be so, to my latest age,
Adds joy to duty, makes me glad to pay   (70)
Such honours to thee as my numbers may;
Perhaps a frail memorial, but sincere,
Not scorn'd in heav'n, though little notic'd here.
   Could time, his flight revers'd, restore the hours,
When, playing with thy vesture's tissued flow'rs,
The violet, the pink, and jessamine,
I prick'd them into paper with a pin,
(And thou wast happier than myself the while,
Would'st softly speak, and stroke my head and smile)
Could those few pleasant hours again appear,   (80)
Might one wish bring them, would I wish them here?
I would not trust my heart – the dear delight
Seems so to be desir'd, perhaps I might. –
But no – what here we call our life is such,
So little to be lov'd, and thou so much,
That I should ill requite thee to constrain
Thy unbound spirit into bonds again.
   Thou, as a gallant bark from Albion's coast
(The storms all weather'd and the ocean cross'd)
Shoots into port at some well-haven'd isle,   (90)
Where spices breathe and brighter seasons smile,
There sits quiescent on the floods that show
Her beauteous form reflected clear below,
While airs impregnated with incense play
Around her, fanning light her streamers gay;
So thou, with sails how swift! hast reach'd the shore
'Where tempests never beat nor billows roar,'
And thy lov'd consort on the dang'rous tide
Of life, long since, has anchor'd at thy side.
But me, scarce hoping to attain that rest,   (100)
Always from port withheld, always distress'd –
Me howling winds drive devious, tempest toss'd,
Sails ript, seams op'ning wide, and compass lost,
And day by day some current's thwarting force
Sets me more distant from a prosp'rous course.
But oh the thought, that thou art safe, and he!
That thought is joy, arrive what may to me.
My boast is not that I deduce my birth
From loins enthron'd, and rulers of the earth;

But higher far my proud pretensions rise –   (110)
The son of parents pass'd into the skies.
And now, farewell – time, unrevok'd, has run
His wonted course, yet what I wish'd is done.
By contemplation's help, not sought in vain,
I seem t' have liv'd my childhood o'er again;
To have renew'd the joys that once were mine,
Without the sin of violating thine:
And, while the wings of fancy still are free,
And I can view this mimic shew of thee,
Time has but half succeeded in his theft –   (120)
Thyself remov'd, thy power to sooth me left.

It can be noticed that, although the painting is overtly a consoling object because it imitates so deceptively and so well, the speaker's first reaction states its inadequacy: 'Oh that those lips had language'. This inadequacy appears to be allowed for in the moderate claim made for the consolation which the picture eventually provides: 'Thyself remov'd, thy power to sooth me left'. However, this equilibrium is never a stable compromise. The poem is frail beyond even its own clichéd description of itself as a 'frail memorial'. Within a fiction of recovering a lost contentment the speaker has lived over again a childhood largely of discontentment. It will be useful here if we adopt Michael Riffaterre's terms by which he divides a text between its *meaning* (the information conveyed at a mimetic level by its variety of detail) and its *significance* (the 'indices of indirection' conveyed at a formal level by displacement, distortion or symmetrical repetition).[71] Given that distinction the instabilities of Cowper's poem become more explicit. For the poem's meaning is the consolation of remembered joy. Its significance is the repetition of remembered anxiety. Its meaning is a narrative of checks and balances. Its significance is a pattern of further decomposition.

Cowper's poem works along two narrative lines. The first is the identification of the picture with the mother, the replacement of her absence by its presence. This narrative depends upon a convention of representation by which difference is abruptly stated as identity: 'Those lips are thine', 'thou art she', 'My mother! . . . say'. These phrases constitute a first narrative line in which the poem enables the speaker to write as if he were in conversation not with the picture (as at first he is – 'Oh that those lips had language') but with his mother (as he is later on – 'My mother! . . . say').

Second, there is another narrative line about what is recollected within that 'conversation'. The recollection includes incidents from childhood, incidents which are recurrent or unique. The variety of detail of that childhood falls both before and after the final loss, the mother's death. The incidents within this narrative of childhood include watching from the nursery as the hearse leaves the family home; going to school each morning; being put to bed each night. These incidents, although they are like the portrait insofar as they are overtly signs of the mother's presence, are in each case incidents either of her loss or on the threshold of her absence. All the other events of the poem (with the exception of the child's playing with the flowers of his mother's dress, an incident we will discuss later on) are also acts of farewell: the loss of the family home, the death of the poet's father.

In the two narrative lines, both in that about the portrait and in that about remembered childhood, the mother is absent. Childhood is remembered as a sequence of loss, and the mother as always about to be lost. The happiness of her brief presence is always the consequence of her threatened departure, of the fact that she is as a rule not there. The two narrative lines, therefore, join each other: the portrait of the mother now soothes him in precisely the same way as the actual mother had done. Both console by virtue of a presence which is no more than the shadow of an absence. The speaker by foregoing the mother manages his own 'pleasure' without 'violating' hers. In the representational portrait memory is faced by an irreconcilable choice. Either the canvas-and-pigment amount to an index (the painting is here because the mother is dead), or they amount to an icon (the mother is here because the painting 'immortalize[s]' her).

In delaying this choice for the speaker about how to read the painting, one important detail is the 'maternal smile' on the face which the portrait represents. Such a smile can provoke two opposite indications which in the poem run the risk of damaging each other. Either it is a smile of absorption, signifying that the mother is happy being dead, being by herself; that is, the smile as an index of her being lost to him.[72] Or the smile is directed towards the viewer, towards him; that is, the smile is an icon of her pleasure in being with him. The smile indicates either one or the other, and it cannot at once indicate both. It is either inward and private, or outward breaking through the painting's glaze.

A first suspicion about the smile occurs in line 27. It is

explained that the face smiles now because it had wept before on behalf of the distressed child/poet. Separation had caused sorrow. Coming together, the receipt of the painting, now brings joy. We might expand the verses and say that the mother appears now to want to be, to enjoy being and to have regretted not being with the child. She is with him now and, therefore, she smiles. This first reading of the portrait as an icon is strengthened by the incident of his playing with the flowers of his mother's dress, which the speaker celebrates later on. The parenthetic lines, 78–9, affirm an absolute presence of voice, touch and smile. The memory of the mother is of her being happier because she is with the child. However, the lines are not as stable as this reading suggests. It is the only such incident in the poem. The use of parenthesis, the prominence given to the phrasing of 'the while' (ending a line, rhyming, and repeated by the periphrastic 'those few pleasant hours'), limit the celebrations for this unique, brief and atypical moment.

It is, therefore, not surprising that the hesitations which disrupt these lines are accentuated in the lines that immediately follow (80–7). This happens in such a way as to re-direct the idea of the smile signifying that she is happy with the child, towards the opposite idea of the smile signifying that she is happier by herself. The set of images which had clustered around the domestic and had dominated the poem until now are abruptly changed. In their place now it is an exotic south-sea climate that 'smiles', and the mother's gorgeous reflection, no longer a portrait looking outward, regards itself in the mirror of the sea. This image both of pleasure and of distance is followed (88–107) by the assertion that the son is absolutely separated from the mother ('compass lost'), in contrast with the father's absolute presence to her ('anchor'd at thy side'). The smile upon the portrait now signifies not maternal concern for the child/poet but, instead, it appears as an index of their separation:

> the thought that thou art safe, and he!
> That thought is joy, arrive what may to me.

This same conflict is repeated in other sequences of lines in the poem, and, as such, it gives us some explanation for their syntactic oddity.

For example, lines 11–20 are about the speaker's obligation to write a poem as a response to the painting. The perplexity of these lines is once again about the identity/difference of the painting and what the painting represents. The portrait is interpreted as asking for a poem about 'a mother lost so long'.

> I will obey, not willingly alone,
> But gladly, as the precept were her own.

The syntactic oddity here is in the way that, although the final clause directs us to read that the speaker will obey *not only* willingly *but also* gladly, the metrical expectations and the syntactic order prepare us for a quite different reading: namely, that the speaker is *alone* not by his own choice but by hers. This discrepancy allows two widely different statements, both of which we will see supported elsewhere in the poem. They might be paraphrased as follows: (i) I will obey and I will write the poem willingly and also gladly because she requested it; (ii) I will obey, although I am not alone of my own will – however, I am glad about it because it is her will.

These perplexities are useful insofar as they permit Cowper to release the poem's two different purposes. The first of these is that of a polite, fairly public, occasional poem. Such a poem distances the speaker from his topic by means of the fiction of the 'speaking picture' and also it dramatises the speaker's 'sincere' or 'artless' refusal of this convention in favour of the notion that it is his mother, and not the painting, who speaks to him. The second purpose lacks this format of self-control. For, in addition to the identity of the portrait and the mother, the poem is also controlled by the sequence of childhood separations of which the picture itself is merely another repetition. Within this second purpose the moment of writing is not a moment of self-control and recollection, but a further deceptive incident in the remembered sequence of separations and absences. Therefore, the moment of writing is no different in its perplexity from each moment of childhood and anxiety. No less than the portrait's gaze at the poet, the mother's gaze at the bed-time and school-time child, her smile, her very presence, is now and always has been an index of her absence. 'That face renews my filial grief . . . thou art she'. The two purposes of the poem intersect. The polite fiction of her presence repeats the anxious memory of her absence.

The disparate statements of the poem are brought together in relation to this unspoken recognition that the mother is and always has been happier out of his sight. That is the poem's significance. The portrait, its face and its smile conceal and reveal that recognition. Is she smiling as if to herself? Is she smiling as if at him? The poem diffuses this choice across its narratives and analogies in such a way that it can only appear in moments of syntactic perplexity, or also in moments of semantic contradiction.

An inspection of such a semantic contradiction will show us how it is that the memories of the speaker depend upon his *not* confronting directly a recognition of the mother's original separateness. The semantic knot is tied by the repetition of one term in a single pair of lines about the memory of his mother's death (39–40). The speaker recalls how he had, in the days after she died, expected to see her at any moment. However, he,

> disappointed still, was still deceiv'd;
> By disappointment every day beguil'd.

These lines were emended by Cowper in one MS by his replacing 'disappointment' in the second line above with 'expectation'. Such a revision highlights the discrepancy that occurs in the unrevised version which we quote above and which was twice published by Cowper. The unrevised version might be paraphrased as follows: 'in spite of constant disappointment I was, nevertheless, duped'; this is followed by: 'on account of disappointment I was constantly duped'. The second half of the statement (of which the poem as a whole is an extended version) flows from the first, but semantically reverses it. Taken together the two halves of the statement indicate how a strategy of disappointment is a *sine qua non* of the poem. Disappointment is the necessary condition of both the narratives of the poem, in spite of their insistent consolations. It is because of this that the one brief 'while' that his mother appeared happier with the child is put in its place (by an extraordinary argument and displacement of pronouns in which 'what we call here our life is such, / So little to be lov'd, and thou so much'). And the place for that singular moment is in parenthesis! By this strategy of disappointment pleasure is averted by being halved. Desire, by possessing only the image of its object, rids itself of guilt.

It is by eliciting this significance of the poem, its necessary condition of disappointment, its radical pessimism about the flexibility of the self, that we can decide why Cowper chose to write about a picture. Because of its representational convention the portrait (and the interpretation of the portrait) is determinate. The smile *has to be* related to a source which the speaker already knows about, a happiness which produced it. The image of the young mother *has to be* accepted, as we say, for what it is. Assumptions about original-and-image form the convention upon which the poem is writable and readable. The picture appears to enforce a 'momentary dream, that thou art she. / My mother!' For the purposes of a polite fiction this dream, which identifies the original with its image, appears as a *consequence* of the speaker's looking at the portrait. However, the opposite is true: looking at the portrait is the consequence of the dream.

The use of a portrait to support this perplexity is more fully understood if we look at the most recent commentary on the matter by Sir Joshua Reynolds. In his penultimate discourse at the Royal Academy in 1788 Reynolds had continued in the relatively expansive and enquiring manner which characterises the discourses throughout the 1780s. Having established earlier the distinctions between higher and lower styles of painting, he had been emphasising more recently the centrality of genius (Discourse 11), the relative unimportance of particular methods (Discourse 12), the affinities of painting with other, non-mimetic arts (Discourse 13), and some characteristics of modern painting as exemplified in the work of Gainsborough (Discourse 14). Finally, Reynolds argues in 1790 (Discourse 15), his purpose overall had been 'to distinguish the greater truth from the lesser truth; the larger and more liberal idea of nature from the more narrow and confined; that which addresses itself to the imagination, from that which is solely addressed to the eye'.[73]

Such an argument gives a relatively low status to what Reynolds terms imitation: that is, to representations of local scenery, still life, and so on. It gives a relatively high status to what Reynolds terms the poetical: that is, to a representation of ideal and mythical subject-matter in the grand style. The first requires little and the second requires much adherence to (or, in its other sense, imitation of) learned models such as Michelangelo, Poussin and Raphael.

The scale of value so presented gives an edge (and also a touch of condescension) to Reynolds's admiration for Gainsborough. To pay such homage to a contemporary artist was itself a breach in the decorum of the *Discourses*.[74] However, given Reynolds's admission that in the eighteenth century the grand style, 'the language of the Gods now no longer exists, as it did in the fifteenth century', it is likely that amongst the moderns we will find ourselves often 'preferring genius in a lower rank of art, to feeblenes and insipidity in the highest'.[75] Therefore, it is useful to study Gainsborough, although his style of painting 'did not require that he should go out of his own country for the objects of his study; they were everywhere about him; he found them in the street and in the fields'.[76]

Gainsborough, therefore, is not grand and poetical. He is 'faithful' towards his restricted subject-matter. His distinction and the controversial nature of his work both lie in his peculiar and 'novel' manner of execution. Reynolds's difficulty is precisely with

all those odd scratches and marks, which, on a closer examination, are so observable in Gainsborough's pictures, and which even to experienced painters appear rather the effect of accident than design; this chaos, this uncouth and shapeless appearance, by a kind of magic, at a certain distance assumes form, and all the parts seem to drop into their places; so that we can hardly refuse acknowledging the full effect of diligence, under the appearance of charm and hasty negligence. That Gainsborough considered this peculiarity in his manner and the power it possesses of exciting surprise, as a beauty in his works, I think may be inferred from the eager desire which we know he always expressed, that his pictures, at the Exhibition, should be seen near as well as at a distance.[77]

It is, of course, quite appropriate to a representational convention that Gainsborough should have wanted his pictures seen from a certain distance. But that he should also wish them to be seen up close is to emphasise an indeterminacy and mobility, an uncertainty of actual representation, by virtue of the plasticity of the roughened medium. This is to disturb and enlarge the activity of looking at a picture in much the same way as we shall later notice Thomas Twining disturb and enlarge the activity of listening to music. The spectator's subjectivity is brought into play insofar as the painting's composition explicitly depends upon the spectator's choice and situation. In the simplest terms, it leaves something for the spectator to do, something decisive. To incorporate that activity into a convention of representation is to displace the balance of original and image. We have already seen

John Gregory and others insist that 'a certain distance' is required in representation and that we must prevent images being brought 'too near the eye'. It is for Reynolds a confrontation with a paradox that encourages him finally to decide that Gainsborough's 'want of precision and finishing', however desirable for its quality of lightness, is inadvisable.[78]

This paradox is one between a faithful likeness and the imperfect texture of an image. It becomes a crisis when Reynolds comes to consider that epitome of representation: the portrait.

Now Gainsborough's portraits were often little more, in regard to finishing, or determining the form of the features, than what generally attends a dead colour; but as he was always attentive to the general effect, or whole together, I have often imagined that this unfinished manner contributed even to that striking resemblance for which his portraits are so remarkable. Though this opinion may be considered as fanciful, yet I think a plausible reason may be given, why such a mode of painting should have such an effect. It is presupposed that in this undetermined manner there is the general effect; enough to remind the spectator of the original; the imagination supplies the rest, and perhaps more satisfactorily to himself, if not more exactly, than the artist, with all his care, could possibly have done. At the same time it must be acknowledged there is one evil attending this mode; that if the portrait were seen, previous to any knowledge of the original, different persons would form different ideas, and all would be disappointed at not finding the original correspond with their own conceptions; under the great latitude which indistinctness gives to the imagination, to assume almost what character or form it pleases.[79]

Gainsborough's practice of working the surface of the picture forces Reynolds's idea of representation into an absurdity. The spectator's relative freedom in relation to the picture immediately becomes an anxiety about the picture's primary purpose, which is (largely for commercial reasons) presumed to be wholly in its relation of image to original. What Reynolds wishes to inhibit in the way we look at pictures ('the great latitude which indistinctness gives to the imagination') is what James Usher and others wish to encourage in the way we listen to music.

William Cowper looks at his poem's portrait entirely within the presumption of faithfulness which Reynolds defends. Both poet and painter assume that a portrait is to be a precise and finished image. Indeed precision and finish replace the stability of the original which it represents. Both Cowper and Reynolds also indicate some tension in maintaining that assumption: Reynolds in his provisional attraction to the imprecise and unfinished effects of Gainsborough's work; and Cowper in his memories of the instabilities of the past which the fixed image of the portrait replaces, but which its uncertainties repeat.

We have found in the hesitations of Cowper's poem that the material presence which it describes is itself a part of the same structure of representation, the same disappointment and deception, the same substitution of an image for its object. The strategy of the poem is to avoid a recognition that the material presence which the portrait appears to represent had not been adequately present at all. It is by reason of the principle of representation, which for Reynolds and for Cowper is epitomised by portrait painting, that this evasive strategy can take place. The portrait constitutes the mother: a presence which appears to determine the portrait in every detail, and which now insists that its determinate interpretation can be no more than 'this mimic show of thee'. In spite of its unpromising tone 'this mimic show of thee' is a phrase that comforts, because as a way of looking at the painting it guarantees to the final 'thee' a presence more absolute than any other strategy throughout the poem can sustain. The iconic/indexical convention of the portrait, therefore, produces a comfort which, in its recurrent perplexities of memory and disappointment, the poem appears to disturb by calling into question the idea of faithful imitation upon which the portrait depends. There is in this poem by Cowper a crisis in that idea of imitation which the portrait constructs, and which the poem (in spite of its intentions) deconstructs.

We need not extend in any detail our analysis to such poems as 'Alexander Selkirk', 'The Poplar Field', 'Yardley Oak' or 'The Castaway'. It will be clear in any reading of these poems that they also elaborate a process of memory as disappointment. Consider, for example, the words of Alexander Selkirk:

> When I think of my own native land,
>   In a moment I seem to be there;
> But alas! recollection at hand
>   Soon hurries me back to despair.[80]

No verses could more strongly contrast with those by Blake about the complexities of the imprisoned bird's song: the music of the relatively autonomous power of imagination. It is, therefore, more useful to analyse, by way of contrast with Cowper's figure of painting as despair, his own use of an image of music. This image of music is put to work by Cowper also in contexts that mediate memory and disappointment. Its uses are infrequent, but they are strikingly different from the use of the figure of the portrait.

We can consider first the sixth book of *The Task* and its use of an image of music developed according to the outlines of Hartley's theory of vibrations and association:

> There is in souls a sympathy with sounds;
> And, as the mind is pitch'd, the ear is pleas'd
> With melting airs, or martial, brisk, or grave:
> Some chord in unison with what we hear
> Is touch'd within us, and the heart replies.
> How soft the music of those village bells,
> Falling at intervals upon the ear
> In cadence sweet, now dying all away,
> Now pealing loud again, and louder still,
> Clear and sonorous, as the gale comes on!
> With easy force it opens all the cells
> Where mem'ry slept. Wherever I have heard
> A kindred melody, the scene recurs,
> And with it all its pleasures and its pains.[81]

This verse-paragraph goes on to include memories once again of his parents. But in this instance the poet speaks of the mind as something comprehensive and rapid. It reaches toward a more obscure sense of regret, not for what fullness has been lost but for what is never fully possessed.

> But not to understand a treasure's worth
> Till time has stol'n away the slighted good
> Is cause of half the poverty we feel,
> And makes the world the wilderness it is.[82]

This relationship, at once more indirect and more equivalent, between the present and the past is not developed further in *The Task*. Unlike those lines in a MS version of *The Prelude* in which Wordsworth constructs a double uncertainty about

> what there is
> Of subtler feeling of remembered joy
> Of soul & spirit in departed sound
> That can not be remembered[83]

Cowper's poem ensures a pattern for the past and the present by comparing both with the cyclic order of the seasons. This cyclic pattern is available to moderate the inner 'wilderness' into something almost bearable.

I can find only one instance, and indeed only one image, in

which Cowper proposes, as did Blake, a negative and relatively autonomous relationship between the imagination and its environment. The image occurs, again, in the context of disappointment and the consolations of time. The image constitutes one brief poem, 'To the Nightingale which the author heard sing on New-Year's Day, 1792'. It will, again, be best to reproduce this brief poem in full.

> Whence is it, that amaz'd I hear
>   From yonder wither'd spray
> This foremost morn of all the year,
>   The melody of May?
>
> And why, since thousands would be proud
>   Of such a favour shown,
> Am I selected from the crowd
>   To witness it alone?
>
> Sing'st thou, sweet Philomel, to me,
>   For that I also long
> Have practis'd in the groves like thee,
>   Though not like thee in song?
>
> Or sing'st thou rather under force
>   Of some divine command,
> Commission'd to presage a course
>   Of happier days at hand?
>
> Thrice welcome then! for many a long
>   And joyless year have I,
> As thou to-day, put forth my song
>   Beneath a wintry sky.
>
> But thee no wintry skies can harm,
>   Who only need'st to sing,
> To make ev'n January charm,
>   And ev'ry season Spring.[84]

The speaker in this poem might well be the one to whom Blake's songster sings from its golden cage. The question is again about why one would sing in adversity, in the absence of any reason and sense. What is this song without a source, this song which, both in its singing and in its listening, constructs the source it lacks?

Two-thirds of the poem is made up of such exclamatory questions: whence and why? The analogy between the bird's song and the poet's work is an explicit one; the difference between them remains implicit. How great this difference is remains uncertain. It appears as a difference in the strength or persuasive lyricism of their 'poetry'. The negative relationship between the bird's delighting voice and its wintry occasion constructs the idea of a relatively autonomous poetry. Also listening to the bird's song 'misrepresents' the season in which it is heard. Such an idea of poetry is one, as we have seen above, which no convention of realistic painting could give to Cowper. Instead, this poem raises the possibility described by James Usher that 'an object has been there which was not represented by a sensible idea, and which makes itself felt only by its influence'. Also, it raises the possibility described by Chabanon that in unhappy circumstances song is not constrained to repeating anything except gaiety. The analogy of the nightingale's musical performance involves notions of the indeterminate and undetermined workings of an 'image' which Cowper's poem is scarcely willing to admit.

Once again it is a syntactical perplexity which allows Cowper some breathing space. The final stanza of the nightingale poem runs together two statements which normally must be kept separate. First, there is the statement that winter need not matter to a nightingale because he can survive by song alone ('Behold the lilies of the field . . .'). Second, there is the statement that winter need not matter to a nightingale because he can transform it by his song into a paradisal garden (the magic of the music of Orpheus).

These conventions – first, a benevolent Providence; second, a metamorphic imagination – become complicated when Cowper presents them to us in one sentence. Either of them alone is unacceptable to him. The first is unacceptable to his faith. The second is unacceptable to his poetics. Therefore, in this final stanza neither idea is given emphasis insofar as both are placed so close to each other that each remains unclear. No reader could interpret the poem either as a decision in favour of the creative imagination, nor as a decision in favour of an absolute benign Providence. The reader can, instead, only hesitate in an indecision between both.

3

WILLIAM WORDSWORTH

Responding to suggestion: Thomas Twining

Thomas Twining (1735–1804) understood himself to be a 'modernist' in his preferences in music. Twining, the eldest son of the founder of the successful tea-merchandising company, chose to adopt the life of a country clergyman and scholar instead of that which lay open to him in the family business. A younger brother, Daniel, entered commerce; and we know much about Thomas Twining from his correspondence with Daniel.[1] The other chief correspondent in Twining's life was the historian of music, Charles Burney. Burney made use of Twining's scholarship and modern tastes especially in the writing of the early volumes of his history.[2] According to one of Twining's letters, written from his living near Colchester, the most celebrated event in his life was to attend one of Haydn's London concerts.[3]

As a student and fellow at the University of Cambridge from 1755 to 1763 Twining had taken part in the musical life of the colleges. He recalled later in a letter to Burney the influence of the poet Thomas Gray in encouraging a preference for recent and contemporary music.[4] Gray's modernist tastes are not recorded in his published writings; the case is otherwise with Twining. His major work is the critical edition of *Aristotle's Treatise on Poetry, Translated: with Notes on the Translation, and on the Original; and Two Dissertations, on Poetical, and Musical, Imitation*. Twining completed this work in 1784 and it was published in 1789.[5]

In the second of these dissertations Twining analyses the position of contemporary forms of music in the light of a critical account of Aristotle and of classical definitions about the arts and representation. An admirer of Diderot, Condillac, D'Alembert, and later of Lessing, Twining approaches his work on Aristotle as 'an example of *un-idolatrous* editorship', fair, rational, and up-to-date.[6] However, in spite of this approval for the enlightenment, Twining liked to idolise some anti-rationalist pleasures in music. Indeed, his private notes and letters often read like those, as it were, of *Rameau's Nephew*. A letter to Charles Burney catches the tone of his enthusiasms:

> It was Mr Gray, principally, who made me first turn my back upon all this, by his enthusiastic love of expressive and passionate music, which it was hardly possible for me to hear and see him feel without catching some of his prejudices. For Pergolesi was his darling; he had collected a great deal of him and Leo in Italy, and he lent me his books to copy what I pleased. This was the bridge over which (throwing bundles of old prejudices in favour of Corelli, Geminiani, and Handel into the river) I passed from ancient to modern music. I let my ears and my feelings carry me which way they pleased, and soon renounced what was once my creed – that the Pergolesis and the Leos had carried vocal music to its utmost perfection, and that nothing was to be done after them.[7]

This application of the idea of progress to musical taste resulted in Twining's continuous appreciation for contemporary music and especially for instrumental music and for Haydn.

It is true that Twining, in spite of the minor place conventionally assigned him, has been recognised for his 'modernism'. His position as a friend and adviser to Burney has been generously acknowledged in Roger Lonsdale's biography of Burney. Histories of literary criticism have found in Twining's critical theory, in his attitude to classicism, in his literary tastes, and in his enthusiasm for mountain scenery, indications of a pre-Romantic. Writers on comparative aesthetics have discussed the contribution made by Twining's published writings to eighteenth-century ideas about the arts. More recently, Twining has been credited with a notion of imitation which is important in the development of an eighteenth-century theory of signs. However, it is also as a 'modernist' that Twining has been condemned. Leo Spitzer, in his article on the collapse of the allegorical significance of the concept of *Stimmung*, singles out as culprits not only eighteenth-century epistemology in general but also Twining in particular. In the edition of Aristotle Twining rejects archaic accounts of music and myths about music (indeed Burney's history is especially indebted to him here). Twining includes in his rejection Spenser's description of the choir of nature. Spitzer finds in this response a narrow and literalist rationalism.[8]

There is, therefore, an ambiguity in Twining's account of the arts, an obscurantism and a rationalism unstably at work. This is precisely indicated in his decision to include an essay on music in a critical edition of Aristotle's *Poetics*. It is an ambiguity in Twining's work which emerges also as that between the musical

enthusiast and the man of letters, the analyst and the man of
sensibility, the correspondent of the celebrated Heyne of Göttingen and the retiring country clergyman. The apparatus to the
edition of Aristotle emphasises one side of these opposites: the
critical scholar. The accompanying dissertations on poetry and
music emphasise the other side: the private enthusiast. We shall,
therefore, find it useful when analysing the contradictions
encountered by Twining to consider also his unpublished papers
and correspondence.

We can first examine these contradictions in a sermon by
Twining which we learn from his letters to have been of especial
importance to him.[9] It was delivered at Colchester on 19 May
1790, a year after the edition of Aristotle was published. The aim
of the sermon was to define the limits of reason in reading the
bible, a contribution to the Socinian debate. The letters make it
clear that Twining's faith and orthodoxy were far from confident
as he attempted to mediate between two conventional approaches
to reading the bible: (i) as a system of natural morality; (ii) as an act
of revelation. In order to find some middle ground between the
two, Twining distinguishes between an 'unintelligible proposition' and a 'mystery'. In the first of these we do not
understand the terms; in the second we do not understand the
relation between the terms. Twining adds that instances of
mystery, clusters of uncomprehended relationships, are an
everyday experience. They ought not to be meddled with by the
mind.[10]

Twining was familiar with, and almost nonplussed by, David
Hume's essay 'On Miracles'.[11] In the sermon he is clearly evading
the problem Hume had isolated: namely, that the criteria of
eighteenth-century empiricism had nothing positive to say about
religious experience and faith.[12] Twining simply decides that
certain objects of knowledge are analysable, and certain others
are not. Despite the otherwise consistent praise and defence of the
encyclopedists we also find in Twining this rejection of rational
analysis. In this instance the restriction on reason is equated with
faith. Elsewhere it will be equated with pleasure.

The argument used in the sermon of 1790 can be quite directly
related to a letter which Twining wrote as early as 1763, the year
in which he left the university and renounced his future in the
family tea business.

there is no kind of investigation so tempting & pleasant, as that of *things which can never be* found. Search for a thing that *may* be found out, & ten to one but you find it presently; & then, after a little compliment to your sagacity, all your pleasure is over! the happiness of *thinking one's self near finding anything*, is, I have observ'd, greater than that of *having found* it & this happiness, a man that is wise enough to pursue *unattainable* things, may enjoy all his life.[13]

Like James Usher, Twining is in love with whatever recedes from his knowledge of it. This is what gives an edge to his thought. It is, therefore, not surprising that reputable critics have praised Twining's edition of Aristotle as the best critical edition in English, and the accompanying dissertations as among the most incisive eighteenth-century criticism.[14] For Twining also argues that 'The critic, who suffers his philosophy to reason away his pleasure, is not much wiser than the child, who cuts open his drum, to see what it is within that caused the sound.'[15] Instead of this being an excuse for lazy thinking, it becomes for Twining a principle by which he can intelligently define musical pleasure, on the one hand, and the relationship between music and the language of poetry, on the other.

In this way Twining differs from James Usher, and the difference emerges especially in Twining's interest, not only in the problem of the signification of music, but also in the experience of music itself. A large and practical knowledge of music, constant friendship with the greatest musicologist of the day, an active participation in concert life, are all evidence of Twining's practical interest in music. He is an avid listener and an eager performer. His detailed knowledge appears in long analyses of specific pieces of music.[16] His contemporary taste is seen in his defence of modern instrumental music.[17] His original intelligence can be found in the application of his sensibility for music to arguments about its modes of signifying.

Sensibility is a notion to which Twining gives precise attention. Music, he writes, is 'a highly sensible pleasure (for sensual is ambiguous)'.[18] The first occasion on which we find him exploiting that contrast as part of a larger and more specific aesthetic is the arrival in his home of a marvellous novelty, the pianoforte. He writes to Burney in 1774:

I am much pleased with the tone of it, which is sweet and even; in the pianissimo it is charming. Altogether the instrument is delightful, and I play upon it *con amore*, and with the pleasure I expected. If it has defects which a good harpsichord has not, it has beauties and delicacies which amply compensate, and which make the harpsichord wonderfully flashy and insipid when played after it; though for some purposes, and in some of my musical moods, though not the best I confess, I might turn to the harpsichord in preference. There are times when one's ears call only for harmony, and a pleasant jingle; when one is disposed to merely sensual music, that tickles the auditory nerves, and does not disturb the indolence of our feelings or imagination. But as soon as ever my spirit wakes, as soon as my heart-strings catch the gentlest vibration, I swivel me round incontinently to the pianoforte.[19]

For Twining, with all his ironic humour, the piano appears to allow a deeper level of feeling and a more active imaginative response, both of which would otherwise tend to be unexpressed. This notion is worth pursuing further. On the one hand, it is part of that popular attitude which eventually makes the harpsichord redundant as a concert instrument. On the other, it explains to us how Twining locates in that popular change a new perception of musical sound and a new concept of its modes of signifying.

Twining attributes his preference for the piano to a new relationship which it enables between the music and the listener. The piano, because of the character of its sound, facilitates a richer subjectivity. The technical basis for this aesthetic, along with some apparent paradoxes, emerges when Twining puzzles about the harmonic imperfections of different instruments.

Imperfection comes [he writes in 1783] when we modulate into other keys – when we want the same *sound*, to do in different relations: the mechanism of our instruments forces us to want this: The pretended imperfection of *nature* is more or less according to the instrument we measure it by: believe the Harpsichord and other instruments where *all* the sounds are fixed – nature is a mere bungler. Ask the fiddle, where *some* sounds only are fixed – it will speak a little better of her. Ask the *voice*, if Nature is imperfect, – it will not know what you mean.[20]

Twining's exposition involves contrasts between the harmonic imperfections of keyboard instruments, the lesser imperfections of stringed instruments, and the possible perfect intonation of the human voice. However, the piano, being banged not plucked, with its consequently 'complex' sound in contrast with the 'brightness' of the harpsichord, is unlike other keyboard instruments insofar as it approaches the tone of the human voice. Its sustaining power and its power of relative dynamic modulation, combined with perfections and imperfections of temperament, make it the ideal musical instrument.[21] Twining's comments on the different values of different instruments are in response to discussions about the possibility of perfect temperament. His objection is to a science of acoustics, the purpose of which was to produce instruments of more and more controllable and mathematical perfection in performance.[22] Twining has occasion in his letters to argue against some of these popularised experiments, especially against those of Robert Smith.

In particular Twining condemns Smith for the attention he devoted in the *Harmonics, or the Philosophy of Music Sounds* (1749) to the construction of instruments which made perfection of intonation possible. It is fascinating that Twining first raises this issue in the context of dispelling what he understands to be the religious superstition of the seventeenth-century view of consecutive fifths as a sacrilege. That kind of allegorical sanctity is, according to Twining, an absurdity. Whatever the ear confirms is good, and any specific rules ought to be flexible. It is for this emancipation from an allegorical way of interpreting music that Leo Spitzer has criticised Twining and the eighteenth century in general. We can, however, notice a difference within the century itself. Certainly, the natural science of acoustics substitutes an iconography of the calculus in post-Newtonian work on music and musical instruments.[23] However, in place of that old and now obscure allegory of the sacred, Thomas Twining substitutes a new obscurity of sensibility.

Consider, for example, Twining's preferences within the different kinds of harpsichords available on the market:

Don't let it be one of Dr. Smith's *perfect monsters*, that will check me in my extempore ramblings. I *work* out my *own* modulations with fear and trembling upon those harpsichords. They were not made for lovers of *Music*, but for lovers of *sound*, as Dr. Smith was, who, I believe, would have heard the worst music with much the same pleasure as the best, provided the ratios of the intervals were but right.[24]

The result of such theoretically perfect construction is not *tune* but *being in tune*. By way of contrast, Twining decides that the listening ear should not be so much *perfect* as *strong*. The listener ought to be prompted to be responsive, and not to '*hear* so *literally*'.[25]

Twining finds some small support for this view in the aesthetics of the Abbé Dubos, who had argued that music is something which we rather feel than hear.[26] To illustrate this idea, which repeats the earlier contrast between the sensible and the sensual,

Twining returns to the differences between the harpsichord and the piano. He distinguishes between these two major keyboard instruments by basing his preference upon Rousseau's defence of melody as a pure and original invention which contrasts with 'Harmony *ready* invented to one's hand'.

Upon a *harpsichord* . . . this support of harmony, batteries, and poddlediddle basses etc. seems necessary, at least in movements that are not rapid. The Pianoforte will bear simple melody much better, to be sure; but even here, I find myself always supposing the instrument only a good sort of succedeneum for 2 instr.'s of more *perfect* expression, or 2 voices. I continually find myself singing when I play E. Bach's music – a key'd instr. that can *sustain* & vary a tone is a great desideratum that still remains to be supplied.[27]

On one side, therefore, we have harmony, the harpsichord, the literal ear, sensuality. On the other side, we have melody, the piano, the responsive ear, sensibility. Nature and voice are equivalent. To Twining there appears to be a difficulty insofar as he is arguing within a contrast between the mathematical basis of temperament and its perceptual basis, for he can equate his notion of perfect 'natural' intervals with neither of these. One result of this is that he must not only define the material nature of musical sound to be imperfect, but he must also declare that this imperfection, this lack of mathematical precision, is the better part of music. 'Imperfection' is the opportunity for 'strong' listening. The quality of sound on a piano, because of its imprecision, offers the larger access to subjectivity. The relatively 'perfect' harpsichord offers less.

Twining states these ideas most fully when he is arguing not only against contemporary techniques in acoustics but also against his friend, Charles Burney. Burney had pointed out the apparent contradictions in Twining's first hypothesis, and in 1777 Twining replies:

So you won't hear of *dissonant Harmonics*? . . . I cannot find the expression in Rousseau, where I thought it was . . . we both are agreed, I imagine, that Harmonics – *the Harmonics* of a sound, are (as Rousseau defines them *art. Harmonique*) *tous les sons concomitans* etc. . . . how it is certain that among these aliquot parts, not only *many wou'd* be dissonant, if heard, but *some* that *are* heard are dissonant: ex gratia – the aliquot $\frac{1}{7}$ which, in the lower strings of a Harpsichord, often prevail over *all* the other Harmonics, so as to bother one, (me, at least, for *one*) in tuning . . . That there are *dissonant Harmonics* therefore, you will not dispute; only you think the expression shocking, and doubt whether anybody has ventured upon it. I shou'd be sorry to *swear* that it is not an unhappy audacity of my own coining. Yet I seem to remember it; & when I get to some books at Fordham I will try to find it . . . I acknowledge it does not *sound* prettily. At the same time, if I had occasion to talk of those *dissonant* sounds, I sh'd be puzzled to avoid the expression, while *Harmoniques* continues to be the only technical, usual, term for *all the sounds* that accompany a note, consonant or dissonant. Perhaps *resonance* wou'd do?[28]

Twining's memory had not entirely failed him. Returning to his library in the village of Fordham he would have found that he had slightly misquoted Chabanon. The *Observations sur la Musique* (1769) argues that 'Les législateurs en harmonie ont, il est vrai, capitulés avec l'oreille pour lui faire admettre les accords dissonans.'[29] Yet Twining's lapse of memory produces a more useful term than any of these: *resonance*. For resonance is an aspect of sound, its materiality, which Twining can approve. His emphasis upon it obviously relates to his preference for the pianoforte and his doubts about harpsichords. A 'perfect' ear cannot, but a 'strong' ear can cope with resonance.

D'Alembert had similarly noticed the difference between the perceptual and the mathematical basis of musical pleasure. In his argument against Rameau's mathematical basis for a theory of harmony, D'Alembert observes how

Il entrera toujours dans la théorie des phénomènes musicaux une sorte de métaphysique que ces phénomènes supposent implicitement, et qui porte son obscurité naturelle.[30]

For D'Alembert these observations do not in any way undermine the principle that music is an art of imitation. They merely criticise the exaggerated claim by Rameau that the perfection of musical composition would follow from the mathematical analysis of harmonic sounds. Twining, however, makes use of D'Alembert, as he also makes use of Chabanon, in order to advance a more general and extraordinary epistemological argument.

Twining argues that the pleasure and signification of music depend upon an inadequacy or imprecision in the very material of its sound. The act of listening (which is perceptual) and the source of pleasure (which is signification) are imposed one upon the other. It is not surprising that Twining's argument includes a preference for instrumental over vocal music. For instrumental music has the extra 'inadequacy' of its significance being in no way given, except by one's listening to it. So great is Twining's preference that we read in a letter of 1769 how, on hearing 'the grand, fuguing, learned, style' of Handel, 'I knew nothing of the words, and heard it as instrumental music'.[31]

This is all a part of Twining's sense of the modern. Writing to Burney about the advantages of writing a history of *this* age of *real* music, he ridicules the antiquarians. Tactfully he chooses for special contempt the antiquarianism of Sir John Hawkins, whose history of music had been published shortly before the first volume of Burney's.[32] Burney rises to the bait:

> The Knight's reasoning abt. musical Expression is curious. For my part I think good Music well executed wants *no words* to explain its meaning to me – it says everything that the Musician pleases . . .[33]

Even in opera, *pace* Addison, the music and not the words matter. As far as Burney is concerned, even Handel's 'Return God of Hosts' may just as well be a supplication to his mistress.[34]

The energy with which Twining defends mere instrumental music indicates how he sees himself writing at a point in time when a whole burden of received opinion, from Aristotle to Rousseau, had to be cast off. Again he writes in notes on a letter to Burney:

> Those who talk of instrumental Music i.e. of Music by itself, as *unmeaning* (Plato de Leg. lib. 1. quoted by Dr Brown p. 47 Rousseau, Art. Sonate) and expressing nothing, forget that if that was the case, it could not possibly *add* expression to verse. If it cannot move the passions separately, it cannot conjointly. If it assists the [poetry], it must be by some strength of its own which it brings with it. Dr B[urney] p. 208 speaking of the Latin Mottets, because the words are unintelligible to the greater part of the hearers, says there is a total separation of *sense* from *sound*. If by *sense* he means the *particular ideas* of the words, it will be true; but neither can the *music with* the words, express those *particular ideas*; at best it may seem to do it; all it can *really* do is to excite affections or a *temper*, similar to those of the words; and that it can do without the words, else how could it do it *with* them.[35]

These notes apply the general observations we have seen developed in James Harris, in Charles Avison and Edmund Burke, in such a way as to collapse the conventional principle of representation in music and also in language. The figure of the responsive listener becomes especially important. First, the listener participates in the pleasure of filling out the material sound; second, the listener participates in the pleasure of filling out the signification of the music.

Twining brings these two responses of the active listener together in the second dissertation accompanying his edition of the *Poetics*: 'On the Different Senses of the Word, Imitative, as applied to Music by the Antients, and by the Moderns'. Out of the ideas sketched throughout his papers and correspondence he makes one principle that will support an aesthetics of music. The intention of this dissertation, according to his letters, was to be 'rather philosophical, than *critical*; to consider what Music *can* do, and how, rather than what she has done'.[36]

Twining argues that the conventional opposition between 'imitation' and 'expression' is not open to our choice between either one or the other. What the ancient authors, who knew only vocal music, meant by 'imitation' is what modern authors mean by 'expression'. However, it is Twining's conclusion that the ideas and affections produced by music are too indeterminate to be classified under either term.[37] By getting rid of the terms of dispute he clarifies a new and positively stated aesthetic.

First in a footnote, and subsequently in the final passages of the dissertation, Twining elaborates precisely the two aspects of musical pleasure which he had developed in the correspondence with Burney. He defines the interplay between the listener's subjectivity and the music, and also states the logical primacy of instrumental music. First Twining comments on 'the vague and indeterminate assimilations of Music purely instrumental'. In order to support this pleasure with some epistemological basis, he adds the following note:

Music is capable of raising *ideas*, to a certain degree, through the medium of those *emotions* which it raises *immediately*. But this is an effect so delicate and uncertain – so dependent on the fancy, the sensibility, the musical experience, and even the temporary disposition, of the *hearer*, that to call it *imitation*, is surely going beyond the bounds of reasonable analogy. Music, here, is not *imitative*, but if I may hazard the expression, merely *suggestive*.[38]

In a similar way to the hazard of the word 'resonance', so also with 'suggestive' the experienced uncertainties of music become the key elements of its description. By abolishing the terms 'imitation' and 'expression' the new term removes the emphasis both from the world the music might be thought to represent and from the feelings it might be thought to articulate. Both these sources of meaning are displaced. In their place the *listener* is placed as the centre. Even when the older terms re-occur, as they must, the structure of listening as 'suggestive' produces pleasure and significance:

> whatever we may call it, this I will venture to say, – that in the *best* instrumental Music, expressively *performed*, the very indecision itself of the expression, leaving the hearer to the free operation of his *emotion* upon his *fancy*, and, as it were, to the free *choice* of such ideas as are, *to him*, most adapted to react upon and heighten the emotion which occasioned them, produces a pleasure, which nobody, I believe, who is able to feel it, will deny to be one of the most delicious that Music is capable of affording. But far the greater part even of those who have an ear for Music, have *only* an *ear*; and to *them* this pleasure is unknown.[39]

Such a description of the role of the listener is a radical shift in the epistemology of aesthetic pleasure. The activity of the listener produces a response which appears both dialectical and free. The mind and feelings of the listener seek an image outside themselves in music. The perception of that uncertain and empty sign hurries the listener back upon his own subjectivity. The pleasure lies in the excess of signification over and beyond the initial and incomplete sign the music had offered. The meaning of music depends upon the enigmatic character of its signs which, instead of replacing a source which they would imitate or express, turn the listener's attention to his own inventive subjectivity. To hear literally, to demand words accompanying the instruments, to rely on instruments of mathematical control, to dislike resonance, is to dismiss that whole process of suggestion. For Twining the structure of listening to music and the completeness of its pleasure depends upon the incompleteness of music in terms both of its signs and of its material sound.

Music as tabula rasa: Adam Smith

In order to understand better the ideas of Thomas Twining and also the consequences of those ideas, it is useful to contrast Twining's aesthetic with that developed according to the theory of the association of ideas. Twining's admiration for the suggestive character of music is an admiration for something less precise than anything produced by the otherwise similar theory of association. Among those who maintained that theory, the notion that music is obscure usually resulted in its being placed (as we have noticed with John Baillie) in the category of the sublime. This was done not so much for emotive as for epistemological reasons. Distinctions of the kind made by Twining were ignored: all music and all instruments and all styles were treated as if they were of a piece.

In the *Essays . . . on Taste* (1790) Archibald Alison writes that 'the sublimity of . . . sounds is to be ascribed not to the mere quality of the Sound, but to those associated qualities of which it is significant'.[40] Alison grants that he knows nothing about music and he borrows from Rousseau's argument that music imitates speech. Music, he asserts, is expressive by virtue of its association with 'signs in the human Voice'. Without words 'music can express nothing more particular than the Signs themselves'. Alison, therefore, arrives at two different responses to music which, in contrast to their function in Twining, remain quite unrelated to each other. The first response is the perception of a texture of related sounds. The second is the perception of meaning by an abstract and fairly uncertain act of association of music and speech-sounds.[41]

Alexander Gerard had arrived at a similar position in his *An Essay on Taste* (1759; revised 3rd edition, 1780). The representational arts depend, for Gerard, upon the theory of association and the same theory explains

> also the sublime in music: it seems to be derived in part from the length and gravity of the notes; the former constituting a kind of amplitude to the ear; the latter contributing to that composure and sedate expansion of the mind which attends the perception of sublimity: and it is then completed, when the artist, by skilfully imitating the sublime passions, or their objects, inspires those passions into his hearers, and renders them conscious of their operation.[42]

Although Gerard recognises an 'exquisite' and 'inexpressible' delight which arises merely from the structure and order of a musical composition, he argues independently that music is best when according to a principle of association it is 'applied to a determinate subject'.[43] This unrelatedness in their responses to music is evidence of how theories of the arts which, like those of Alison and Gerard, are based on the theory of association, remain ill at ease with music. As Alison puts it, there appears to be for sounds no 'kind of established Imagery in our Minds'.[44]

A similar, if less forceful, difficulty extends to language and to poetry. This is evident at least in the appendix which Gerard added to the third edition of *An Essay on Taste* in 1780. Revising his earlier decisions, Gerard is eager to admit that words are signs without resemblance to objects. They are, therefore, not mimetic in any simple sense. They only become mimetic, indeed, when they combine to form the 'subject' of a poem. It is this which constitutes the imitation. Gerard's definition is a strikingly promising one: 'The subject of every poem is to a certain degree a *fable*; and to the very same degree, it is an imitation.'[45] The structure of the relation between the parts of the poem must therefore decide its meaning.

It is precisely at this point in the discussion that Adam Smith, in one of the most intelligent essays on music in the eighteenth century, intervenes. 'The subject of a composition of instrumental Music is a part of that composition; the subject of a poem or picture is no part of either.'[46] The structure of the relation between the parts becomes therefore the all-in-all of music. The other arts either imitate or express something which lies outside themselves. Music is, therefore, self-contained in a way in which the other arts are not. Smith, taking the notion of the empty sign no less seriously than those who precede him, finds in that emptiness a formula by which the other arts, and not music, appear 'incomplete'. The very title of Smith's essay, 'Of the Nature of that Imitation which takes place in what are called the Imitative Arts' (1795), indicates an objectivity and a sense of irony. In this essay we find clear statement of an idea of music which, if it is supplemented by Twining's aesthetic of the 'suggestive', amounts to that which is available to the poetics of the early Romantics.

This essay on the arts by Adam Smith takes its place among his other writings on the 'Philosophical Subjects' of perception and language. In either case Smith elucidates the condition of a structure or grammar without which knowledge and communication would be impossible. 'The Invention, therefore, even of the simplest noun adjective must have required more metaphysics than we are apt to be aware of . . . that of prepositions would be accompanied with yet more.'[47] So argues *A Dissertation on the Origin of Languages* which describes the history of languages as the assignation of names to things *and* as the formation of classes, species and general abstractions.[48] In Smith's work the general abstractions are thought to be not logically but historically prior to the particular. Language, he argues, needs to be 'thoroughly mixed and blended with the correlative object' it names.[49]

Language can achieve this by using, for example, inflected verbal forms. Smith argues on an assumption that words are more diverse and pleasurable insofar as they are indices of the things which they so variously represent. Therefore, the essay regrets the simplification of grammar that has caused 'the prolixness, constraint and monotony of modern languages'.[50] In order to make his audience more 'apt to be aware of' the structured content of knowledge, and in order to provide contemporary evidence of vital and complex structures, Smith must look beyond language-in-use. He must look to the history of languages, and also to non-verbal 'language'.

For example, in an essay 'Of the External Senses', Smith amends Berkeley's comparison between the 'language' of the eye and verbal language. Berkeley had argued that, 'As, in Common language, the words or sounds bear no resemblance to the things which they denote, so, in this other language, the visible objects bear no sort of resemblance to the tangible object which they represent.'[51] Smith, however, argues that the language of the eye has a superior quality, 'a fitness of representation' by virtue of its more consistent and less abrupt grammar.

In this language of Nature, it may be said, the analogies are more perfect; the etymologies, the declensions and conjugations, if one may say so, are more regular than those of any human language. The rules are fewer, and those rules admit of no exceptions.[52]

In this description we find a grammar of representation which exactly fits its correlative grammar of interpretation. This 'fit' is more or less exact in perception and in language.

In Smith's analysis of the arts we again find an emphasis on grammars and structures. However, there is the important difference that the mind is here required to be more conscious of its own process of interpretation. Some provision must then intervene between the 'languages' of perception and their 'fitness of representation' in order to allow the process of interpretation to be foregrounded. It appears to Smith that the arts, and specific modes within each art, are important insofar as they are structures which can make us aware of the mind's processes. It is not some single 'meaning' which is to be noticed, but instead the process of noticing that meaning and also the correlative activity of the artist in the producing of the art-work.

In order to facilitate this process the work of art must contain a sort of discrepancy. Smith argues that painting and sculpture are satisfying more or less according to the amount of difference or discrepancy that exists in them between 'the object imitating, and the object imitated'. It follows, therefore, that

> The proper pleasure which we derive from those two imitative arts, so far from being the effect of deception, is altogether incompatible with it . . . The nobler works of Statuary and Painting appear to us a sort of wonderful phaenomena, differing in this respect from the wonderful phaenomena of Nature, that they carry, as it were, their own explication along with them, and demonstrate, even to the eye, the way and manner in which they are produced. The eye even of an unskilful spectator, immediately discerns, in some measure, how it is that a certain modification of figure in statuary, and of brighter and darker colours in painting, can represent with so much Truth and vivacity, the actions, passions, and behaviour of men, as well as a great variety of other objects.[53]

The observer of a statue or of a painting does not, therefore, see x as equivalent to x^i. The observer, instead, perceives the way and manner in which x can be imagined as equivalent to x^i. By virtue of its difference or discrepancy, both of medium and of formal elements, the statue or painting is an occasion for a reflective act of interpretation.

This is an aesthetics of anti-illusionism. As such it is highly appropriate to certain transformations in late eighteenth-century art, which we shall discuss later on, transformations which have been analysed especially by Dora and Erwin Panofsky and by Robert Rosenblum.[54] Their work has directed attention towards the importance of pure linearity and abstractionism, the creation of a *tabula rasa*, in such painters as William Blake, John Flaxman and Francis Towne. One logical consequence of Smith's essay is to find painting to be, in terms of its necessary formalism and anti-illusionism, more 'abstract' than sculpture.[55] Another consequence is to find instrumental music to be the epitome of such abstract formalism and anti-illusionism: the *tabula rasa*.

For instrumental music, instead of making the mind reflect upon the ways in which one object is recognised via modifications to another, makes the mind of the listener reflect only upon the ways of recognising order and method in the composition. This is as much as to say that the mind is to reflect upon itself. For the order and method of the composition become correlative to the listener's anticipation and memory. In this way a 'full concerto of instrumental Music' presents an object so agreeable, so great, so various, and so interesting, that alone, and without suggesting any other object, either by imitation or otherwise, it can occupy, and as it were fill up, completely the whole capacity of the mind, so as to leave no part of its attention vacant for thinking of any thing else. In the contemplation of that immense variety of agreeable and melodious sounds, arranged and digested, both in their coincidence and their succession, into so complete and regular a system, the mind in reality enjoys not only a very great sensual, but a very high intellectual pleasure, not unlike that which it derives from the contemplation of a great system in any other science.[56]

This aesthetics of music brings us to a momentary conclusion. In his essay Smith rebuts some terms used previously to explain the indeterminacy of music. For example, he argues against Twining that melody and harmony 'in fact signify and suggest nothing'.[57] Also he argues against the conventional idea, expressed in relation to music by Sir William Jones, that the arts operate by sympathy. 'Whatever we feel from instrumental Music', writes Smith, 'is an original, and not a sympathetic feeling: it is our own gaiety, sedateness, or melancholy; not the reflected disposition of another person.'[58]

Reading empty signs: Campbell, Stewart and de Gérando

Aesthetics is a discourse which is contingent on many aspects of life. I have described the reception of instrumental music within a society, and within a climate of opinion, that defines music by a set of concepts which we can summarise in the notion of the 'empty sign'. It is not likely that practices of language, of literature, of poetics, will fail to touch upon these elements of an aesthetic. Pictorialist assumptions about language had worked well for empiricist notions of words. A concept of the 'empty sign' can, dialectically, oppose that convention. James Usher asserts the latent capacities of the mind which empiricism does not account for. His notion of music subverts that convention about images and ideas which support the 'philosophy of the ideas of sense'. He points the way forward to a notion of subjectivity more unstable even than that implicit in the principle of association. In Usher's aesthetic music epitomises an effect that can touch upon all kinds of desire. Music is the empty sign correlative to the mind's active dissatisfaction with its usual environment. Music promises, suggests, withholds. The epistemology of music's uncertainties is developed for its own sake by Thomas Twining and, more decisively, by Adam Smith. Its subversion of the principles of imitation is seen nowhere more clearly than in the conclusion to Twining's second dissertation, immediately preceding the text of the *Poetics*. For it is an extraordinary way of introducing Aristotle to assert that, although painting and sculpture are in a sense imitative arts, if we apply to poetry and to music

the same general denomination of *Imitative Arts*, we seem to defeat the only useful purpose of all classing and arrangement; and, instead of producing order and method in our ideas, produce only embarrassment and confusion.[59]

This appears to close a long chapter of Aristotelian poetics. Twining makes many restrictions on the ways in which poetry can be called imitation: restrictions which exclude the lyric poem in particular, and all poetry in general (except impersonative dramatic speech). Yet it is not his purpose to equate his ideas about music with those about the language of poetry. In no way does he argue that with poetry 'the very indecision itself of the expression . . . produces a pleasure' which would be the special pleasure of language.[60]

However, in order to understand the solutions to difficulties in poetics and literature which can be elaborated by means of such notions as are common in theories of music, we need look no further forward than 1796. In that year in his Preface to his *Poems on Various Subjects* Samuel Taylor Coleridge introduces the problem of privacy and the individual author's relation to the public reception of his poetry. He presents the not unusual title of his collection as itself an index of the problem:

Poems on various subjects written at different times and prompted by very different feelings; but which will be read at one time and under the influence of one set of feelings – this is an heavy disadvantage.[61]

This introduces an argument designed by Coleridge to defend the supposed egotism of 'effusions' against condemnation by such writers as Charles Churchill. Coleridge appeals to the public as 'a number of scattered individuals' who may each enter sympathetically into the poet's egocentricity.[62] This egocentricity is, he claims, his difference from the fashionable poets of the day who 'avoid the word *I*' and repress it the more urgently it would be uttered.[63]

Coleridge's argument assumes that language can become a transparent medium between individuals. The fallacy of such an assumption was bluntly presented to Coleridge by the critics of his slim volume.[64] It is therefore interesting to look at the way he adjusts his argument (as well as the contents of the volume, now entitled simply *Poems*) in order to meet the attack. In 1797 he silently emends the Preface to the first edition and shifts the burden of intelligibility away from transparent language and towards the activity of reading. Poems on various subjects, prompted by different feelings, but read in one situation and under one state of feeling, are now no longer admitted to carry of themselves a disadvantage. Or, if they do, it is one for which the reader must compensate. For 'the supposed inferiority of one poem to another may sometimes be owing to the temper of mind, in which he happens to peruse it'.[65]

Such a concept of the act of reading, which vacillates between the subjectivity of the author and that of the reader, and which locates obscurity in the reader's changefulness instead of, for example, in the verbal allusiveness or incoherence of the poem,[66] is unthinkable within previous conventions of a rhetoric of poetry. It is unthinkable that Pope or Goldsmith would relate the merit of a poem to the relative states of feeling of a reader. There had, instead, been a set of agreed public effects in the reading of a poem, be it satire or elegy or ode.[67] Coleridge's concept of the effusion, of the lyric poem, robs that rhetoric of its central principle: specificity of intention and effect. Not only must that rhetoric be replaced if the reader's understanding of a poem 'may be owing to the temper of mind, in which he happens to peruse it', but also ideas about language must be re-defined in this poetics of the young Coleridge.

Eight years before Thomas Twining completed the writing of his edition of the *Poetics* George Campbell (1719–96) had provided the framework for such a re-definition of how language communicates. Campbell, a student at Aberdeen and Edinburgh, principal and professor at Marischal College, remained close to the common sense school of Thomas Reid. His work on language, *The Philosophy of Rhetoric* (1776), was given great prominence by Dugald Stewart during the 1790s. A second edition appeared in 1801 under the influence of Stewart's enormous prestige.[68]

Campbell's theory of language is a re-reading of commentaries by Berkeley, Hume and Burke. Burke's decision that words do not raise specific ideas in the mind had diverted into aesthetics one aspect of a critique by Berkeley of general abstract ideas. In *The Principles of Human Knowledge* (1710) Berkeley attributes to the power of abstract ideas the despondency and failure of the sciences. Inner contradiction and paradox darken and entangle the understanding of all thinking men with such abstractions as 'substance', 'matter', 'absolute space', and so forth. Therefore, writes Berkeley,

I come now to consider the *source* of this prevailing notion, and that seems to me to be Language. And surely nothing of less extent than reason itself could have been the source of an opinion so universally received . . . if there had been no such thing as speech or *universal* signs there never had been any thought of abstraction.[69]

Berkeley avoids some implications of this analysis and extricates thought, or reason, from the priority of language by viewing words only as instruments. His critique of abstraction, therefore, entails no analysis of language itself, but only of assumptions about language. Berkeley does analyse the assumptions, first, 'that every name has, or ought to have, only one precise and settled signification', and second, 'that language has no other end but the communicating our ideas'.[70] Against the first assumption Berkeley argues that,

It is one thing for to keep a name constantly to the same definition, and another to make it stand everywhere for the same idea; the one is necessary, the other useless and impracticable.[71]

Against the second assumption he argues that communication is not 'the chief and only end of language'. More frequently, more casually and familiarly, 'the hearing of sounds, or sight of the characters, is oft immediately attended with those passions which at first were wont to be produced by the intervention of ideas that are now quite omitted'.[72] As an example of this more familiar mode of language Berkeley, with his peculiar and ironic economy, gives us the tag 'Aristotle hath said it'. Such a tag serves no purpose of information; it serves rather to encourage 'the motions of assent and reverence in the minds of some men'.[73]

    The solution Berkeley proposes is, none the less, embarrassingly evasive:

Whatever *ideas* I consider, I shall endeavour to take *them* bare and naked into my view . . . so long as I confine my thoughts to my own ideas divested of words I do not see how I can be easily mistaken.[74]

Faced, as Coleridge will be, with this problem of privacy, of communicating by means of language thoughts and ideas (such as those which are unfamiliar and 'ascribe everything to the immediate operation of Spirits') Berkeley agrees with Bacon that one must 'think with the learned, and speak with the vulgar'. The business of communication then shifts from the writer to the reader. The reader, if fair and also ingenious, 'will collect the sense from the scope and connexion of a discourse, making allowance for those inaccurate modes of speech which use has made inevitable'.[75]

The Philosophy of Rhetoric takes up Berkeley's arguments under the heading: 'The nature and power of signs, both in speaking and in thinking'. [76] Campbell's central point includes the dismissal of the possibility that we can think with the learned and speak with the vulgar. The reason for this can be found in how

it may be observed, that we really think by signs as well as speak by them . . . we should never be able to proceed one single step in thinking, any more than in conversing, without the use of signs.[77]

It is with this decisive and alarming refusal to separate language from thought that Campbell approaches the problem of writer and reader, the problem of interpretation.

The problem, in the form he gives to it, has all the marks of a Coleridgean query: 'What is the Cause that Nonsense so often escapes being detected, both by the Writer and by the Reader?' Campbell concentrates his argument on discourse which is relatively abstract and difficult, because it is in that kind of writing that misinterpretation is most likely. However, the problem remains in principle a more general one.

That mere sounds, which are used only as signs, and have no natural connection with the things whereof they are signs, should convey knowledge to the mind, even when they excite no idea of the things signified, must appear at first extremely mysterious.[78]

These comments about language recall, in their choice of terms, Usher's comments about music. However, Campbell is on more promising ground. He is able to discuss language according to an additional convention by which language consists of 'sounds considered as signs'. Of course, no similar interpretative convention applies with music. It is that convention which allows us to analyse the material and structure of a language as something distinct from its signified content.

The relationship between one word and another, which is constituted by usage and by structure, becomes in this view more important than the relationship between either the things signified or 'between words and things'. It is the relationship

which comes gradually to subsist among the different words of a language, in the minds of those who speak it, and which is merely consequent on this, that these signs are employed as signs of connected or related things . . . Hence the sounds considered as signs will be conceived to have a connection analogous to that which subsisteth among the things signified; I say, the sounds considered as signs: for this way of considering them constantly attends us in speaking, writing, hearing, and reading. When we purposely abstract from it and regard them merely as sounds, we are instantly sensible, that they are quite unconnected, and have no other relation than what ariseth from their similarity of tone and accent . . . Hence the words and names themselves, by customary vicinity, contract in the fancy a relation additional to that which they derive purely from being the symbols of related things. Further this tendency is strengthened by the structure of language.[79]

In language, therefore, relationships which appear to specify a signified content overlap and merge with relationships of usage and structure.

Campbell's analysis of this complexity leads him to a recognition of the ways in which thinking *acts upon* signs. Interpreting, writing, reading, are complex activities. In reading, for example, geometrical figures 'the mind with the utmost facility extends or contracts the representative power of the sign, as the particular occasion requires'.[80] Whatever the difference between these signs and the words of a language, 'There is . . . a difficulty in explaining this power the mind hath of considering ideas, not in their private, but, as it were, in their representative capacity.'[81]

Campbell highlights the *power* of the mind in order to dismiss the explanations offered by Locke and by Hume to account for representation. With a radical misreading of *The Principles of Human Knowledge* Campbell attributes to Berkeley an understanding of interpretation which, he exclaims, even Berkeley's admirers have overlooked. For, in Berkeley, Campbell asserts, 'not only words but ideas are made signs'.[82] Communication in language is now understood according to a convention which does not distinguish in any simple way between words and ideas. In contrast with the representational convention proposed by Locke, in which 'The use of words is to be sensible marks of ideas, and the ideas they stand for are their proper and immediate signification',[83] Campbell cites Berkeley on both words and ideas as signs. Both are '"nothing but the capacity they are put into by the understanding of signifying or representing many particulars;" and, if possible, still more explicitly, "the signification they have is nothing but relation:" no alteration of their essence, "that, by the mind of man, is added to them"'.[84]

The interpretative mind is, therefore, far more flexible, powerful and free in its activity upon these signs/ideas than it is under a convention in which each word has a 'proper and immediate signification'. It is along the lines of this analysis by Campbell that Dugald Stewart develops a theory of language and interpretation. As early as 1792 Stewart argues that 'words are the sole object about which our thoughts are employed'. It is language which facilitates the capacities of thought and which gives to the mind 'a sentiment of its own power'.[85]

The difficulties implicit in these ideas will form the basis of Stewart's decisive interest in the work of the French idéologue, de Gérando. Also, with de Gérando's assistance, these ideas will be used to resolve the two major contradictions in Stewart's work: first, that between the opposite but equal values of imaginative and philosophical thought; second, that between a 'sensationalist' theory of language and a 'conceptualist' theory of interpretation. In Stewart's analysis of these contradictions we shall find a strong connection between the notion of the empty signs of music, elaborated by Twining and Smith, and the notion of poetry and language, initiated in Coleridge's Prefaces of 1796 and 1797, and further elaborated in the 1800 Preface to Lyrical Ballads.

The first volume of Stewart's Elements of the Philosophy of the Human Mind appeared in 1792. Its arguments are developed and revised throughout the Philosophical Essays (1810) and also in the later volumes of the Elements which appear after 1813.[86] The contradictions in Stewart's thinking appear most strongly in 1792 and they are brought to a relatively clear resolution in 1810. It is during this period that de Gérando is important to Stewart. It is also during this period that Stewart is important to our understanding of Coleridge's and Wordsworth's poetics.

The design of the first volume of the Elements is a sequence leading from the relatively less to the relatively more complex powers of the mind. The order is as follows: Perception,

Attention, Conception, Abstraction, Association, Memory, Imagination. Each of these involves another which precedes it. Imagination is the most complex and involves a 'combination' of all the previous powers. Perception is the least complex. However, it also requires more than a simple model of interpretation to describe it. An habitual confusion of ideas and words has led writers after Locke to ignore the complexity even of perception.

The greater part of metaphysical language, concerning perception in general, appears evidently, from its etymology, to have been suggested by the phenomena of vision. Even when applied to this sense, indeed, it can at most amuse the fancy, without conveying any precise knowledge; but when applied to the other senses, it is altogether absurd and unintelligible.[87]

For Stewart the consequences of this analogy between perception in general and the visual appears to have been of the greatest importance. It is, for example, at the basis of Hume's scepticism. For the visual analogy encourages the difficulty in connecting two principles: first, that all our distinct perceptions are distinct existences; second, that the mind never perceives any real connection between distinct existences.[88]

The strategy which Stewart adopts in order to undermine this scepticism is, therefore, to alter the visual analogy. He reinterprets it according to another analogy: that of hearing. Consequently perception appears to offer and to require a more flexible response from whomever is perceiving, listening or seeing. To use the analogy with hearing is to notice that,

in a concert of music, a good ear can attend to the different parts of the music separately, or can attend to them all at once, and feel the full effect of the harmony . . . the mind is constantly varying its attention, from the one part of the music to the other, and . . . its operations are so rapid as to give us no perception of an interval of time.

The same doctrine leads to some curious conclusions with respect to vision. Suppose the eye to be fixed in a particular position, and then the picture of an object be painted on the retina . . . the mind does at one and the same time perceive every point in the outline of the object (provided that the whole of it be painted on the retina at the same instant,) for perception, like consciousness, is an involuntary operation. As no two points, however, of the outline are in the same direction, every point, by itself constitutes just as distinct an object of attention to the mind, as if it were separated by an interval of empty space from the rest . . .

If these observations be admitted, it will follow that, without the faculty of memory, we could have no perception of visible figures.[89]

This relatively complex dependence of one mental activity upon others, even in a simple act of perception, is developed by Stewart in such a way as to emphasise the variety and indeterminacy of *all* acts of interpretation.

In the instances of imagination and of language this indeterminacy is so radical that it will require, in place of a theory of representation, a new notion of interpretation and of reading. Stewart dismisses the conventional priority of representation or imitation in each and all of the arts. Imitation, he writes, is at most a means to an end. That end is the artist's purpose 'to speak to the imagination of others'.[90] However, so radical is the indeterminacy of imagination and of language that, for Stewart in 1792 as for Coleridge in 1796, communication appears wholly uncertain. In poetry that uncertainty becomes a part of a reciprocal and dynamic relationship between writer and reader.

In Poetry, and in every other species of composition, in which one person attempts, by means of language, to present to the mind of another, the objects of his own imagination; this power is necessary, though not in the same degree, to the author and the reader . . . the imaginations of no two men coincide . . . the agreeable impressions which they feel, may be widely different from each other . . . In poetry the effect is inconsiderable, unless upon a mind which possesses some degree of the author's genius . . . and able, by its own imagination, to co-operate with the efforts of the art.[91]

Stewart's emphasis is, to a degree greater than that of Campbell and almost equal to that of Twining, precisely upon the activity of the auditor/reader:

according to the different habits and education of individuals; according to the liveliness of their conceptions, and according to the creative powers of their imaginations, the same words will produce very different effects on different minds . . . It is therefore possible, on the one hand, that the happiest efforts of poetical genius may be perused with perfect indifference by a man of sound judgement, and not destitute of natural sensibility; and on the other hand, that a cold and common-place description may be the means of awakening, in a rich and glowing imagination, a degree of enthusiasm unknown to the author.[92]

Stewart insists, in parallel with his replacement of the visual analogy for perception by that of hearing, that the analogy of poetry with painting must therefore be abandoned even where the poet and reader coincide in their idea of the poem.[93]

In order to signal the end of pictorialism Stewart returns to the terms in which he had described the shifting and complex activity of even simple perception. He takes as an example of the kind of reading/writing he admires the first six lines of Thomas Gray's poem 'The Bard': 'On a rock whose haughty brow . . . with haggard eye the poet stood'. What interests Stewart is the almost instantaneous creation of two perspectives: first, vast (a whole landscape); second, more precise (a close-up of the bard's face). Stewart comments,

In general, whoever examines the play of his imagination, while his eye is employed either in looking up to a lofty eminence, or in looking down from it, will find it continually shifting the direction of its movements; – 'glancing' as the poet expresses it, 'from heaven to earth, from earth to heaven.'
Of this mental process we are peculiarly conscious in reading the descriptions of poetry.[94]

In painting, Stewart argues, this 'quick and varied succession' is impossible.[95]

The process of a shifting and flexible response, which Stewart describes as that of reading, listening and, by extension, of non-pictorial vision, is central to the whole enterprise of his work. The first contradiction we have noticed in this work is that between the opposite but equal values assigned to both philosophical and imaginative modes of thought. In the first volume of the *Elements* Stewart asserts that this 'faculty of imagination is the great spring of human activity, and the principal source of human improvement'.[96] However, earlier in the same volume he also writes that,

the perfection of philosophical language, considered either as an instrument of thought, or as a medium of communication with others, consists in the use of expressions, which from their generality, have no tendency to awaken the powers of conception and imagination; or, in other words, it consists in its approaching, as nearly as possible to the language of algebra. And hence the effects which long habits of philosophical speculation have, in weakening, by disuse, those faculties of the mind which are necessary for the exertions of the poet and the orator.[97]

The development of philosophy, therefore, involves the destruction of the imagination. Yet the imagination is that kind of thought which is the most lively and productive.

The desire, described by Wilkins, Leibnitz and Condillac, for a language of philosophy as pure and instrumental as that of algebra, and the contemporary, contrary desire for a primitive and highly figured language of imagination, found in Gray and in James Macpherson, confront each other most brutally in Stewart.[98] On the one hand, he provides a rationale for figurative language by noticing the active mode of interpretation it exercises. On the other hand, he recognises what Campbell also had described:

we *think*, as well as *speak*, by means of words . . . The effects, therefore, of ambiguous and indefinite terms are not confined to our communications with others, but extend to our private and solitary speculations.[99]

This indicates the extent and the irreducibility of the contradiction. Faced by that, Stewart calls in aid from de Gérando.

Stewart's familiarity with de Gérando's writing developed through the 1790s, particularly during the years of Stewart's travels in France.[100] In the *Philosophical Essays* of 1810, in spite of a pretended disregard for the tradition of the *philosophes*, Stewart makes the claim that he finds in de Gérando one who might well have written the *Elements*. It is the French *idéologue*'s work on signs and on language which accounts for this coincidence of interests.

In the years 5 and 6 of the new republic L'Institut National de France invited studies of the question: 'quelle a été l'influence des signes sur la formation des idées'.[101] De Gérando responded with a four-volume essay which, amongst much else, places the ideas of music we have found from Usher and Chabanon to Smith, in the context of the ideas of language we have found in Campbell and in Stewart. De Gérando's huge essay reduces itself to a single powerful assertion that revises what had amounted during the eighteenth century to almost a consensus about what John Locke had called σημειωτική, or *the Doctrine of Signs*.

Les signes enveloppent en quelque sorte, de leur influence, toutes les facultés de notre esprit, ils se mêlent à toutes nos opérations. La question de la perfectibilité de la raison humaine embrasse à son tour toute l'étendue de nos connoissances. En semblant ne demander qu'un traité sur les signes, on demande en effet un traité complet de philosophie.[102]

De Gérando is, therefore, critical of Locke for not providing a history of the institution of signs; and he is critical of Condillac for not analysing the interaction between signs and thought. However, he subscribes to their tradition of enlightenment. His main objection is to the assumption, also supported by that enlightenment, that intellectual and scientific progress is available 'par un moyen aussi simple que la réforme des langues'.[103]

De Gérando, therefore, decides upon the indeterminacy of all signs and, in consequence, revises the conventional analogy of language with the pictorial.

Il ne suffit plus de fair connoître un objet, il faut annoncer quel est son rapport avec notre bien-être. Il ne suffit plus de peindre un fait; il faut exprimer encore s'il sert d'objet au désir . . .[104]

In phrases which can be applied directly to Coleridge's first prefaces, de Gérando insists that all signifying is

toujours relatif à la disposition où nous nous trouvons nous-mêmes. Ainsi, un même signe n'agira point de la même manière ni sur un individu en divers instans, ni sur divers individus; par une raison semblable, l'usage d'un certain système de signes n'entraînera pas les mêmes conséquences chez les divers peuples, ne chez un même peuple en différens siècles.[105]

Within this principle which applies to all signifying, he nevertheless makes distinctions which reply to the contradiction we have found in Stewart between the relative value of the discursive and the imaginative. In relating this contradiction to a theory of signs de Gérando offers some solution to his Scottish contemporary.

For de Gérando divides signs into two main kinds: *signes figurés*, or metaphors; and *signes arbitraires*, or abstract terms. His great innovation is to remark the fundamental similarity between these two modes. In the first place, de Gérando notices the pleasures of metaphor:

pendant que le signe figuré détermine d'une manière trés marquée le caractère dominant de l'idée, et ses dimensions principales, il laisse dans une sorte de vague les confins qui la terminent . . . l'imagination aime à errer, et la vue des limites lui deplaît et la réfroidit.[106]

In the second place, similarly, abstract terms by their abridgement of concrete detail leave the mind (as Burke's *Enquiry* had already noticed) with no image of what it names. In consequence,

le mystère et l'obscurité . . . l'excitent, en effet, à de plus grands efforts. Nous détournons les yeux de ce qui frappe nos regards; nous poursuivons l'objet inconnu sur les voiles dont il s'enveloppe.[107]

Therefore, both figurative and abstract signs equally provoke the mind. So also, although to a lesser degree, the other modes of signs ('analogous' and 'indicative') which complete de Gérando's categories stimulate an interpretative activity. In this way both the philosophic and the imaginative show their power 'par l'imperfection même de leur langage'.[108]

Because signs and words are all-enveloping and all-contaminating, the powers of the mind must depend upon the inefficiency, discrepancy and indeterminacy of words and signs in operation. The notion of the relatively empty sign passes, therefore, from music to language. Its usefulness is, once again, to indicate the autonomous power and pleasure of the mind. The analogy between language, poetry and music becomes now a feature of their common use of empty signs.

It is not surprising to us at this point, therefore, that de Gérando has a lot to say about music. He defines it as a form of primitive speech, a 'langage des sons', which is related to the imagination in much the same way as 'articulate' speech is related to philosophic method. In spite of the apparent conflict between the 'observation calme et rigoureuse' of philosophy and the 'rêverie' of music, both share a common ground similar to that described by Adam Smith.

les lois de l'harmonie sont de veritables méthodes. Il y a donc dans la musique une sorte de philosophie cachée qui se mêle à ces impressions si vives qui nous affectent; elle exerce notre esprit pendant qu'elle parle à notre âme; elle veut que nous pensions pour bien sentir.[109]

The hidden philosophy within music applies, in particular, to large instrumental forms. Their structure, what Coleridge will call their 'principles of form',[110] is relatively unimpaired because of the abstract and empty medium of sound.

For de Gérando music performs, in relation to the mind, an activity similar in practice and identical in principle to that of language.

Nous devons donc regarder la musique comme un des moyens les plus propres à développer et à entretenir les facultés de l'imagination dans un individu, comme dans une nation . . . elle doit multiplier les liaisons d'idées, leur donner une plus grande force, et favoriser ainsi, dans l'imagination, cette faculté d'énergie qui la rend capable de former des conceptions étendues.[111]

Interpreting suggestion: Stewart and Brown

After his reading of de Gérando, Stewart defines more extensively and with more optimism the function of signs, figures and categories, not only in thought but in experience itself. Language envelops not only solitary speculation but also solitary perception.

In consequence of the generic terms to which, in civilized society the mind is early familiarised, the vast multiplicity of things which compose the furniture of this globe are presented to it, *not* as they occur to the senses of the untaught savage, but as they have been arranged and distributed into parcels or assortments by the successive observations and reflections of our predecessors.[112]

The recognition of the function of categories and of the 'prison-house of language' develops in Stewart's work without any consequent pessimism. In part this is because Stewart is blandly confident that we are improving the accuracy of the categories as science improves. However, in the meantime, the imperfection of language and its figurative arrangements provoke an activity of interpretation which, like de Gérando, Stewart elaborates upon principles which had previously been used to explain the pleasure of music.

This is a resource which solves the contradictions Stewart encounters. For with it he can attack the sensationalists and materialists after Locke and Diderot, on the very ground which such writers as Joseph Priestley and Erasmus Darwin had selected as its best defence: a sensationalist theory of language based on etymological analysis and the researches of John Horne Tooke.

John Horne Tooke's *A Letter to John Dunning* (1778) and his *The Diversions of Purley* (Vol. I, 1786, Vol. II, 1798) comprise an extraordinary philological exploration intended to uphold the kind of nominalism advanced by Hobbes, and to expose, according to Stewart, 'the imaginary power of *Abstraction*'.[113] This intention, insofar as it takes language as its evidence, looks back to Diderot's reading of Locke's notion of the sign. According to Stewart's translation:

Every idea must necessarily, when brought to its state of ultimate decomposition, resolve itself into a *sensible* representation or picture . . . Hence an important rule in philosophy, – That every expression which cannot find an external and a sensible object to which it can thus establish its affinity, is destitute of signification.[114]

The Diversions of Purley give to this principle an historical version by tracing in all parts of speech whatsoever, in prepositions, conjunctions, verbs, their etymological source in a name for a sensible object. Stewart's resistance has the interesting strategy of accepting the evidence of Horne Tooke pretty well as it stands. He then transforms its implications so that they serve to defend his own philosophy of the active powers of the mind.

There is an irony, therefore, when Stewart in 1810 invites the

'English physiologists' to turn away for a moment from 'the medullary substance of the brain', so that they may consider instead 'the phenomena of thought' that is language as it is described by Horne Tooke.[115] This is no more than to invite Priestley and Darwin from their laboratories into their libraries. The only correction to Horne Tooke which Stewart offers is to point out that the etymological root of a word is not its correct literal meaning: 'spirit' is not the same as 'breath'. This is easily done by borrowing the principles of Campbell's *Rhetoric*. The two signs are different because they are not given to interpretation as the same. Interpretation is contextual, a matter of selection and of choice.

If many have not noticed this problem it is because they have overlooked the decisive importance of interpretation: 'Many authors,' writes Stewart, 'have spoken of the wonderful *mechanism of speech*; but none has hitherto attended to the far more wonderful *mechanism* which it puts into action behind the scene.' Horne Tooke may have shown the imperfect, awkward and material character of language, but these inadequacies are turned by Stewart to serve his own purpose instead of 'the ultimate purpose to which they had been supposed to be subservient'.[116]

Stewart is, therefore, quite happy to admit, beyond even the extravagant claims of his opponents,

how much more imperfect language is, than is commonly supposed, when considered as an organ of mental intercourse. We speak of *communicating*, by means of words, our ideas and feelings to others; and we seldom reflect sufficiently on the latitude with which this metaphorical phrase ought to be understood. Even in conversing on the plainest and most familiar subjects, however full and circumstantial our statements may be, the words which we employ, if examined with accuracy, will be found to do nothing more than to suggest *hints* to our hearers, leaving by far the principal part of the process of interpretation to be performed by the Mind itself.[117]

Interpretation is astonishing because the mind is presented only with inadequately precise signs. The inadequacy of the signs, or, to use the term first hazarded by Twining and here adopted by Stewart, their mode of *suggestion*, is both the occasion and the evidence of the activity and energy of the mind.

The notion of suggestion continues to describe something which is less precise than that of association. For the mechanism of association described by Hartley had implied a relatively fixed order of sensations any one of which may produce a repetition of their original sequence in experience. Suggestion implies no such repetition of previous items. According to a disciple of Stewart, Thomas Brown, in an essay 'On Suggestion and its difference from Association', we should enquire

> whether the laws that regulate recurrence be laws of *association*, in the strictest sense of that word, as expressive of some former connecting process, – or merely laws of *suggestion*, as expressive of the simple tendency of the mind, in the very moment in which it is affected in a certain manner, to exist immediately afterwards in a certain different state.[118]

For Brown suggestion is the central process of the mind. Although this process is mechanical it releases the mind from the more fixed mechanism of a repetition of associations. In this way, Brown argues, the poet can produce and vary metaphors 'though there may never have been in the mind any proximity of the very images compared'. Association implies metonymy. Suggestion implies metaphor. Without a previous contiguity there is, none the less, 'a proximity as real in the mixed suggestions of ideas and emotions'.[119] Metaphor constitutes the essence of poetry. It is produced by a process of suggestion, which is at the centre of all thinking and constitutes its mobility and instability.[120]

If language were representationally efficient this activity of the mind would remain unused or imperceptible. It is, writes Stewart against the sensationalists, 'a fortunate circumstance, when the words we employ have lost their pedigree . . . the obscurity of their history prevents them from misleading the imagination, by recalling to it the sensible objects and phenomena to which they owed their origin'.[121] The useful imperfection of language, its obscurity, is therefore its secondariness to whatever original condition its naming has replaced. To recognise this secondariness, by which language is not an imitation or an expression of ideas and feelings, is to avoid the error 'of considering language as a much more exact and complete picture of thought, than it is in any state of society, whether barbarous or refined'.[122] This returns us to the most important contradiction which Stewart's writings confront: the simultaneous praise and dispraise of the imagination, its simultaneous primitive and enlightened status.

This conflict is eased by the use of de Gérando's equation in principle of the figurative and the abstract sign. That equation gives the strategy by which to disarm Horne Tooke; it gives also a place to imagination in the processes of philosophy. For Stewart can now encourage the use of figurative language in the writing of philosophy. This is a strategy which will '*vary*, from time to time, the metaphors we employ, so as to prevent any one of them from acquiring an undue ascendant over the others, either in our own minds, or in those of our readers'.[123] We have encountered this strategy in the *Elements*, where Stewart had substituted for the analogy of seeing, with perception in general, the analogy of hearing and of music. Now the strategy has become systematic. It elaborates the obscurity of language. By this method of shifting and varying the figures of the discourse Stewart keeps at the centre of his philosophy a practice which demonstrates its main argument: the very writing calls into play the active powers of the mind.

Before language, music called those powers into play – and also afterwards. Stewart's disciple, Thomas Brown, describes music as a 'language' not of words, which are the 'murmurs' of feeling, nor of 'echoes' which are dim repetitions or associations of memory. In a poem, 'To the Spirit of Music', he describes this art, instead, as a 'language' separated from its objects. Music is, therefore, a set of 'dark' signifiers which are delightful and which can have no fixed signifieds.

TO THE SPIRIT OF MUSIC

Wake me not, with bliss I cannot name,
   Wake me not, to passions thus unknown! –
Say, – But O! how sweet that *stranger-tone*!
Say, what happier realms its language claim!
Com'st thou, from those moon-light shades so dear,
   Love's still shades, where only murmurs rise,
   And, when joy o'erpowers the whispering eyes,
Speak faint words, which but the heart can hear;
Or, where far, in memory's sunless isle,
   Echoes only live of raptures past,
   And, each mingled cadence wildly cast,
Half with thought the doubtful soul beguile? –
No! – A wanderer thou, from native heaven. –
   Truths, of holiest power, thou fling'st around.
   Angels hear, and learn. – To us the sound,
Dark, but O how sweet, alone is given.[124]

The creative reader: Wordsworth's poetics

Coleridge had looked for an interpretative response, similar to that described by Stewart, from readers of his *Poems on Various Subjects*. The Preface of 1800 to *Lyrical Ballads*, the two parts of the 'Essay on Epitaphs' (1810), and the 'Essay Supplementary to the Preface' of 1815, develop this notion of interpretation and imply its connection with Wordsworth's poetry.

In 1815 Wordsworth argues that the poet confronts the fixed and oppressive associations that cling to language. The business of poetry is to dissolve these stabilities, 'but they retain their shape and quality to him who is not capable of exerting, within his own mind, a corresponding energy'.[125] Again, Wordsworth writes that a reader's

> ability to enter in the spirit of works of literature must depend upon his feeling, his imagination, and his understanding – that is, upon his recipient, upon his creative or active and upon his judging powers, and upon the accuracy and compass of his knowledge – in fine, upon all that makes up the moral and intellectual Man.[126]

Only interpretative power can remove the language of the poem from conventionally fixed associations. Both writer and reader must together take advantage of the 'sad incompetence of human speech'. According to this model of composition, language and interpretation, it no longer appears scandalous for Coleridge to have argued that the merits of a poem can depend upon the reader.

Like Stewart, Wordsworth converts the 'incompetence' of language into a positive value. This conversion can tell us much about the mode of language which characterises Wordsworth's poetry. It can tell us again much about how Wordsworth's poetry is *not* based upon a theory of 'self-expression', but upon a theory of language which places poetry at the centre of the relationship between language and society. Poetry is so placed because the conditions of interpretation are social practices. The connection between his poetic use of language and that idea of interpretation is most clearly seen in the 1800 Preface.

Although the Preface does not confront the relationship between a poetic use of language and the other social uses of language, it does aggressively declare that the poems which follow demand an analysis of the conditions of their interpretation. Such an analysis would be impossible without 'pointing out, in what manner language and the human mind act and re-act on each other, and without retracing the revolutions not of literature alone but likewise of society itself'.[127] This extension of ideas about language into ideas about social change is something which the Preface develops in relation to the poems, not directly but through a series of oppositions. In opposition to the lyrical ballad is placed a contrasting set of language-uses. There is the 'gaudiness and inane phraseology' of much modern verse; there are 'arbitrary and capricious habits of expression'; there are 'gross and violent stimulants' of the press, towards which literature itself has tended; there are 'many expressions, in themselves proper and beautiful, but which have been foolishly repeated by bad Poets'; there are the habits of 'poetic diction'; there are 'transitory and accidental ornaments'.[128]

It is a strong paradox that all of these uses of language are classified by the Preface together with an original and primitive language of feeling. The gaudy, violent and ornamental, *and also* the original language of strong feeling, are in opposition to the mode proposed for Wordsworth's own poems. The Preface places together both the original primitive language of passion *and* the mimicry of that kind of densely figurative language in over-refined verse. There is, first, the densely figurative mode of language of the 'earliest poets of all nations', and second, the language of poets who 'set themselves to a mechanical adoption of those figures of speech'. These can be seen as one and the same from the point of view of contemporary interpretation. Or, more precisely, they appear the same because both defeat interpretation.

The Reader or Hearer of this distorted language found himself in a perturbed and unusual state of mind: when affected by the genuine language of passion he had been in a perturbed and unusual state of mind also: in both cases he was willing that his common judgement and understanding should be laid asleep . . . The emotion in both cases was delightful . . .[129]

It is precisely in this way that Wordsworth defines his own poetry as secondary to the spontaneous language of feeling which primitive poetry must, and refined poetry pretends to, repro-duce. For Wordsworth the poet is decisively aware of the secondariness of his mode of language: the Wordsworthian poet knows 'that no words, which *his* fancy or imagination can suggest, will be to be compared with those which are the emanations of reality and truth'.[130]

Wordsworth recognises a mode of language which 'most often, in liveliness and truth, falls short of that which is uttered by men in real life'. This implies also his defence of metre and verse. Insofar as the language of poetry can, as it were, slip back into an excess of real excitement, its secondariness can be protected by 'the tendency of metre to divest language, in a certain degree, of its reality, and thus to throw a sort of half-consciousness of unsubstantial existence over the whole composition'.[131]

This secondariness of the poem, its difference from any reproduction of the real language of feeling, is not a part of the sequential argument of the Preface. It is, instead, the argument within its oppositions. Those oppositions are, on the one hand, between modes of language which act to inhibit 'the discriminating powers of the mind, and, unfitting it for all voluntary exertion, to reduce it to a state of almost savage torpor'; and, on the other hand, the modes of language of the Wordsworthian poet whose main ability is 'a greater promptness to think and feel without immediate external excitement', and whose poetics require of the reader no less than the same. The secondariness of this mode of language is that which allows the reader to perceive 'similitude in dissimilitude'. And that 'principle is the great spring of the activity of our minds'.[132]

It is, therefore, the admission that the poet's language is relatively inadequate in terms of imitation or expression which constitutes the social value of the poet's work. The destabilising of any continuity between experience and language provides the reader with the opportunity of an imaginative response which otherwise and elsewhere is ruined by modes of language which are too specific.

Given the large-scale parallel of Stewart's arguments about language and interpretation with those of Wordsworth, it is not surprising to find also that at least one important part of Wordsworth's poetic practice follows principles which Stewart advises. We recall the admiration in Stewart for a shifting and varying succession which constitutes perception. We recall also the principle of altering the metaphors and analogies in discourse so as to allow no one to dominate. In both models the process of interpretation is made uncertain and, therefore, energetic.

It is noticeable how both these principles quite fully describe a characteristic of Wordsworth's poetic practice. This coincidence can be well illustrated by a reading of two or three excerpts from different stages in the writing of *The Prelude*. Consider first an incident described in the version of 1798/9:

> ere the fall
> Of night, when in our pinnace we returned
> Over the dusky lake, and to the beach
> Of some small island steered our course with one,
> The minstrel of our troop, and left him there
> And rowed off gently while he blew his flute
> Alone upon the rock – oh, then the calm
> And dead still water lay upon my mind
> Even with a weight of pleasure, and the sky,
> Never before so beautiful, sank down
> Into my heart and held me like a dream. [133]

The terms of a figure of analogy – lay upon, weight, sank down, held – appear in a linked sequence by which one might expect a continuity between the natural scene (the surface of the water) and the perception of that scene (the consciousness of the mind). However, the terms of the sequence do not connect in such a way as to maintain a continuity. Instead of the scene lying upon and, by its weight, sinking into consciousness, the figure of analogy shifts and alters in such a way as to suggest and then to disrupt that most likely interpretation.

There is in the figure no consistency of tenor and vehicle. Some things have weight, but they lie upon; other things have no weight, but they sink and support. No connective ground of analogy is maintained, although a conventional form of analogy is suggested. The reader must, therefore, co-operate with the text by responding to its incompleteness. Stewart had taken as his model of all active interpretation the relationship of the listener to a piece of music. His description, which he also applies to the reader of poetry who must possess 'some degree of the author's genius', can be applied to the reader of *The Prelude*:

the mind is constantly varying its attention, from the one part of the music to the other, and . . . its operations are so rapid as to give us no perception of an interval of time. [134]

The device which we have noticed in the passage from Wordsworth quoted above can be found to operate also throughout larger sections of his poem.

For example, through its revisions from 1799 and 1805 to 1850, the passage of the poet's memory of 'spots of time' maintains a similar pattern of variation and discrepancy in repetition. Consider the non-alignment of the following sets of 'descriptive' lines. Each of the two pairs occur very close to each other.

1 (a)   I saw
  A naked pool that lay beneath the hills,
  The beacon on the summit, and more near
  A girl who bore a pitcher on her head
  And seemed with difficult steps to force her way
  Against the blowing wind.

 (b)   the naked pool,
  The beacon on the lonely eminence,
  The woman and her garments vexed and tossed
  By the strong wind.

2 (a) I sate, half-sheltered by a naked wall;
  Upon my right hand was a single sheep,
  A whistling hawthorn on my left, and there,
  Those two companions at my side, I watched
  With eyes intensely straining as the mist
  Gave intermitting prospects of the wood
  And plain beneath.

 (b)   the wind, and sleety rain,
  And all the business of the elements,
  The single sheep, and the one blasted tree,
  And the bleak music of that old stone wall,
  The noise of wood and water, and the mist
  Which on the line of each of those two roads
  Advanced in such indisputable shapes . . .[135]

In both pairs the items are enumerated and qualified in a manner which both constitutes and avoids repetition. Uncertainty is brought forward, therefore, as a central element in the writing and the reading of the poem. First, the girl is signified by the pitcher which she carries; second, a woman by the turmoil of her dress. First, the hawthorn whistles and the wall is naked; second, the hawthorn is blasted and the wall plays a bleak music. First, the mist separates so that other things can be seen; second, it takes on its own forms and shapes and intentions. Pictorialism is in this way dismissed, and replaced by a preference for a dynamism of uncertainty, variation and repetition. What Stewart describes as the 'ubiquity' of the poet's anti-pictorialist eye now becomes a principle of all the senses.[136]

In Wordsworth's verse the result is a shifting instability, without any reliable identification of image and object, and open discrepancies within the language and structure. *The Prelude's* account of the hawthorn, the stone wall, the single sheep, corresponds, the poem tells us, to the time of Wordsworth's father's death. The contrast between Wordsworth's written memory of loss and that of Cowper could not be more striking. The poem by Cowper on his dead mother's portrait structures the relationship between memory and loss in terms of the representationalist model of image and object. Its strategy includes the identification of these with each other, of the portrait with the mother. The principles of pictorialism, therefore, define the functions of memory for Cowper, whereas, for Wordsworth, principles of variation and uncertainty replace the pictorial.

'Unknown to me,' writes Wordsworth, 'the workings of my spirit thence are brought.' In contrast with the analogies of the full and determinate signs of the visual and the pictorial, it is by means of the empty and indeterminate signs of music that we have found such an activity of consciousness first described. Since Usher and since Twining the whole aesthetics of music is an aesthetics of an active consciousness. An exact contemporary of the early composition of *The Prelude*, de Gérando, insists first, that objects must be registered in relation to our desire; second, that the imagination is dispirited by any limits placed before it. Therefore, the imagination desires to follow that which causes it to wander. The empty signs of music are, he argues, most appropriate to the enlargement and pleasure of the imagination. It is music which

doit multiplier les liaisons d'idées, leur donner une plus grande force, et favoriser ainsi, dans l'imagination, cette faculté d'énergie qui la rend capable de former les conceptions étendues.[137]

It is, therefore, an aesthetics of music which constitutes the best contemporary description of Wordsworth's poetic practice.

One further example, also from *The Prelude*, will show us again 'cette faculté d'énergie' which music produces in consciousness. In this instance we will notice in particular the strategy, by which the effect is achieved, to be one of altering the figures or metaphors of the passage in such a way as to make interpretation dizzy with uncertainty. The passage elaborates, in this way, the strategy advised by Stewart of using *'obviously inconsistent metaphors'* in order to prevent any one figure dominating the mind of either writer or reader. Consider the following celebrated passage from Book VI of *The Prelude*:

> The immeasurable height
> Of woods decaying never to be decayed,
> The stationary blasts of waterfalls,
> And in the narrow rent at every turn
> Winds thwarting winds, bewildered and forlorn,
> The torrents shooting from the clear blue sky,
> The rocks that muttered close upon our ears,
> Black drizzling crags that spake by the way-side
> As if a voice were in them, the sick sight
> And giddy prospect of the raving stream,
> The unfettered clouds and region of the Heavens,
> Tumult and peace, the darkness and the light –
> Were all like workings of one mind, the features
> Of the same face, blossoms upon one tree;
> Characters of the great Apocalypse,
> The types and symbols of Eternity,
> Of first, and last, and midst, and without end.[138]

Irrespective of the multiplicity and paradox within the scene described, the passage depends upon the process which elaborates on what the description can be 'seen as'. It is an extraordinary variation of analogies. The passage brings forward face and mind and tree and apocalypse as a group of remarkable differences maintained only by a simple assertion of their identity. The process by which these differences accumulate is similar to Brown's principle of 'suggestion' rather than to any principle of association. Indeed, the things connected are so unalike and apparently unfixed that it is the process itself, the energy which can bring them together, which is foregrounded, rather than any one of the figures which the process discovers.

Conventional procedures of representation are dismissed by these practices, which can only be understood according to models of open interpretation such as those offered by Usher, Chabanon, Twining and Adam Smith. The connections between these models of the empty sign and models of language are most firmly established by de Gérando and by Stewart. Music and language show how the mind desires to go beyond the limit of the signified. In place of that limit, music and language can present the multiplicity and emptiness of the material signifier. It is in this way that Wordsworth, whatever his antipathy to actual music, recognises a 'natural music':

> Oh 'tis a joy divine on summer days
> When not a breath is stirring, not a cloud,
> To sit within some solitary wood,
> Far in some lonely wood, and hear no sound
> Which the heart does not make, or else so fit[s]
> To its own temper that in external things
> No longer seems internal difference
> All melts away, and things that are without
> Live in our minds as in their native home.[139]

Just as these lines recall the notion, most clearly stated by Adam Smith, that it is our own feelings and not those communicated by another that we experience when we listen to music, so also other lines by Wordsworth recall Twining's, Smith's and de Gérando's insistence that the structure and order of music is a kind of *philosophie cachée*. We read in the first book of *The Prelude* that

> The mind of man is fram'd even like the breath
> And harmony of music. There is a dark
> Invisible workmanship that reconciles
> Discordant elements, and makes them move
> In one society.[140]

Of these various connections between Wordsworth's thinking and that of others on aesthetics, poetics and music, it seems to me most important that we notice the similar practice of interpretation which Wordsworth's poetic practice, on the one hand, and a contemporary aesthetics of the empty signs of music, on the other, both demand.

It is interesting to notice, therefore, the way in which Wordsworth describes even seeing as if it were hearing. In this he repeats an emphasis on that varying and uncertain activity of the mind which Dugald Stewart, in particular, had highlighted.

> I stood
> Within the area of the frozen vale,
> Mine eye subdued and quiet as the ear
> Of one that listens, for ever yet the scene,
> Its fluctuating lines and surfaces,
> And the decaying vestiges of forms,
> Did to the dispossessing power of sight
> Impart a feeble visionary sense
> Of movement and creation doubly felt.[141]

4

SAMUEL TAYLOR COLERIDGE

Finding a place for music

As with his writing on so many other topics, Coleridge's statements on music are fragmentary and scattered. Nevertheless, they can be shown to have certain consistencies in their principles and in their development. Coleridge's speculations on music are applied by him to questions of general aesthetics and to the consequences of an aesthetic. Those speculations, therefore, demonstrate their specific importance in the context of Coleridge's thought about the arts, and they demonstrate their specific meaning in the context of notions and assumptions about music which were current at that time. Coleridge's writing about music can, when so understood, both clarify his other writings and bring to them a new emphasis.

Writers from James Usher to Thomas Twining had juxtaposed ideas of music with ideas of the other arts. In this way they had established a thorough relationship (even when it was one of contrast) between the epistemologies applied to the different arts. They had, therefore, made possible the kind of analysis of 'Art' as one single process which often marks the period of early Romanticism. Specifically with regard to music, Coleridge inherits from those English, Irish and Scottish writers the notion that this art, of all the arts, is most abstract in character.

Coleridge, therefore, shares the notion of music as the most ideal of the arts insofar as it is least impeded by its medium of empty signs. Coleridge describes a tendency of all the other arts in terms of this ideal character of music. Such a concept of music is available to compensate, as it were, for restrictions which the media of the other arts impose upon them. It was available to Coleridge not only through the writings of Twining and Smith, for example, but also through a large body of sermon literature.[1]

When Coleridge came to arrange a hierarchy of the arts according to the amount of ideality each allows, music came out on top. That was in 1818. The principle of relative ideality derives in part from Schiller and Schelling. When Hegel, according to this same principle, arranged historically a corresponding hierarchy of the arts, poetry, and not music, came out on top as the most ideal and Romantic art. That also was in 1818.[2]

This similarity and this difference clarify the distinct contexts which each writer occupied. Coleridge's and Hegel's principle for distributing the arts is basically the same: they have it from the same source. The actual order of the arts is different in each. This also largely coincides with the source of their assumptions: in this instance, the sources are different. For Coleridge the inherited notion of music answers to his two main criteria of a work of art. These are, first, that it exhibit method and, second, that it counteract the tyranny of the imageable and the oppressive criteria of visuality.[3] These requirements (first, that the aesthetic object be distinct and, at the same time, imply the infinite ground of its conception; second, that art counteract the conventions of rationalist empiricism and the epistemology of the 'idea') were issues which Coleridge had to fight to establish. Hegel could take them for granted. If Kant was at this time a novelty in Britain, he was already a matter of course in Germany.

Coleridge argues that music is 'of all the others . . . the best symbol of the Idea . . . for it is, as far as sight is concerned, formless, and yet contains the principles of form so that in all civilized language we borrow the names of elements of proportion from it'. This is the central character of music and it is this which places it above the other arts.[4] Although the other arts are also a mediation between a thought and a thing, they are by contrast more troubled by a confusion of method and have too great a 'reliance on the immediate impressions of the senses'.[5] Painting, because of Coleridge's assumptions about the visual, and poetry, because of Coleridge's notions of language, are more or less inhibited. Some kinds of music can also rely too much upon a material medium. But music alone, in its principles and in its empty signs, can be free.

Music is prominent in Coleridge's writings because of its proximity to abstraction. The continuity of his idea of music with that of, for example, Dugald Stewart is obvious. It is a different idea of music in almost every respect to the idea of music described by Kant as late as 1790, and which was available to Coleridge in the second book of the *Critique of Judgement*.[6] For

Kant music rates highly among the arts in point of sensuous charm, but lowest in respect of any moral or intellectual aspect. It is (to reverse Twining's terms) not sensible but sensual. It is an agreeable, not a beautiful art. Unlike poetry and painting (the arts of speech and the formative arts) its materials or content exclude it from any relation to cognition.[7]

This evaluation of music remains dominant in German aesthetics until after Hegel. Schelling in the *Philosophy of Art*, which he wrote during the years 1802 to 1805, substitutes for Kant's threefold classification of the arts a twofold division between the arts of the real and the arts of the ideal. Although he describes music as that which 'representing pure movement, is above all others the art which strips off the bodily', music does not fall into the class of the ideal arts. The class of the real, incorporating Kant's groupings of the arts of form and of the play of sensations, includes music, painting and sculpture.[8] This evaluation does not change, at least with respect to music, even when we consider the examples of Schiller, Körner or Goethe. Although each of these can argue in some way that music is the purest of the arts and maintains the same opposition between the sensual and the ideal, they each conclude with an emphasis quite different from that of Coleridge. For example, Schiller writes that 'even the most etherial music has, by virtue of its material, an even greater affinity with the senses than true aesthetic freedom really allows'.[9] W. H. Wackenroder and Ludwig Tieck will, as we shall notice below, offer Coleridge materials for an alternative view of music. But it is, in any case, a view already available in Britain. Coleridge's ideas of the texture of musical sound and of the structure of musical composition are continuous with Twining's analysis of 'resonance' and with Smith's description of the 'discursive' form of music. Working within these ideas, therefore, Coleridge conceives of music more as an abstract than (as Kant had considered it) a sensual art.

Arthur Schopenhauer, whose aesthetics of music appeared in 1819, a year after Coleridge delivered the *Philosophical Lectures*, does indeed produce an idea of music comparable with that of Coleridge. For Schopenhauer music is quite unlike the other arts insofar as it is non-representational. For this reason (developed, as it is, through Schopenhauer's concept of music as an embodiment of *der Wille* itself) he defines music as absolutely distinct from the other arts. Unlike Coleridge, therefore, Schopenhauer excludes music from his systematic aesthetics by absorbing it entirely within his metaphysics. Of music as an art Schopenhauer writes,

It stands quite apart from all the others. In it we do not recognise the copy, the repetition, of any Idea of the inner nature of the world. Yet it is such a great and exceedingly fine art . . . that in it we certainly have to look for more than that *exercitium arithmeticae occultum nescientis se numerare animi* which Leibnitz took it to be.[10]

Schopenhauer therefore parodies Leibnitz in such a way as to arrive at a new definition: *musica est exercitium metaphysicae occultum nescientis se philosophari animi.* His view of music in relation to the other arts is also entirely anti-Kantian: 'for those others speak only of the shadow, but music of the essence'.[11] Comparable as it is with Coleridge's high view of music, this description by Schopenhauer may itself be indebted to a similar tradition. As a student in England for three months in the first years of the nineteenth century Schopenhauer had not only acquired an entire fluency in the language but had also in particular been a student of music while learning the flute. However, by placing music outside the field of the other arts Schopenhauer does not attempt, as Coleridge does, to find a single ground upon which to base a unified aesthetic.[12]

The notion that music is a kind of abstract thought is a widespread one in Britain. It is shared by William Hazlitt as much as by Coleridge. For Hazlitt music is in no way tied to particularity or to the contingent. It is, for Hazlitt, no casual mark of Jeremy Bentham's character that the jurist intersperses his hours of work with his favourite art of music. Bentham's mode of thought and mode of relaxation equally illustrate to Hazlitt a frigid and calculating habit of abstraction.[13]

It is with the same derogatory enthusiasm that Coleridge attaches a large significance to the prominence of sculpture in France and in societies which sanction the slave trade.[14] Both writers correlate modes of thought with forms of art. They are in general agreement about the character of the particular arts, but they are not in agreement about the value of each art. Both agree that music is the most abstract of the arts, the most independent of particularity. But each draws a different consequence and, therefore, each evaluates music in an opposite way. Coleridge falls in with the German principle of ideality but not with Kant's or

Hegel's description of the particular arts. Hazlitt falls in with Coleridge's description of the particular arts but not with the principle of ideality. Hence the difference in their evaluation of each art.

Coleridge and Hazlitt are instances of a decisive moment in the history of theories of the arts in England. They stand out as contrasts, one against the other, at the moment when the very term *aesthetic* first designates a philosophical enquiry.[15] It is at this time also that music comes to supplant painting as an habitual analogy for the arts of language.[16] It is not surprising to find that it is at the point where theories of the arts constitute one important claim by the critical idealists against the criteria of empiricism that music comes into prominence. Coleridge is the most important writer on aesthetics to place music as an art which, in matters of the first importance, stands above all the others. For Coleridge the characteristic nature of music is the proper tendency of all the other arts. And the other arts are all the better insofar as they realise that tendency.

Coleridge's analysis of the arts is one large part of his analysis of mediation. The overall problem of the mediation of thought and thing, in such a way that the one would both incorporate the other and render itself explicit, is a problem which brings together Coleridge's writings on epistemology, on literature, and especially after 1818, on the relationship between metaphysics and social history. The problem of mediation brings together his analysis of imagination, of the symbolic, of the allegoric, and his revision of eighteenth-century theories of the sign.

Throughout Coleridge's work, even as one area of his interest supplants another, the analysis of mediation remains a major concern and a strong link between each part of his thought. Despite the break in 1818,[17] when it is apparent that he shifts his attention away from literature and the arts and towards metaphysics and religion, music remains an important intellectual and emotional interest. This is in contrast with the other arts and even with literature, and it serves to indicate the important place which music comes to hold in Coleridge's thought.

Coleridge's practical contact with music had not been enormous. His opportunities to discuss his interest in the theory of music were, arguably, less frequent than his opportunities to do so with painting. It is, nevertheless, certain that his enthusiasm for music was greater than his enthusiasm for painting.[18] In the other arts, except of course in literature, he took no substantial interest.

Coleridge's interest in music is in some contrast with that of his literary contemporaries. In contrast with that of Wordsworth, his interest in music is particular and practical. Both writers make numerous allusions to music throughout their poetry, but it is Coleridge whose allusions reflect a contemporary enthusiasm.[19] There is an anecdote from the spring of 1823 which summarises the contrast between the two men. They were together one evening at the house of Charles Aders where regular small concerts were held. Coleridge, as usual, settled in and enjoyed the music. Wordsworth fell asleep.[20]

Coleridge's interest in music was more persistent than that of Charles Lamb. More than a biographical anecdote tells us this. Although Lamb's derisive lines on the currently popular figures in music have affinities with Coleridge's derisive 'Lines Composed in a Concert-Room', the other writings of Elia show little avidity for music or for ideas about music.[21] In contrast with Hazlitt, who condemned music all at once, Coleridge discriminates between composers. Hazlitt's condemnation is of all kinds of music because music itself 'is of too high a sphere'.[22] Coleridge's judgements are particular, a mixture of approval and disapproval.

Some music is above me; most music is beneath me. I like Beethoven and Mozart – or else some of the aërial compositions of the elder Italians, as Palestrina and Carissimi. – And I love Purcell.[23]

This example of Coleridge's fairly informed and catholic taste is from a conversation of 1833. A few years earlier he would not have forgotten to include Cimarosa as another favourite. For Rossini he had developed a contempt.[24] Coleridge's tastes, therefore, are in the tradition of the enlightened concert-goers of his day represented also by the reviewer of Haydn in the *Morning Chronicle*, and by William Shield with whose music Coleridge was familiar. Coleridge has more to say about music than Keats or Byron or Shelley. Thomas De Quincey has a comparable enthusiasm for music, but his idea of it is quite different.[25]

The friendship between Coleridge and the Evans sisters is the occasion for our knowledge about his practical interest in music before his arrival at Cambridge. During his time at the university he attended concerts, took violin lessons ('to render my ear callous' to other violinists in the building), and formed a friendship with Charles Hague, who was later to become professor of music at Cambridge. By 1794 we hear of plans made by Coleridge with one of the Clagget brothers (most likely Charles), who ran a popular London concert-rooms,

to write a serious Opera, which he [i.e. Clagget] will set . . . the rules for adaptable composition which he has given me are excellent.[26]

Clagget also set four songs for Coleridge. However, after 1794 we hear no more of this projected opera.

Coleridge's humorous and dilettantish intention – with 'wild music [to] accompany myself on my Violin. Ça Ira!'[27] – gives way to a more conceptual interest in music. This is not to say that Coleridge lost any of his enthusiasm for actual musical perform- ance. In Cambridge he is amused by his extravagant regret at missing Mrs Billington in the oratorios. He is amused also at his own musical experiments. In London, by 1804, he is again amused that he is now an 'exquisite Judge of Music', and he is impressed that by hearing Mrs Billington sing during her benefit concert he has 'acquired a new sense'.

Nevertheless, Coleridge's practical involvement with music cannot have amounted to a great deal. Later on in life he wished that he had acquired a 'technical knowledge of Music'.[28] During the last decade of the eighteenth century the intention to speculate and to let others play the instruments takes over from the earlier and more practical flirtation. Afterwards, Coleridge's attention to music remains specific, but it is defined also by his other speculative interests. His thought about music becomes a part of his other thought.

Statements about music emerge in almost every part of Coleridge's writing. Through isolated jottings in the Notebooks, through the poems, through his writings on the imagination, on language, and on the arts in general, through his own most valued work on method and in his lectures on the history of philosophy, there is a prominence of ideas about music which is at once extensive and desultory.

It does not take away from the importance of these statements about music that they are desultory or that they are as often exclamatory as methodical. That is a characteristic of much of Coleridge's more innovative thought. It is not surprising that any attempt to place music at the centre of a more general aesthetic would be relatively incoherent. The peripheral position of music in any major theory of the arts before the nineteenth century and also the ultra-conservative writing by the musical establishment at the turn of the nineteenth century are impediments to including music in any new theory of the arts. One effect of the description of music which we find culminating in Adam Smith is to isolate music from the other arts because it is radically non-representational. Also a contemporary figure such as William Crotch, currently professor of music in Oxford and afterwards first principal of the Royal Academy of Music, made matters worse. Crotch's lectures at Oxford and in London are an attempt to give music what, in comparison with the other arts, it appeared to lack: that is, a set of classical models. The published summary of his lectures is placidly out of date and applies to music, as late as 1831, the supposed advice of Joshua Reynolds that one should have a cautious respect for classical models.[29]

It is probable also that we may exaggerate the nature of the contemporary popularity of music. Any brief survey of the literary reviews shows that music was in no case considered there as one art among equals. The appearance of the first great music magazines in the first quarter of the century shows a relative growth in public interest in music. The appearance, also during this period, of programme notes shows that such public interest intended to be informed.[30] However, in relation to the prestige of literature, the position of music can be clearly estimated. For the literary reviews show a smaller respect for music than do the music reviews for literature.

It is, therefore, not remarkable that Coleridge's use of ideas about music is desultory and unstable. What is remarkable is that music could have any place at all in a theory of the arts *which proposes one concept as their common ground*. Coleridge's intention is to describe 'the Affinity of the Fine Arts to each other, and the Principle common to them all'.[31] At the turn of the nineteenth century music is the test case of such a consistent aesthetic. It is an index of the scale of Coleridge's re-orientation of the arts upon a new common ground that he at once accepts the concept of music as empty of representation, and also that he intends to overcome the division within the theory of the arts which this concept of music had produced.

The circumstances of the Royal Institution lectures of 1808 indicate one purpose throughout all the desultory jottings. The lectures as they were delivered were an unsuccessful and abbreviated version of an original intention to lecture on the fine arts in general. The fact that this 'would require references and illustrations not suitable to a public lecture Room' deterred Coleridge. The more simple plan was to bring under the heading of poetry alone

the whole result of many years' continued reflection on . . . the source of our pleasure in the fine Arts in the antithetical balance-loving nature of man, & the connection of such pleasure with moral excellence.[32]

To consider this intention of Coleridge is to bring into focus a considerable amount of his other writings over those many years.

From jottings before 1808 in the Notebooks (in particular, from recent notes made during his travels in Malta and Italy) to the lectures on philosophy of 1818 we find a continued, if not a continuous, reflection on poetry, music and painting. All in all, during the period from 1800 to 1818 the arts are the main correlative of Coleridge's moral epistemology. After that, religion supplants them, although music remains relatively important. Until 1800 poetry and painting are an habitual pairing, if always a problematic one. By 1818 it is poetry and music which predominate.

It is as well to contrast the extremes of Coleridge's attitudes to music and to point up the changes. In 1797 he writes some 'Lines to W[illiam] L[inley]', one of the gifted musical family of Bath. In these lines Coleridge expresses some indecision because the serene ideality of the music excludes common suffering. In the same year he praises William Lisle Bowles's sonnet on 'sad and sweet' music as the only poem he has read which suits his own experience of music.[33] However, by 1799, Coleridge is again on the attack. His 'Lines Composed in a Concert-Room' make the conventional eighteenth-century contrast between primitive and sophisticated music. The poem favours the 'genuine power' of an old blind musician and of natural music over 'intricacies' in scented rooms.[34] However, throughout Coleridge's subsequent writings on music, only the contrast between the ideal and the sensual aspects of music implicit in that primitivism remain.

One contemporary equation of music with ideality was a religious one. Bowles himself, in a pamphlet in defence of oratorios, was to argue that 'of all the arts of man, music is the only one associated in our minds with the pure joys and happiness of heaven.'[35] For another contemporary clerical writer, an *adagio* by Mozart reveals these same latent feelings of a divine kind. However, a well-executed piece of ingenuity does not.[36] Richard Eastcott of Exeter quotes an eminent divine in defence of Montesquieu's claim that music alone does not corrupt men.

Of all the enjoyments of sense . . . music is the least sensual . . . its charms being calculated to inspire, a just idea of him, who formed the heart, to a relish of such delights.[37]

Writing in the last decade of the eighteenth century, Eastcott thought that music was put to profane uses. Coleridge's writings after 1800 are distinguished by his appreciation of the quality of music in actual performances and composers, and also by his use of this sense as a part of an epistemological analysis beyond the scope of the loosely associationist thinking of the religious advocates.

Words and the 'Tyranny of the Visual'

The religious defence of music promotes the associationist principle summarised by Alison:

The sublimity of . . . sounds is to be ascribed not to the mere quality of sound, but to those associated qualities of which it is significant.[38]

That principle led Alison to regret the limitations of purely instrumental music because of its restricted signification. In order to understand Coleridge's praise of music and his application of that praise it is useful to notice another writer of the Scottish Enlightenment who is not an associationist, who predates Alison, and whose thought on music is far closer to that of Coleridge.

Thomas Robertson, Fellow of the Royal Society almost from its inception in 1784 and Honorary Doctor of Divinity at Edinburgh University seven years before his death in 1799, proposed *An Inquiry into the Fine Arts* in many volumes. Only one was published, and that one in 1784. Robertson's work has received minimal attention.[39] This is not because the one volume he published 'is incomplete – it does, for example, include a substantial introductory essay. That one volume has been ignored rather because it deals with that peripheral feature of contemporary aesthetics: music.

Robertson's argument constitutes an attack on the inhibiting principles of imitation in all its forms. Such an attack can only undermine even an associationist aesthetics. All the arts, writes Robertson, ought to incorporate, in place of *la belle nature* or *la nature embellie*, the *'bello ideale';* that beauty, which is independent and uncopied; *created* by the idea of the Fine Artist.'[40] Robertson rejects Charles Batteux's arrangement of the arts according to their function of imitation. Instead, he divides them into two groups: 'those which make an impression chiefly upon the Body, and . . . those which make an impression chiefly upon the Mind'. Music is placed among the arts of the body, and poetry alone as the art of the mind. However, in contrast with other contemporary aesthetics, the difference between them is only relative. All the arts 'possess, in some degree, and probably great ones, certain inherent and independent powers in themselves'. None of the arts, therefore, need derive their strength by means of either imitation or association. To this extent the arts have dignity. Aristotle's definitive statement about imitation is not a confusion of terms (as Twining was to argue) but 'an inaccuracy in his very thinking'. Music has more clearly than the other arts a 'something else', an independent power, which Robertson leaves unanalysed.[41]

The fact that Robertson turns first to music after announcing a rejection of imitation does not surprise us. Nor need it be surprising that he, thereafter, abandons his programme. Some years earlier, in 1772, the orientalist Sir William Jones had argued that, although painting and to a lesser degree poetry involve imitation, all the arts have a 'nobler origin' which is typified by music.[42] Robertson rejects even such a residual primitivism as that. Indeed, his theory is interesting largely because of his 'modernist' approach to music.

It is by this modernism that Robertson provides definitions of music which indicate correlations between the arts such as Coleridge elaborates. This applies in a number of instances,[43] but it is nowhere more important than in Robertson's equation between the character of modern music and the spirit of the modern age. Haydn, after all, was one of his favourites. The relationship between art and society which Robertson proposes is a brusque development of that implied by Adam Ferguson and other Scottish historians during the second half of the eighteenth century. It is a stronger version of that which we noticed in James Usher. It is strikingly unusual in Britain in 1784. In history, writes Robertson,

the whole body of the people . . . unseen, direct every progress; and always, at last, in the season of crisis, publicly take the lead. Their spirit, their turn of thinking, their pleasure and pains, are subtle topics of consideration; but they must be considered, if we are either to understand or to treat of human affairs.[44]

A study of the fine arts among the social history of a people will, therefore, often 'unriddle the rest'. Such specific analysis is the more necessary because no two cultural or historical moments, argues Robertson, are even similar to each other.

No rise and no fall is like another . . . Different countries rise in their turn to grandeur; but a different spirit and manners rise with them. How vain, then, an abstract comparison of Ancient and Modern Music; and how absurd, to blame one for not resembling the other . . . Modern music . . is highly suited to modern times: the spirit of our age is of a more refined and general kind; and does not in the Arts, fix upon particular sentiment and passion. Above all, this is the case in Religious music . . .[45]

The significance of music derives, therefore, from the sensibility of the time that produces it. It is in its turn an index of the spirit of its age. That Robertson found in the concertos of the Earl Kelly (who had his style from Mannheim) an expression of contemporary Scotland, need not cause us to disregard the strength of the basic framework.[46]

For, freed from the principle of imitating nature, the arts in general can now be integrated into a synthetic history which, in a more systematic form, Coleridge will encounter in the work of Schiller and A. W. Schlegel. The usefulness of Robertson's idea of music can be seen from his interpretation of the way in which the modern period has separated instrumental music from words. In place of the more usual contrast between sense and sound, or in contrast to James Beattie's *Essay on Poetry and Music* (1776), which regrets that 'music without poetry is vague and ambiguous',[47] Robertson attaches significance to the formal separation itself.

Is mere sound a thing of nought? Does it not place an image before you? Do you not see it passing by? its very speechlessness filling you with attention?[48]

Robertson's *Inquiry* accepts the emptiness and ideality of music, correlates them, and attaches to contemporary instrumental music a formal significance. This is a strategy which Coleridge will develop.

Henry Nelson Coleridge recalled that his uncle differentiated between Beethoven and Mozart, on the one hand, and Rossini, on the other, because the Germans involved thought and the Italian 'mere addresses to the sensual ear'.[49] The best music, according to Coleridge, is sacred. In his comments on the debate about oratorios, to which Bowles had contributed, Coleridge brings together an evaluation of sacred music and a theoretical argument about the arts. The universality of music makes it the best expression of the 'grand simple Thoughts' of religion. Its use in public worship counteracts the 'individual and dividious self'. Only the modern puritan Wesleyite could find such music theatrical.[50]

Coleridge extends his defence of music to include Robertson's distinction between imitation and ideality in the arts. Nor is music conceived of in terms of a primitivist naivety. Instead, it stands for the arts in which action becomes symbolical.

Man is the only animal who can *sing*; music is his invention, if not God's Gift by Inspiration / for unlike painting it is not an imitative Art – To man alone it is given to make not only the air articulated, and the articulated Breath a symbol of the articulations & actualities of his Heart & Spirit, but to render his gestures, his postures; & all his outward Habiliments symbolical.[51]

The difference which Coleridge notes here in 1810, that music comes *ab intra* and not *ab extra*, confirms an idea of the first importance. His subsequent attack on Schlegel's characterisation of Christian art as allegory, in which visual forms are translated into ideas, has its source in such a difference. It is to confirm the same idea that Coleridge inserts a sentence of his own into his transcriptions of Schelling's lecture on the relationship between the plastic arts and nature. The sentence is a decisive one: the poet 'must out of his own mind create forms'.[52]

The disjunction of the imagination from its objects is precisely what Schelling's essay strives to overcome. This purpose is one which is also important to Coleridge. However, it is also for Coleridge a risky approximation to pantheism in its identifying the imagination with the forming power of nature. We shall consider this further later on.[53] In the language of Coleridge's epistemology the forms of art in which an intransigent pantheism is present are those in which visual and accidental associations of language conceal an explicit activity of the mind.

For Schelling it is painting, but not sculpture, which fulfils the requirement that thought remain explicit.[54] For Coleridge it is music and, with more complication, also poetry which 'presumes no disjunction of Faculty – simple *predomination*' of the mind over its materials. This accounts for other additions to his notes from Schelling's lecture. The music of savages, he writes, insofar as it is imitative cannot be called music in its proper sense. So much for Rousseau's primitivism. Properly speaking, music and poetry are the human arts because their products are from the mind. However, of the two,

Music is the most entirely human of the fine arts, and has the fewest *analoga* in nature . . . that man is designed for a higher state of existence . . is deeply implied in music, in which there is always something more and beyond immediate expression.[55]

Such a definition brings together at once Coleridge's terms of analysis. There is the actual interest in music as an art; there is an aesthetics; there is a metaphysics. The figure of music, alone among the arts, can easily relate all three.

In the 'Essays on the Principle of Method', written in 1818, Coleridge brings together for the purposes of his general philosophy his appreciation of music and of its explanatory use. Placing the 'Method in the FINE ARTS' as a mediation between his Kantian opposites of the ideal order of Law or of Reason, on the one hand, and the practical order of Theory or of Understanding, on the other, he defines how art has a place in the two orders.

Relationships of theory are provisional, and, as for example in medicine, they are constituted by one practical point of view. Art includes these insofar as we have some previous experience of the materials of art in their practical relationships. Art also includes the order of reason,

For in all, that truly merits the name of *Poetry* in its most comprehensive sense, there is a necessary predominance of the Ideas (i.e. of that which originates in the artist himself), and a comparative indifference of the materials.[56]

By this double aspect art links the two orders of the reason and of the understanding. It is at this point in 1818 that music and poetry are placed side by side. And so it is that Coleridge continues immediately to explain that,

A true musical taste is soon dissatisfied with the Harmonica, or any similar instrument of glass or steel, because the *body* of the sound (as the Italians phrase it), or that effect which is derived from the *materials*, encroaches too far on the effects from the *proportions* of the notes, or that which is *given* to Music by the mind.[57]

The distinguishing element of music, therefore, is its accessibility to reason. Timbre, or the body of the sound, appears to limit this element when the music is played on certain kinds of instruments. This notion of timbre needs to be contrasted with Thomas Twining's notion of resonance, which, at first, it appears to resemble.

In Twining's view, what the mind 'gives' to the music becomes apparent in the imperfect harmonics of an instrument's 'resonance'. For this reason the piano is preferred to the harpsichord. Listening to a piano we, as it were, have to give more order from the mind in order to compensate for the imperfections of the sound. In Coleridge's view, on the other hand, it is the too great completeness of the material sound which inhibits the mind. This is not a simple contrast between the two writers. Both of them agree that the mind 'gives' order to the music. Both of them agree that this distinguishes music most clearly from the other arts, and also that this distinguishes good music from bad. Coleridge's complaint is, however, against timbre (or certain qualities of timbre) and not against resonance. The apparent contrast with Twining is a result of Coleridge's wish to locate the inadequacies of certain music in the unusual materiality of its sound.

Coleridge's insistence that the value of music, its access to reason, depends upon the distinctness of the proportioned notes of the scale emphasises a European prejudice. Roman Jakobson has described the opposition between what the European ear finds as the distinguishing element in a melody and what the African ear selects. For the European the melody becomes a different melody when the relationships on the musical scale are altered so as to re-arrange the sequence of notes. The European is then disposed to notice a distinguishing or decisive difference between two melodies. For the African, on the other hand, it is not the changes of relationships along the scale which differentiates one melody from another; it is the change of timbre. It is, simply, the change from one instrument to another. The '*body* of the sound', as Coleridge describes it, is an accidental difference (and sometimes a regrettable one) only to the idealising, European ear.[58]

There is an illustrative local parallel to Coleridge's distinction between the body and soul of music, that is between timbre and proportion. In 1780 an obscure apothecary, one John Elliot, published his *Philosophical Observations*. Elliot is (to re-work Coleridge's joke) a metapothecary, if not a metaphysician. In his *Observations* Elliot claims to be the first to account for timbre or, as he calls it, 'the *mode* of sound . . . this curious phenomenon' of difference between two instruments playing the same note.[59]

This *je ne sais quoi* presents a problem in Elliot's analysis of how we see and hear. His solution is a revealing one. Vision and hearing, he argues, are the pure senses. They, unlike the senses of direct feeling, act by a 'mediation of unison vibrations'. Elliot performs a number of painful experiments (rubbing and prodding the eyes and the ears) in order to deprive these senses of their correspondent external vibrations. He concludes from this research that there are 'innate' colours and sounds which his experiments have, as it were, stimulated and made apparent. The innate colours and sounds are the pure tones.

No such purity is allowed to the other senses. Their sensations are altogether external, material and impure. However, the sense of hearing can impair its purity by one aspect of sound, that of timbre. For 'the sense of feeling . . . seems to have a greater share in these modes, insomuch that the mixture of the sounds and their being heard as one, depends on it, and not on the innate sounds'.[60] The same separation of the materiality of the sound from the proportion of the notes accounts for Coleridge's assumption. More important, the *psychological* description of music, that when it is not overwhelmed by the body of its sound it is a simple equivalence of 'outer' with a prior 'inner', corresponds to Coleridge's *critical* decision that music makes explicit the creative power of the mind.

It is according to this critical description that music is differentiated from the other arts and from language. Coleridge's well-known dictum, that art is the figured language of thought, implies that the difference between the arts is their greater or smaller mediation of the ideal without its apparent loss. Music answers most easily to the requirement that the 'inner' become explicit through the 'outer'. Except where the timbre of the sound predominates, music, unlike the other arts, takes for its material that which is unimpaired by our prior experience of it in the realm of 'theory' and of the practical understanding.[61]

In the same year as the publication in *The Friend* of the essay on the principle of method, Coleridge develops from these notions of music his clearest statement about its place in culture and among the arts in general. It is in the fourth of the *Philosophical Lectures*, a series delivered from 1818 to 1819, that music comes to represent the proper purpose of the arts and, especially, to subvert the tyranny of visual forms. We shall best be able to understand this development if we consider first an earlier and simpler desire by Coleridge to be rid of an epistemological problem. For it is in the face of this problem, and according to the peculiar terms of his epistemology, that Coleridge evaluates each of the arts and attributes to each a correlative mode of thought.

The reason why music is described in 1818 to be the first among the arts appears in 1804 with Coleridge's desire, in the composition of poetry, to avoid the pictorialism of words.

Soother of Absence / O that I had the Language of Music / the power of infinitely varying the expression, & individualizing it even as it is / – My heart plays an incessant music / for which I need an outward Interpreter / – words halt over & over again![62]

With something of an ironic parallel, William Lisle Bowles reminisced about the composition of his fourteen sonnets. He had fashioned them 'from the natural flow of music in which they occurred to me'.[63] For Bowles, in contrast with Coleridge, words were no impediment.

The epistemological problem which Coleridge faces has two interdependent aspects: first, an uncertainty about the capabilities of words; second, a conviction that the imagination must avoid definite, visual forms. Both aspects face Coleridge for the first time at the end of his stay in Germany. Both emerge clearly in 1800 with the writing of the Preface to the second edition of *Lyrical Ballads*, and also with the intention (which supplants a proposed 'Life of Lessing') to write what eventually becomes the *Biographia Literaria*.

In the letters to his wife and to his friend, Thomas Poole, about his journey from Göttingen to the Hartz mountains, Coleridge worries incessantly about his 'misery of words'. Things are individual, but words are arbitrary and general. Language may serve as a means of personal and private recollection, but his wife and Poole know nothing of this foreign countryside. Therefore,

I could half suspect that what are deemed fine descriptions, produce their effects almost purely by a charm of words, with which & with whose combinations, we associate *feelings* indeed, but no distinct *Images*.[64]

In 1800 Coleridge gets in touch with the painter, Henry Howard, in order to experiment on the benefits each might derive from the other. It is only later that the awareness of the 'misery of words' conflicts with the second aspect of the problem, the tyranny of the visual.

For the tyranny over the imagination of visual forms is also met with at the end of Coleridge's stay in Germany. Its most important early statement is Coleridge's letter of 1799 to Josiah Wedgwood about the reasons why slaves came to be treated more humanely under the Roman emperors. The first reason for this, Coleridge argues, is simply the economy of supply and demand. A restriction on slave-trading resulted in improved conditions for those already in ownership. The second reason is a more complex one.

This second reason has to do with changes in the current mode of thought and, therefore, in its correlatives of the political and the aesthetic. The sheer size of the empire, Coleridge argues, made a national form of religion, with one mythology of definite images and incessant associations, incongruous. Christianity, which is the world-religion of Asia 'divested of Asiatic forms & ceremonies', had met therefore with little opposition. Although in France a 'Passion for Statues &c' (and after his journey to Italy Coleridge would add the Catholic emphasis on pictorial icons) is again smuggling 'a sort of Idolatry into the feelings', the overall trend of history has seen the abolition of that oppression of the imagination. In consequence, Rome freed her slaves, and, between 1200 and 1300, the rest of Europe did likewise.[65]

Such a conjunction of ideas, translated into an evaluation of the different arts in British aesthetics, can only be quite different from that in Schiller and in Schlegel. The problem of the definite and of the visual allows, for Coleridge, a different cultural value to the various arts. Despotism – its social and political reality in the form of the slave trade or of the children used in the cotton factories – takes a particular form in Coleridge's epistemology.

Despotism is the specific consequence of a systematically visual empiricism. In Coleridge's thought this gives a value to such opposites as antique/Christian, Classic/Romantic, naive/sentimental which often reverses the value given to them by his German contemporaries. In each case the developments of a synthetic history of correlative forms of thought ensures this difference. Such forms of thought, whether they be art, religion, politics or philosophy, are superimposed one upon the other in Coleridge's description of history as the progress of one mind. They are again superimposed in his opposition between an historical philosophy and chronological history. At any one moment of history the state of the arts, of politics, of language and of worship can be understood, therefore, as differentiated acts of the one predominant form of thought.[66] The arts are in this way implicated in the state of politics, of religion and of philosophy to which they correspond.

These correspondences are not rigid, but they are sufficiently fixed in Coleridge's mind to make it impossible for him to accept the evaluation of the arts put forward by his German contemporaries. Coleridge, because of his analysis of the political character of the pre-Christian (and modern) era, could in no way propose with Schiller a return to the serenity of classical sculpture. Nor could he, because of his resistance to the predominantly visual criteria of Anglo-Gallic empiricism, give to painting the kind of prominence of 'first among the arts' given to it by Schlegel.[67] When Coleridge, as we shall see, did come to modify his criticism of painting he did so according to non-pictorialist principles. At any rate, both painting and sculpture are two arts so implicated in the negative side of his epistemology that Coleridge can by no means use either of them in order to describe the proper tendency of art in general.

The arts and the mediation of ideas

The attack on the criteria of empiricism constitutes a central focus of Coleridge's major writing on both politics and aesthetics. For this reason music, which we have seen to undermine empiricist thought from Usher to Stewart, serves to connect Coleridge's aesthetics and politics. This is nowhere as clear as it is in *The Statesman's Manual* and in the *Philosophical Lectures*. Subsequently, the attack on empiricism becomes a matter of religion and of metaphysics. The attack constitutes Coleridge's Kantian intention, in the MS 'Logic', that the domains of Reason and of Understanding should be mediated but not confused. In the MS 'Of the Divine Ideas' and in the final dictations to J. H. Green it is the assertion that the mind implies a ground of action wider than any mere equivalence between its activity and that of nature. In these ways Coleridge could name not only Anglo-Gallic empiricism but also Schelling's transcendental idealism as forms of contemporary materialism and also as forms of implicit pantheism. The extremes of the dialectic are, finally, alike. The arts are one possibility of mediation.[68]

It is Coleridge's general principle that the forms of theology, of science and of politics are modified by a prevailing philosophy. They can be understood as indices of that philosophy.[69] In *The Statesman's Manual* he argues that political and civil revolutions are found to coincide with revolutions in metaphysical systems. In a later marginal note to this text he adds that the history of the fine arts is equally related to the history of philosophy.[70] *The Statesman's Manual* is Coleridge's most cohesive and eloquent description of the 'mediatory power' of the imagination and of its relation to philosophy, religion and science. The attack on the 'Idolism of the unspiritualised understanding' is here most systematically applied to an opposition between contemporary philosophy, with its criterion of visuality, and religion which ought to be a synthesis of reason and imagination. Insofar as theology itself, however, is modified by the philosophy of the day, Coleridge avails himself also of this concept of the symbolic and of the arts in order to save his radical definition of the 'Idea' with which this text concludes. For this purpose, which gives the possibility of a form of mediation which might avoid the contagion of empiricism, it is to poetry and to music that Coleridge turns. Music is a 'living Educt of the Idea'. Plato's language, therefore, is more like music than it is like words as they are now understood.[71]

It is in the lecture on Plato, the fourth of the *Philosophical Lectures*, that Coleridge gives to that moment when the Idea first enters the fine arts the same date which he had given, in 1799, to the abolition of slavery. The other arts are more or less modified by this event, but music alone represents it in its very character. It is in this lecture that Coleridge makes full use of what he had added to *The Statesman's Manual* about the arts and their relation to a prevalent philosophy. Also it is in this lecture that he concludes by placing music above all the other arts by reason of what is most important in any art: its capacity to mediate and make explicit the ideal.

Coleridge introduces these arguments by noticing that

All great and bold ideas in their first conception, in their very nature are too great for utterance . . . If I be required to mention facts I think that this will be most convincing: I speak of the connexion of speculative opinion, especially of the Platonic Idea with the fine arts.[72]

Despite the restrictions of their media, the work of Giotto and of Cimabue and also a mural of about 1300 in the Campo Santo at Pisa mark the character of the Platonic renascence in Italy. The grace and symbolic import of these paintings is not 'outraged' by the 'mere superficies and stiff lines' of 'any distinct palpable visible forms'.[73]

The achievement of these painters, by which they overcome the restrictions of merely visual media and exceed the 'visible', is more than the achievement of a particular historical moment. In terms of Coleridge's evaluation of the arts and of their place within a moral epistemology this achievement of the Platonic renascence is the goal of the arts in general. For

The mind always feels itself greater than aught it has done. It begins in the act of perceiving that it must go beyond it in order to comprehend it; therefore it is only to that which contains distinct conception in itself, and, thereby satisfying the intellect, does at the same time contain in it a plenitude which refuses limitation or division, that the soul feels its full faculties called forth.[74]

It is to this definition of, amongst much else, the ideal art object that music corresponds. Coleridge need only elaborate the kind of perceptions we have already met with in Smith and Stewart. For Coleridge, it is not music considered merely as sound, as it was for such a writer as Usher. Nor is Coleridge's idea of music figured in the trope of the Aeolian harp. He had come to reject that image for the very reason that the music of that instrument could not imply 'distinct conception in itself'.[75]

Music, instead, comes from and is given order from within. In the same way as years before, in 'Dejection: an Ode', Coleridge had contrasted the Aeolian harp ('Which better far were mute') with another music ('from the soul itself must there be sent / A sweet and potent voice, of its own birth, / Of all sweet sounds the life and element! . . . All melodies the echoes of that voice'),[76] so also in this philosophical lecture he identifies 'joy' with such a composed music. For Coleridge, 'joy' is an element that has a 'distinct conception in itself'. Therefore, it is not in mere sound or in mere natural music that the ideal of art is found. It is to be found instead in actual music as it is composed and performed.

The correlative of that power of the mind, its productiveness and productive receptivity, 'which is the source of all that we really enjoy or that is worth enjoying', is the man-made music of Coleridge's own practical experience. Therefore, the lecture on Plato concludes:

> How an Idea acts on the mind we may perhaps best learn from that which is as far as sight is concerned formless, and yet contains the principles of form so that in all civilized language we borrow the names of the elements of proportion from it – I mean music. Truly it is an innocent, affecting Delight which we have in pure sounds – an infantine Joy . . . If we sink into music our childhood comes back with all its hopes and all its obscure reminiscence and with it faith, a reliance on the noble within us on its own testimony. We feel ourselves moved so deeply as no object in mortal life can move us except by anguish, and here it is present with Joy. It is in all its forms still Joy.
>
> We feel therefore that our being is nobler than its senses and the man of genius devotes himself to produce by all other means, whether a statesman, a poet, a painter, a statuary, or a man of science, this same sort of something which the mind can know but which it cannot understand, of which understanding can be no more than the symbol and is only excellent as being the symbol.[77]

Whatever the differences in their practical experiences of music, there is an extraordinary continuity between these definitions by Coleridge in 1818 and the definition by Usher in 1767 that music 'is sufficiently perceivable to fire the imagination, but not clear enough to become an object of knowledge'. Coleridge has, more than anything else, elaborated upon that definition in such a way as to include ideas about the intellectual and imaginative form and precision of music, and, therefore, to rescue the arts from notions of the sublime and the obscure. Music, that is, allows Coleridge to find an instance of the relationship between the discourses of imagination and of reason.

It is important, therefore, not to be misled by the fact that Coleridge in this passage uses some plagiarism from Wackenroder's *The Marvels of the Musical Art*. It is unlikely that the reader will be misled if we notice what Coleridge adds to his selections from that text. Wackenroder had written of music, childishness, and incomprehensible joy.[78] Coleridge adds to this how music constitutes a critique of contemporary philosophy. It does this by being, in respect of the visual, without form, while it is, in any other mode, the very ground of all forms. Thus Wackenroder's exclamations become part of a consistent argument about the evidences of philosophies. That argument places Coleridge and the terms of Coleridge's epistemology in the tradition especially of Dugald Stewart.

Coleridge also gives a political extension to this argument. The other arts and even the art of the statesman, the domain of the understanding, is (as theory is to reason) merely symbolic of what is figured in the art of music. Music alone is the forming mind itself mediated through a plenitude of empty signs. It is this possibility of art that Coleridge applies, in these lectures and in his other writings, to moments of political emancipation. Such emancipations are of many kinds: from the slavery of a national religion; of the cotton-children from the terms of their employment; of the modern empirico-mechanist from the 'despotism of the eye'.[79]

It is possible to hazard a date for Coleridge's preference for music above the other arts. We have seen that up to 1800 he had been enamoured of music but suspicious of it. This was nothing if not conventional. He had also attempted to compensate for apparent inadequacies in the resources of language by enlisting the help of a painter. In February of 1804, before his departure for Malta and Italy, he took part in musical life in London. After hearing his old favourite, Mrs Billington, he announced that he had acquired 'a new sense'. What exactly that new sense might be he does not explain. However, in the same year, at the opera in Syracuse, Coleridge noticed how the words and the music of a quintet appeared as fellow-combatants in a kind of love quarrel. The words were not 'interpreters' of the music, but both were 'one, and not one', united, separated and re-united 'till at length they die away in one Tone'.[80]

It is according to this perception that we can understand Coleridge's note, made in the initial stage of his journey to the Mediterranean, 'Soother of Absence / O that I had the Language of Music . . . words halt over & over again!' It seems to be of the first importance that this reflection about the inadequacies of language is itself a note about the autobiographical poem, 'Soother of

Absence', which Coleridge long proposed and failed to write. The hypothetical desire for a language of music is, therefore, a comment on an intractable problem with words. For this problem, if not the language of music, perhaps the 'music of language' will provide an answer.

It has been noticed in one recent analysis of Coleridge's poetic practice how the 'music of language' is not a vacuous phrase when applied to the function of many lines in, for example, 'The Aeolian Harp' and 'Kubla Khan'. It has been argued that the structure of these and other poems by Coleridge imply an excess of language which can be figured in the play of the sensuous material of the signifier.[81] This emphasis on the texture of the sounds of the words, on the 'music of language', gives additional point to the contrast which we made earlier between Coleridge, on the one hand, and Kant and Hegel, on the other, in their evaluations of music and poetry.

For Coleridge is working on the assumption that sound is the most indeterminate and the least sensuous of materials. He is also strongly aware of the ways in which language is socially and historically conditioned so that it is an impediment to thought. A strategy by which language can make self-evident the activity of thought can, therefore, be the development of that aspect of language which is separate from its problems of sense: simply, the sound of language. For Kant and Hegel the immersion in the element of sound is what places music below poetry. For Coleridge, on the other hand, the sound of words abstracts them from their social and historical impediments. This is one basis of poetry because poetry makes its material medium, the sound of the words, explicit. 'The delight in richness and sweetness of sound, even to a faulty excess', is the first symptom of poetic power according to the *Biographia*.[82] It is true that another desire by Coleridge was for a philosophical language so abstract that it could be universally translated. From Leibnitz to Stewart no less had been required. Ironically, it is in Coleridge's comments on Hegel's *Logic* that he admits that such a language is impossible.[83]

'The Sense of Musical Delight'

Coleridge makes his first radical statements about a theory of language in those letters which he wrote at the same time as the composition of the Preface of 1800 and which are familiar to us also as the first hints of the *Biographia*. His first suggestion was to Godwin who, being a 'moralist', should philosophise the philological system of Horne Tooke. Thus, Godwin was to write 'a book on the power of words, and the processes by which human feelings form affinities with them'.[84] This is to ask no more than that Godwin should busy himself in the arguments of George Campbell's *Philosophy of Rhetoric* and anticipate the essay on Horne Tooke by Dugald Stewart. Not many years later Coleridge also abjures the nominalism of the *Diversions of Purley* in favour of the universal grammarians, such as James Harris. Horne Tooke's system, he told Crabb Robinson, is but an 'accidental history of Words', whereas Harris's *Hermes* 'Treated of the essential and logical connections of ideas'.[85] In 1810, the same year as he made these comments and also the same year as the publication of Stewart's essay which turns Horne Tooke against himself, Coleridge praised the stranger etymological work of Walter Whiter because in this system 'words are not mere symbols of things & thoughts, but themselves things'.[86] As if to place the value of the sounds of words on the verge of an absurdity, Coleridge hazards the possibility that, should the work of the universal grammarians and that of the etymologists overlap, the order of things and the order of thoughts would correspond to each other in language by punning.[87] That flagrant conjecture about the sounds of words was an optimistic one, if not altogether unlikely from the author of the 'Logosophia'.

In contrast with the idea that the mind recognises its own activity by virtue of the imperfections of language, Coleridge proposes the notion that language and the mind have a common history and an 'organic' affinity with each other. He had asked Godwin in 1800,

Is thinking impossible without arbitrary signs? & – how far is the word 'arbitrary' a misnomer? Are not words &c parts & germinations of the Plant? And what is the Law of their Growth? – In something of this order I would endeavor to destroy the old antithesis between *Words & Things*, elevating words into Things, & living Things too.[88]

This proposal to Godwin does become shortly his own project: an essay on poetry, 'a disguised System of Morals and Politics', 'a metaphysical Investigation of the Laws, by which our Feelings form affinities with each other, with Ideas, & with words'.[89] If language is not descriptive, how is it not powerless? If it is not logical, how is it more than accidental? If its objects are not imageable nor its laws consistent, how then is it precise? Around these three questions Coleridge indicates a theory of language which both continues and goes beyond the strategies advised by Stewart. Coleridge's emphases on etymology and on the need to desynonymise words show how he recognised that language has a substantial history of its own. One pessimistic answer to this was to respond by rooting out his own cultural biography. Another sign of pessimism was to wish, 'O that I had the Language of Music . . . words halt over & over again.'

Given the first indications of the *Biographia* in Coleridge's letter to Godwin ('elevating words into Things, & living Things too'), it is not surprising that the theory of language it proposes involves a theory of the poetic use of language. For this Coleridge makes use of his assumptions about music in order to define the first mark of imaginative power: 'The delight in richness and sweetness of sound' in language. To have 'music' in the soul is a pre-requisite of the poet. Images and the ability to put images in combinations, these can be acquired,

But the sense of musical delight, with the power of producing it, is a gift of imagination; and this together with the power of reducing multitude into unity of effect, and modifying a series of thoughts by some one predominant thought or feeling, may be cultivated and improved, but can never be learned.[90]

Two main features are involved here: first, the poetic sense of the material, aural character of words, which Coleridge found in Milton as pre-eminently the musical poet;[91] second, the poetic sense of structure which has a unity beyond that of a mere combination of images, and which Coleridge describes in his comparison of *The Tempest* to 'a most finished piece of music'.[92]

These two features in his description of the elements essential to poetic language are the clearest means by which Coleridge defines the kind of abstraction poetry should have. They involve an analysis of the separation of words and things. This analysis is one which Coleridge continues to find useful. It is also an analysis which I. A. Richards has celebrated as the keystone of Coleridge's notion of how poetry works. Richards has also clearly seen that a consequence of Coleridge's analysis is his use of the phrase, 'a sense of musical delight'. For Richards, this is the sense according to which 'The movement of the verse becomes the movement of the meaning.' This contrasts with the words functioning as counterparts of distinct meanings.[93] To identify the words and the thought, however dynamically, as Richards advises, is to ignore the continuing notion of their difference which Coleridge maintains. Language remains for Coleridge a problem precisely on account of his idealism. It had been only in the first place a problem of representation.

That problem of representation has two sides to it: one pessimistic, the other relatively optimistic. If, for example, the description of a multiform ocean of 'cut-glass surfaces' is no more than a 'play of Words', then how can the mind represent anything at all to itself?

O what then are Words, but articulated Sighs of a Prisoner heard from his Dungeon! powerful only as they express their utter impotence![94]

However, in this very exclamation about the incompetence of language there is an indication of the usefulness of Coleridge's perception. For it allows him to analyse instances of representation in which an image can therefore be read as a 'sigh' of oppression. It allows him, for example, to criticise Indian religions as a system 'half-verbal and built on the accidents of language'. Its poetry is an attempt 'to image the unimageable, not by symbols but by a jumble of visual shapes'.[95]

In a similar way, the French language is considered by Coleridge to be anathema to poetry because it has developed so as to confuse ideas, which are relatively obscure, with clear images.[96] By separating word and thing Coleridge, therefore, can treat language as a symptom of cultural history. He can go beyond the notion of etymology and propose, as he did propose, a dictionary on historical principles. Language appears then as the consequence of the mind of the nation which speaks it: the history of 'individual minds, sanctioned by the collective Mind'.[97]

There is optimism in the concept that the laws of language correspond with habits of thought. That optimism continues alongside a pessimism which confronts actual language as an impediment to thought. The contradiction between the two is, perhaps, never clarified. A letter to James Gillman as late as 1827 proposes that the laws of language and of thought are equivalent. It is, therefore, given prominence by I. A. Richards.[98] However,

Coleridge's claim merely begs the question at issue because he stipulates that this applies only if language is used *legitimately*.

The optimism and the pessimism are maintained by dividing between them two different aspects of language: syntax and vocabulary. These come to form the basic antitheses of Coleridge's assumptions about language. The change in his notion about the relative importance of each is indicated by his shift from Horne Tooke's nominalism to the universal grammarians. Syntax, in particular syntax as it has been developed by the Graeco-Roman writers and by the Schoolmen, enables language to be more than an oppressed sigh and to become a flexible operation of the mind and of feeling. This is related, by analogy, to verse in poetry and also to larger-scale structures in the arts. We have noticed in Twining, Smith and Sir William Jones how music is a model of explicit order and method. The value of syntax is usually described by Coleridge either negatively or by analogy with music. Commenting on the famous dictum of Plato's *Republic*, that a change in the form of music marks a disruption in the state, Coleridge interprets Plato by referring to 'the Rhythm, the Tune, of a Nation's thoughts . . . the rhythm of Prose'.[99]

If syntax is the consequence and the occasion of the mind's activity, then vocabulary appears to be relatively inhibiting. Coleridge's history of syntax is a history of the strengths available in language, despite some modern abuses. His history of vocabulary, however, is of something more usually capricious and oppressive. The very inertia of grammatical forms might perhaps appear to offer to syntax a more flexible set of current possibilities than could be available to vocabulary, which changes so much more rapidly. At any rate, the modern history of language as a whole appears to Coleridge to be an unhappy one. All in all, Coleridge describes the contemporary condition of language as marked by an excess of manner in vocabulary, which he attributes to the growth of commercialism since the reign of Charles II, and also as marked by an abbreviation of the resources of syntax.[100] Together these have contributed to an increase of a mode of visuality in the use of language, and this appears to be a correlative of the dominance of empiricism.[101]

To sum all this up Coleridge makes use of a conventional eighteenth-century analogy, most apparent in Rouseau's essay on the origins of language, which parallels the history of words and that of music. He gives to that analogy a new twist by describing the present state of language as a parody of an original music. We have already noticed that Coleridge did not have any confidence in that primitivism, and it is perhaps for this reason that he both advances the analogy and disowns it in the *Biographia*:

In the days of Chaucer and Gower our language might (with due allowance for the imperfections of the simile) be compared to a wilderness of vocal reeds, from which the favorites only of Pan and Apollo could construct even the rude Syrinx; and from this the *constructors* alone could elicit strains of music. But now, partly by the labours of successive poets, and in part by the more artificial state of society and social intercourse, language mechanized as it were into a barrel-organ, supplies at once the instrument and the tune.[102]

The analogy summarises ingeniously how language can write us, think us and speak us. Its pessimism is that of Coleridge's view of 'The unnatural, false, affected Style of the moderns, that makes sense and simplicity *oddness!*'[103] However, it leaves no space for an optimism which Coleridge finds in certain poetic and philosophic uses of language. The evidence for this optimism is found in a more historical version of the past and the present: in the contribution of the Schoolmen, who made language more flexible, and also in the work of certain modern poets who, being relatively inattentive to the image, re-work the devices of composition. This contrasts with other modern poetry with its predominance of 'striking Images . . . Portraiture' and the restrictions of the couplet.[104]

Hence Coleridge's advice to the student of philosophy:

In disciplining his mind one of the first rules should be to lose no opportunity of tracing words to their origin, one good consequence of which will be that he will be able to use the *language* of sight without being enslaved by its affections. He will at least secure himself from the delusive notion that what is not *imageable* is likewise not *conceivable*. To emancipate the mind from the despotism of the eye is the first step towards its emancipation from the influences and intrusions of the senses, sensations and passions generally. Thus most effectually is the power of abstraction to be called forth, strengthened, and familiarised, and it is this power [of] abstraction that chiefly distinguishes the human understanding . . . Hence we are to account for the preference which the divine Plato gives to expressions taken from the objects of the ear, as terms of music and harmony, and in part at least for the numerical symbols in which Pythagoras clothed his philosophy.[105]

The hieroglyph

In terms of Coleridge's pessimism about the condition of language, there is only one adequate analogy with which to describe it. This is the hieroglyph: juxtaposition without connection; distinct visuality without precise knowledge. In order to equip himself with this analogy Coleridge rifled an area of eighteenth-century 'semiology' little used in England, William Warburton's *The Divine Legation of Moses* (1738). This had remained the chief work on hieroglyphs, and, as we noticed in the Introduction, had influenced the idea of the sign in Condillac, Diderot and Rousseau. Coleridge read the *Legation* as early as 1796. He disagreed with Warburton on important principles,[106] but he agreed with Warburton's version of what hieroglyphs had been: sophisticated picture-writing.

Coleridge's history of writing and his application of this to a theory of language derives from the terms of the *Legation*. It is clear that Coleridge returns to Warburton's work when preparing the lectures on philosophy in 1818.[107] Warburton had argued that the interpretation of the bible should take notice of the history of successive kinds of discourse. These kinds of discourse, which can now appear strange, are no more than the correlatives of the different forms of writing which are contemporary with them. The hieroglyph appears in this historical sequence in between picture-writing and the alphabet. The history of these forms of writing is based upon a principle of economy of representation. Each form of writing is, therefore, merely an abbreviation of that which precedes it.

Gilbert Wakefield, a fellow of Jesus College, Cambridge, a Unitarian, whose writings on the Greek language Coleridge was certainly familiar with, gave renewed currency to Warburton's history of writing in 1784. In a paper delivered to the Manchester Philosophical Society, of which Josiah Wedgwood was a member, he both rehearses and revises Warburton's version. Wakefield describes how picture-writing in Mexico had, by the principle of economy of representation, given way to the hieroglyphical writing of Egypt. This had, in its turn, been succeeded by Chinese writing, which, standing in the relation of a *mark* to its object, lies midway between the hieroglyph and the alphabet. In contrast with Warburton, however, Wakefield argues that the alphabet comes into being at a moment discontinuous with what precedes it. Also he argues that, although all forms of picture-based writing may be of human origin, the alphabet has a divine origin. The break in the history between signs which represent things and signs which represent words is shown as a logical flaw in Warburton's account. The transition from representational to abstract script is a fundamental re-orientation of the sign.[108]

The system proposed by *The Divine Legation*, although it is limited to a principle of representation, is a complex one. Representation is divided by Warburton into three orders: *epistolic, hieratic, hieroglyphic*. It is divided into three modes: *curiologic, symbolic, tropical*. It is divided into three tendencies: *communication, secrecy, idolatry*. Graphic writing is not therefore, of necessity, hieratic. It is incidental that it was at the hieroglyphical moment that writing fell a prey to sacerdotalism and secrecy and also became the occasion for idolatry of nature. These things could have happened at any stage.[109]

The alphabet is, according to Warburton's history, no more than another abridgement of the graphic sign. Its additional virtue of avoiding some dangers of idolatry is only accidental. For this reason Warburton has no difficulty about crediting Egypt with both the invention of the hieroglyph and the invention of the alphabet.[110] Wakefield, on the other hand, defends the radical change which the alphabet brings. He, therefore, gives the credit for its invention to the Hebrews.

This disagreement illustrates the use Coleridge makes of a correlation between forms of writing and forms of thought. That correlation itself comes from Warburton. However, the selection of the hieroglyph for particular contempt comes from Wakefield's emphasis on the idolatrous and secretive tendency peculiar to the hieroglyph and absent from the more abstract form of the alphabet. Coleridge's innovation is to make that tendency interdependent with the curiologic and metonymic principles to which an hieroglyphic form reduces language. To bring into subjection to the finite image those 'deep feelings which belong, as by a natural right, to those obscure ideas that are necessary to . . . moral perfection', is for Coleridge the first act of oppression.[111]

In the same way as he had credited the moment of contact

between the Roman and Asiatic–Hebraic with a moral revolution, so also he credits the moment of contact between the Greek–Pythagorean and the Egyptian with a revolution in the idea of language. The abolition of a merely visual natural imagery and the introduction of a connective syntax are the contribution of Pythagoras, of Plato and of subsequent writers.[112] It is not surprising that Coleridge's philosophy of history should place the moment of redemption at the moment of mediation between Greek and Jewish.[113]

The notion of the Egyptian and Oriental hieroglyph is useful to Coleridge because it can be applied to his notion of the modern. After 1810 Coleridge notes apprehensively that his contemporaries set out to justify Oriental forms and devices with arguments that are no better than the 'papistical' slogan, *picturae pauperum libri*. The ancient hieroglyph and the modern habit of thought are superimposed upon each other. Both have fallen into despotism, sensuality, insensibility, and into a form of philosophy which excludes speculation. These are the terms of Coleridge's condemnation of both. There is, for him, no shortage of proofs that 'there is a natural affinity between Despotism and modern Philosophy'.[114]

The terms of Coleridge's epistemology recurrently echo the comparison between the hieroglyph and the modern. He bundles together a host of notions to which he is antipathetic under the concept of visual juxtaposition. The modern philosophers (with the exception of some of the Germans) 'mistake distinct images for clear conceptions'. They impress their readers because they provide a 'system that supplies image after image to the senses, however little connected they may be by any necessary copular [sic]'.[115] The French writers' attempt to destroy connectives in language is the correlative of their attempt to annihilate connections within the order of society.[116] Modern despotism corresponds to oriental hieratic sacerdotalism because in both thought is reduced to a mere repetition of visual images. This is both the cause and the consequence of there being too few men of learning and mass ignorance. The symptom of this mode of thought in poetry is an excess of poetic diction which can be erased only with a diffusion of literacy. Most modern poetry has lost its essence in a repetition of those forms which are 'only hieroglyphic of it'.[117]

The use of the figure of the hieroglyph can both disguise a confusion in Coleridge's epistemology and open up the possibility of a more complex analysis of the visual and of painting. The confusion emerges in the way in which Coleridge uses the terms *concept*, *image* and *word* as if they were interchangeable. For example, he had noted during his first sea-voyage that the 'image' of the ocean was little 'capable of satisfying the obscure feelings connected with words'.[118] In this instance images are visual perceptions and no more than that. Words are in excess of such perceptions by their affinity and association with a subjectivity which the 'image' of the sea disappoints.

However, Coleridge can also claim something which appears to be in contradiction with that relative value of word over image. For example, he notices the advantages for 'one who has been from childhood accustomed to make *Images* the symbols of things, instead of resting on mere Words'.[119] The confusion by which Coleridge can think of words and images as interchangeable in value derives from the Lockean idea of language which he attacks. Coleridge wishes to displace the equation between word and image, but that equation has become so persuasive that he can talk of either words or images as mere picture-concepts in the mind. Under the pressure of that idea of language which applies words only to images, Coleridge uses, on the one hand, the figure of the hieroglyph in order to describe the fate of language; on the other hand, he uses the opposite figure of the material, sensual sound of words, their 'music', in order to release language from its fate under a 'despotism of the eye'.

It is not surprising, therefore, that the reduction of the word to the visual image is noticed especially when words appear in writing and in print. The word as a written mark is likely to have a value even below that of the image. Coleridge's distrust of the figure of the written mark is not, however, an attempt to establish language within a philosophy that would delimit the play of signifiers. Jacques Derrida has equated any derision of writing or any preference for speech with the symptoms of a 'metaphysics of presence' which, by insisting that all signs are substitutes for timeless realities, refuses to allow the play of language. For Derrida a distrust of writing is a refusal to allow, both inside and outside language, the playfulness of material difference.[120] Coleridge's distrust of writing makes it clear, however, that for him the figure of writing is itself an inhibition of difference. The following passage, from a Notebook of 1817, makes it clear that the ideal is protean and multiform.

It is the instinct of the letter to bring into Subjection to itself the Spirit. – The latter cannot dispute – nor can it be disputed for, but with a certainty of defeat. For Words express generalities that can be made *so* clear – they have neither the play of colors, nor the untranslatable meanings of the eye, nor any one of the thousand indescribable things that form the whole reality of the living fuel.[121]

Writing appears, therefore, itself to be a limitation of difference. Coleridge continues to puzzle over the status of the written. In a long and confused, self-confessedly confused, passage he worries out the problem of whether the restrictions apparent in the written might be eradicated by the differences of individual script. On the same principle he praises Milton's strategy of multiplying words by multiplying their written forms.[122] However, it is the *sound* of words and their materiality in that sense, which writing threatens. And it is the sound of words which is the first affection of the poet. Writing can thus serve in Coleridge's epistemology as a figure parallel to that of the hieroglyph. For example, he writes about a contrast between responses to the beauties of a landscape: for a man of mere sense it is no more than what calligraphy is to an illiterate; for a man of piety it is like 'music . . . the rhythm of the soul's movements'.[123]

The passage quoted from Coleridge's Notebook of 1817, about the 'play of colors' and the 'untranslatable meanings of the eye', shows how Coleridge's idea of the visual is opening to possibilities which re-evaluate the status of painting. The visual can now be divided between two opposites: the hieroglyph, on the one hand, and non-pictorial painting, on the other. Words appear to tend toward the hieroglyph. They limit the play of perception. They are discontinuous with how the eye may attach 'meanings' to that perception. The eye, that is released from the discrete and unconnected image, appears to function in a more flexible manner. Dugald Stewart had described how, by analogy with the perceptions of the ear, the perceptions of the eye also can be understood to involve movement, play and recollection.[124] Similarly, Coleridge writes of the perception of a landscape as analogous to the complex preception of music: 'the rhythm of the soul's movements'. This notion of seeing as a more complex sense indicates a new way of seeing painting.

Finding a place for painting

Coleridge's use of the figure of the hieroglyph, and not of painting, as an analogy for restrictive aspects of language indicates a division in his evaluation of the arts. The changes in his description of how the eye sees, for example, a natural landscape relate directly to developments in his appreciation of specific painters. We have discussed the distance which the eighteenth century places between music and painting: one is the art of empty, and the other is the art of full signs. Between these two opposites lies language, which both is and is not representational.

Coleridge's theory of language does away with this direct opposition between music and painting. It does so by introducing the notion of the hieroglyph in place of that of painting. Coleridge was not to know that Champollion's decipherment of hieroglyphs would show them to be a phonetic and not a pictorial system.[125] Coleridge's misreading of the hieroglyph is useful because it provides a critique of eighteenth-century ideas of language by calling into question assumptions about both its representational and structural elements. The hieroglyph, understood as a pictorial sign, highlights language as a sequence of names and diverts attention from language as form. This idea of the hieroglyph is useful also beyond the margins of ideas about language. For a unified aesthetic, which it is Coleridge's aim to describe, relationships must be found between music, the arts of language, and painting. By making the hieroglyph the scapegoat of his anti-pictorialism, and by complicating his ideas of seeing and of hearing, Coleridge prepares the ground for a unified aesthetic.

We can trace this development in Coleridge's changing descriptions of paintings. During his sojourn in Italy Coleridge had at one and the same time attacked the pictorial idolatry of Catholicism and also praised a number of actual paintings as never before. The work of the Platonic renascence modified and discriminated his criticism of painting. Immediately before his departure for the Mediterranean he had familiarised himself with a number of the great English collections. Dunmow, he wrote to Southey, has 'such divine Pictures, & Engravings as have made me almost an apostate to Music'.[126] In Northcote's collection a joint work by Raphael and Veronese caused him to exclaim: 'That is a POEM indeed!'[127] Such equations as these make it not surprising that Coleridge came to find Lessing's *Laoköon* self-contradictory.[128]

In such instances and also in a number of landscape descriptions we find the sense of sight interpreted in a more complex way than simply as a mediator of image and retina. In front of a scene which is highly differentiated, gazing at a star, or staring at a deep blue Mediterranean sky, the objects seen either *'incapacitate'* the sight, or address 'the *Ear* not the *Eye* of the Soul'. They render 'visual impressions the nearest akin to a Feeling'.[129] These statements complicate the idea of seeing by describing it in a negative way. With regard to a re-evaluation of painting this is not likely to be helpful. Such negative descriptions do, however, explain some appreciation by Coleridge of Italian work which quite disregards its compositional features and treats the painting in its visual effects as being in no way different from a clear Mediterranean sky.[130] More positive discriminations about ways of seeing only emerge in Coleridge's writing after his contact with the American painter Washington Allston, in Rome in 1805.

Allston's painting, *Diana and Her Nymphs in the Chase*, is referred to by Coleridge simply as 'Mr. Allston's Landscape'.[131] He disregards what the painting represents in terms of pictorial narrative; his attention is directed instead toward its compositional form. In particular Coleridge comes to admire relations of the painted surface, of colour and structure, independent from relations of mimesis or illusionism. He details relations of 'tone to colors, chiaro-Oscuro to Light & Shade; viz. such a management of them that they form a beautiful whole, independent of the particular Images colored, lit up, or shaded'.[132] The description of Allston's painting is marked by Coleridge's recognition of the independent play of colour, of the subsistence of objects by relationships of colour, and of the variations of tone which connect them on the painting's surface.

The divine semitransparent and grey-green Light on the highest part of the Trunk of this Smoke Tree — Stones that connect the right extremity with the purple rock on the left extremity (— N.B. the color is really grey-paint, but in appearance & so call it, it is grey-blue faintly purplish) — & how by small stones, scattered at irregular distances along the foreground even to one in the very centre or bisection of the foreground, which seems to balance & hold even all the tints of the whole picture, the keystone of its colors . . . the delicate &

o how delicate grey-white Greyhound, whose two colors amalgamated make exactly the grey-blue of the larger & the 12 small stones behind & around them & even the halo (still with a purplish grey) of the crescent carries on the harmony, & with its *bright* white crescent forms a transition to the bright left-hand thick body-branch & trunk of the largest tree . . .[133]

This extraordinary description locates in the very material of the painting a connective principle of mere colour, which can be abstracted from the objects which the painting represents but which always remains a part of its composition. In this way Coleridge can place painting side by side with the other arts, because, like them, it mediates an order given from within. Painting appears to give back to the mind an image of itself, not by visualising a visionary subject, but by its own principles of form. So too does poetry by means of syntax, verse, and sound; so too does music, by its more explicit temporal order. Painting, therefore, appears to have access to the ideal. This is precisely the point which Coleridge makes when he advertises Allston's work in England in 1814.[134] We have observed that to make such an equivalence between the arts, by finding some common principle which their materials and forms share, is to reduce a separation between the arts which had appeared in Lessing and in Adam Smith to be at its widest at the end of the eighteenth century. Indeed, it is clear even in Coleridge's writings, not least because the visual and the ideal are so persuasively opposed to each other, that the relationship which he develops between the arts is a fragile one.

The unstable position of painting is, in the essays in praise of Allston, clear throughout its very justification. Here Coleridge makes use of Kant's criterion of aesthetic disinterestedness in order to eradicate the principle of association which clings most tenaciously to judgements about the visual arts. He cannot, therefore, describe the idealising compositional relations in painting, as he had nine years earlier in Rome, in terms of the mere sensual constituent of colour. Instead he takes up a position, which he was to revert to again in 1818 in his description of the Pisan murals, whereby he abstracts the ideal quality of painting from almost all relation to its visual character. In these essays, therefore, Coleridge illustrates the possibilities of painting by reference to the other arts, to poetry and especially to music: 'each part is . . . as perfect a melody, as the whole is a complete harmony'.[135]

This unstable appreciation of painting by Coleridge is, indeed, reflected again in comments by Allston himself. For example, when Allston had completed his portrait of Coleridge, he wrote that the poet was 'beyond the reach of my art . . . almost spirit made visible, without a shadow of the visible upon it'.[136] Allston appears to be, as it were, under the spell of his sitter's favourite terms. When, for example, he writes about Tintoretto and Paolo Veronese, Allston comments on how

They addressed themselves, not to the sense merely, as some have supposed, but rather through them to that region (if I may so speak) of the imagination which is supposed to be under the exclusive domination of music.[137]

It is, therefore, music which comes to be assumed to be the first among the arts. It is important to notice the persuasiveness of this notion when we come to consider the ways in which Coleridge applies an idea of music specifically to an idea of literature.

Some years after he had stopped writing about the arts in general, Coleridge jotted down the following note about music.

It converses with the *life* of my mind, as if it were itself the Mind of my Life. Yet I sometimes think, that a great Composer, a Mozart, a Beethoven must have been in a state of Spirit much more akin, more analogous, to mine own when I am at once waiting for, watching, and organically constructing and inwardly constructed by, the *Ideas*, the living Truths, that may be re-excited but cannot be expressed by Words, the Transcendents that give the Objectivity to all Objects, the Form to all Images, yet are themselves untranslated into any Image, unrepresented by any particular Object [,] than I can imagine myself to be a Titian, or a Sir C. Wren.[138]

Given these principles which undermine all the other arts, it is not surprising that Coleridge should especially ridicule the realistic and illusionist styles of painting. Of these he most vehemently despised what he called 'Opieism': i.e. the ultra-mimetic copying of everyday life in the work of John Opie (1761–1807). Opie, known as a self-taught primitive, the Cornish wonder, became enormously popular and, in 1805, a professor at the Royal Academy. It has been commented in relation to his work that 'The more positive the subject before him, the better he painted.' To Coleridge he was anathema.[139]

It is, however, also not surprising, given Coleridge's principles about paintings and about hieroglyphs, that his estimate of anti-realist visionary styles should also not be favourable. Although he recognises the extraordinary genius of the painter/poet, William Blake, he regrets his work as a 'despotism in symbols'.[140]

Carl Woodring, in an essay on 'What Coleridge Thought of Pictures', summarises how 'Unsatisfied with surface realism and suspicious of the visionary in art, Coleridge prized above all the ideal.'[141] That 'ideal' is available to Coleridge in the very sensuous material of music. It is however only available in an uncertain view of painting which is most at ease with the Campo Santo murals at Pisa, where the materials of the pictures have become almost invisible.

Structure and texture: a poetics of music

The relationship between music and creative literature which Coleridge establishes is twofold. There is a relationship between the complex temporal order of music and the structure of a work of literature, and there is the 'sense of musical delight' in poetry. Coleridge argues in 1818 that

in all, that truly merits the name of *Poetry* in its most comprehensive sense, there is a necessary predominance of the Ideas (i.e. of that which originates in the artist himself), and a comparative indifference of the materials.[142]

It is the unusual status of music that both its structure and its material appear to Coleridge, and to his age, as if they were equally abstract. It is by contrast with the visual and with the notion of image and idea that the sound of music appears to be uncontaminated with the habit of representation. The sound of music, the sign in music, appears to be without an object and to be, as it were, itself immaterial.

It is only in an unusual instance, such as that of the glass-harmonica, that Coleridge finds in music a disproportion of its materials and 'Ideas'. Generally, the materials of music are, by the very function of sound and of hearing, a mediation without distortion of inner and outer, of subject and object. For these reasons music, unlike any of the other arts, can be usefully related to literature in order to explain, not only the necessary place of structure in imaginative discourse, but also the necessary place of a pleasure in the sounds of words in poetry.

In his lecture on *The Tempest* in 1811 Coleridge takes this play as the example of Shakespeare's drama of the 'ideal'. It is not created in local time or place so much as it is in the imagination. Its language, like that of Milton and of Dante, is not restricted to a specific scenery, nor is its language restricted to any 'dutchified' painting, like that of contemporary writers.[143] Coleridge's description of *The Tempest* emphasises the 'astonishing scheme of its construction'. After dealing with the language of the play it is to this that he turns his attention. In praise of that structure, he claims that 'the same judgment is observable in every scene, still preparing, still inviting, and still gratifying, like a finished piece of music'.[144] Such a statement about the play makes possible the analysis of its wholly formal relationships. Also, such an analysis is directed towards recognising the dynamic by which the play is structured within its own temporality. Coleridge's essay argues that it is possible to achieve a strategic dynamism in language by means of a temporal suspense which has no reference to any time or place. The analogy with a composition of music defines the play in terms which locate the significance of the parts of the play in their relationship to each other. It is not an unlikely coincidence that this essay sees the first critical use by Coleridge of the term 'organic'.[145]

Several comparisons between musical form and organic form were available to Coleridge. A certain Francis Kelly Maxwell, in *An Essay on Tune* (1781), had emphasised the generation of melody from its own inherent principles. That theory was summed up by Thomas Robertson when he defines how

The system of Tune is thus one great indefinite body, depending upon itself: the parts, by their affinities, taking birth from one another: Principals implying and suggesting Adjuncts; and the whole resembling a Body and its Members.[146]

Such a version of melody and of tune derives, as Robertson makes clear, from the harmonic system described by Tartini. Robertson emphasises the central principle of that system: the reduction of *la moltiplicata alla Unita*.[147] It is, indeed, Tartini's system of harmonics that is the only one with which we know Coleridge was familiar.[148] Without doubt, such a theory corresponds to the general application to the principle of beauty which Coleridge borrowed from the schoolmen: 'multëity in unity'. More particularly, the reduction of *la moltiplicata alla Unita* corresponds to what Coleridge had defined in the *Biographia* as that which, in addition to a sense of musical delight, the poet must be born with: 'the power of reducing multitude into unity of effect, and modifying a series of thoughts by some one predominant thought or feeling'.[149]

This principle of composition, which *The Tempest* exemplifies by its complex temporal structure of suspense, recollection and anticipation, is one which Coleridge extends out from literature to the whole concept of interpretation. In this way the structure of *The Tempest* and its abstraction from local time and place becomes a model of how we might interpret our experience in general, but especially our experience of history.

In *The Statesman's Manual* Coleridge advises 'the collation of the present with the past', a reflection on history in 'the habit of thoughtfully assimilating the events of our own age with those of the time before us'.[150] Such a model of interpretation has the advantage of differentiating between the principles, on the one hand, and the influence, on the other, of such related figures as Erasmus and Voltaire, and Luther and Rousseau. The model of interpretation by which the differences and patterns of similarity in history become understandable is described by Coleridge according to that same model of temporal, musical structure.

He explains this view of history by considering history as if it were a symphony by a composer, such as Cimarosa who, as he has

modified the Present by the Past, he at the same time weds the Past *in* the Present to some prepared and corresponsive Future. The Auditor's thoughts and feelings move under the same influence: retrospection blends with anticipation, and Hope and Memory (a female Janus) become one Power with a double Aspect . . . The Events and Characters of one Age, like the Strains in Music, recall those of another, and the variety by which each is individualized . . . renders the whole more intelligible.[151]

Insofar as this structure of intelligibility is found also in the structure of *The Tempest*, we can understand further Coleridge's judgement,

that Shakespeare, no mere child of nature; no automaton of genius; no passive vehicle of inspiration possessed by the Spirit, not possessing it; first studied patiently, meditated deeply, understood minutely, till knowledge become habitual and intuitive wedded itself to his habitual feelings, and at length gave birth to that stupendous power, by which he stands alone, with no equal or second in his own class; . . . with Milton as his compeer not rival. While the former darts himself forth, and passes into all the forms of human character and passion, the one Proteus of the fire and the flood; the other attracts all forms and things to himself, into the unity of his own IDEAL. All things and modes of action shape themselves anew in the being of MILTON: while SHAKE-SPEARE becomes all things, yet for ever remaining himself.[152]

This dialectic between these two poets constitutes in Coleridge's mind the dialectic between the first essential of the poet, a 'sense of musical delight', and the second, 'the power of reducing multitude to unity of effect'. Shakespeare and *The Tempest* correspond to the second. Milton and *Paradise Lost* correspond to the first.

As early as 1807 Coleridge describes Milton as 'the most musical of poets'. He selects a passage from *Paradise Lost* in order to illustrate the peculiar character of the *poematic*, that is of 'poetry independent of the thoughts and images'.[153] Later, he makes use of Schiller's description of Klopstock in order to define Milton as a musical and not as a picturesque poet. To do this Coleridge turns Schiller against himself. It is Klopstock who, in Coleridge's view, forms his sublimities out of mere largeness of images. Milton's poetry, on the other hand, is the 'producing' of his own mind.[154] It is again a praise of Milton when Coleridge notices that his poetry makes no mention of painting, 'whilst every other page breathes his love and taste for music'. According to Coleridge, he no less than Milton was animated to write by listening to music.[155]

Coleridge scans Milton's verse by using musical notation and divides his blank verse line into about fifteen breves.[156] In order to understand how this and its connection with Coleridge's strategy for the composition of *Christabel* are related as instances of Coleridge's claim that in poetry 'the words, the *media*, must be beautiful, and ought to attract your notice',[157] we need to look briefly at a discussion about the importance of the sound of words which took place towards the end of the eighteenth century.

In 1775 Joshua Steele published *An Essay towards Establishing the Melody and Measure of Speech*. Steele contradicts Lord Monboddo's claim that the material sound of words is of no importance. Instead he argues that tonal gradations indicate in speech whatever feelings or significance are attached to the words. The grammarian must learn from the musician. One important purpose of Steele's disorganised work is to supply guidelines for an alternative in English to the Italian recitative.[158]

A number of works elaborate on Steele's work and simplify his notation for recording the intonation of speech. Their intention to provide more specific guidelines is typified in the title of John Walker's contribution to the debate: *The Melody of Speaking Delineated; or, Elocution taught like Music, by Visible Signs, Adapted to the Tones, Inflexions, and Variations of Voice in Reading and Speaking; with Directions for Modulation, and expressing the*

Passions (1787). We have noticed already that Coleridge was familiar with Walker's *Dictionary of the English Language* (1775), which complements Walker's other work insofar as it is a rhyming-dictionary. It is not too fanciful to suggest, in the absence of particular evidence, that the strategy advanced by such writers as Steele and Walker is at the basis of Coleridge's peculiar scansion of Milton.[159] One aspect of this strategy is, of course, the relative unimportance of the number of syllables in a verse-line, in contrast to the relative importance of a fixed number of major stresses. This strategy, adapted by Coleridge for the purposes of *Christabel*, places its innovations within this late eighteenth-century insistence on the similarities between intonations of speech and music.

Perhaps the most consistent way in which Coleridge realised this emphasis on intonation, however, appears in his manner of reciting his poetry in general. Henry Nelson Coleridge has described how his uncle intoned poetry in such a way that

> the verses seem as if *played* to the ear upon some unseen instrument. And the poet's manner of reciting is similar. It is not rhetorical, but musical; so very near recitative, that for anyone else to attempt it would be ridiculous, and yet it is perfectly miraculous with what exquisite searching he elicits and makes sensible every particular of the meaning.[160]

Others give contemporary accounts of how Coleridge read Spenser, Milton and Shakespeare with an intonation that 'almost amounted to a song'. Most thought this excessive. Coleridge himself thought it 'strictly natural', and the necessary substitute for recitative in the reading of poetry.[161]

Hegel considered poetry an art more abstract than music, because language functions as an aspect of sound which denigrates sound and privileges the concepts to which the sounds correspond. In this way, Hegel places his philosophy of the arts within an idealist philosophy which must place language first in the hierarchy of signs, because language appears to be the least material of signs and the most appropriate to represent concepts. Coleridge, on the other hand, has no such confidence in language. The peculiar terms of Coleridge's philosophy, which derive from an attack upon empiricism and a subversion of its criterion of visuality, places the empty sign of music first in the idealist hierarchy of signs.

Coleridge's account of language, therefore, is one which places poetry at the centre of language. Poetry is so placed because a poetic use of language encourages its musical affinities, in particular the pleasure of its mere sound. In this way, language through its use in poetry tends towards becoming a kind of sign which, like music, is not contaminated by 'clear and precise' ideas. In Coleridge's terms the poet is faced by words which 'halt over and over again'. His poetics, with their descriptions of Shakespeare and of Milton, with their innovations in metre, with their extraordinary continuity between imagination and the discourses of philosophy, politics and history, are a poetics which can also be described as a materialist account of language.

This paradox depends altogether on Coleridge's insistence that language must be thought about in such a way that the relationship between signifier and signified does not conceal the material sound of words. To an idealist philosopher, with such a view, language is never a pure translation of concepts. It is, instead, a material medium which relates in a grosser way to whatever the mind is. Coleridge's idealism includes a poetics, not because poetry is a pure utterance of pure mind, but because poetry uses material signs. The liveliness of Coleridge's understanding of Wordsworth, Shakespeare and Milton derives from this extraordinary conflict within the sign in poetry. In order to offer such a poetics Coleridge also needed the empty sign of music.

CONCLUSION

It is possible to be confident about language. William Hazlitt writes,

Words are the signs which point out and define the objects of the highest import to the human mind; and speech is the habitual, and as it were most *intimate* mode of expressing those signs, the one with which our practical and serious associations are most in unison . . . A sound expresses, for the most part, nothing but itself; a word expresses a million of sounds.[1]

For Hazlitt words 'alone describe things in the order and relation which they happen in human life'.[2] For such a writer the analogy between painting and literature asserts this confidence in the capacity of language to record and to specify. Consider, for example, what Hazlitt has to say 'On a Landscape by Nicholas Poussin':

He 'gives to airy nothing a local habitation', not 'a name'. At his touch, words start up into images, thoughts become things. He clothes a dream, a phantom with form and colour and the wholesome attributes of reality. *His* art is a second nature; not a different one.[3]

It has been my argument that in the period from Collins to Coleridge writers, in an alternative convention that is in conflict with the certainties of Hazlitt, explore an uncertainty about language, about its representational and expressive competence. It is true to say that an early Romantic poetic explores, as it were, the excluded middle between the representational and the expressive modes. The analogy for language, under such a sceptical and exploratory gaze, is music. Uncertainties about language are found in different kinds of discourse: in philosophy after George Berkeley, in poetics after Daniel Webb, in aesthetics after James Harris, in semantics after Edmund Burke, in rhetoric after George Campbell. These uncertainties can find a parallel in theories of music. The popular growth of instrumental forms and in particular of large symphonic forms, from Mannheim to Edinburgh to Haydn's London, is the occasion for uncertainties about the meaning of the 'empty sign' of music. These uncertainties are articulated with reference to issues which range from the source and end of music in general to the relative value of specific instruments. Most important, the argument concentrates itself around, not the expressive source of music, but the relationship between the music and the listener; and the argument also concentrates itself around the question of the texture of sound itself. In the discourses of language, be they philosophy, poetics, aesthetics, rhetoric, or the poem, these arguments are reflected in a questioning of the relationship between reader and text and in a questioning of the 'poematic' qualities of the sounds of words.

Studies of the idea of music in the late eighteenth and early nineteenth centuries have over-emphasised either its relation to the notion of 'expression', or its relation to notions of the irrational. The argument put forward by M. H. Abrams, that Romanticism uses an idea of music in order to confirm an idea of unmediated expressiveness, is contradicted by at least two pieces of evidence in what I have written. First, there is Chabanon's perception that

Les Matelots . . . sont gais au moment où ils chantent tristement. Ainsi, la Musique pour eux n'est pas un langage d'expresion: ce n'est pas un Art qui imite, ni qui cherche même à imiter.[4]

Second, we must note the continuity between Rousseau's definition of the musician, as one who is 'affected more by absent things as if they were present', and Wordsworth's definition of the poet, as one who has 'an ability of conjuring up in himself passions, which are indeed far from being the same as those produced by real events'.[5] To take seriously Wordsworth's figure of the poet as conjuror is to recognise the way in which the empty signs of music conflict with notions of sincere expressiveness. In language, tautology is perhaps the closest words can come to being themselves empty signs. It is worth noticing what Wordsworth has to say about tautology in poems:

every man must know that an attempt is rarely made to communicate impassioned feelings without something of an accompanying consciousness of the inadequateness of our own powers, or the deficiencies of language. During such efforts there will be a craving in the mind, and as long as it is unsatisfied the speaker will cling to the same words, or words of the same character.[6]

In such a case, therefore, words stand in place of an absence in the mind and in feelings. They do not name what is 'there'. They conjure up the sensation of what is 'not there'. The poet, like the musician or like the sailor who sings, is relatively free both of self-expression and of mimesis. This possibility had been explored by William Blake. The idea of song in Blake's poetics and poetic practice, his opposition between the unstained shepherd's pipings and the stained voice of the bard, uses contemporary notions about music in order to articulate a conflict between the freedom and the bondage of the imagination. In contrast to this, a poetics which continues within the conventions of representation and of sincerity finds a figure for poetry in the portrait. The conventions of *ut pictura poesis* are simplified in Cowper's addressing a painting as if it were whom it represents. His poem on his mother's picture displays, in all its claustrophobia, the paradox of a representationalist aesthetic before the face of what is 'not there'.

The other side of that paradox is found in the use of music in Gothic literature. This is the place in which we find music tied to notions of the irrational. 'Mad people sing', writes Hazlitt. For him music is 'a mistress whose face is veiled; an invisible goddess'.[7] And, indeed, within a representationalist aesthetic music must so appear. This, curiously, is the key to its elaboration within the Gothic. Consider the case of Maturin's Immalee, transported from her innocent and natural island world to that of Melmoth. In this new and corrupt world where she hears music for the first time, Immalee explains to Melmoth how, for her, melody

raises a form indescribable – not you, but *my idea of you*. In your presence, though that seems necessary to my existence, I have never felt that exquisite delight that I have experienced in that of your image, when music called it up from the recesses of my heart.[8]

The eeriness of what Immalee says is in the gap between what she desires and what we know to be true. That eeriness is made the greater by her confusion between the values of the term 'image' ('experience', 'presence') and those of the term 'indescribable' ('recesses', 'music'). This confusion can be most clearly seen when we notice that in Immalee's sentences 'experience' is *opposed* to 'presence'. Also we notice that the meaning of the music has a secret source, the depths of the heart where what she desires is hidden.

The enigma of the source of music is perhaps its most usual attachment to the irrational in Gothic literature. Consider, for example, this description of a party at Fonthill in William Beckford's memories of his childhood:

Through all these suites – through all these galleries did we roam and wander – too often hand in hand – strains of music swelling forth at intervals . . . Sometimes a chaunt was heard – issuing, no one could divine from whence – innocent affecting sounds – that stole into the heart with a bewitching langour and melted the most susceptible of my fair companions into tears.[9]

The unanswerable question, 'What does music mean?', is at once more plausible and more eerie when it is asked in the form, 'Where does this music come from?' The epistemological problem is then placed in a tiny narrative which appears contrived in order to conceal a mystery. The Gothic convention uses music within such a narrative suspense. It exploits the expressive and representational models of meaning in order to arouse our fear as we approach their limits. It is this which explains their use of music as an index of disorientation. In the *Mysteries of Udolpho* the heroine Emily, is surprised and enthralled by an 'exquisite melody':

While she paused, the music ceased; and, after a momentary hesitation, she recollected courage to advance to the fishing-house, which she entered with faltering steps, and found unoccupied! Her lute lay on the table; every thing seemed undisturbed, and she began to believe it was another instrument she had heard, till she remembered, that, when she followed M. and Madame St. Aubert from this spot, her lute was left on a window-seat. She felt alarmed, yet knew not whither . . .[10]

On the one hand, therefore, we have a representational theory of language and of meaning in general. On the other, we have the subversion of that theory by the Gothic fear of its incompetence. Between these two sides of the same model, in theories of poetics from Collins to Coleridge, we have demonstrated an exploration of the uncertainties of language and the resource which those uncertainties might provide for poetry. Indeed, it is one main strength and interest of the poetry of the period that it includes these uncertainties within itself.

It has seemed to me important that the discussion of music by Collins, Thomas Twining, Adam Smith, Coleridge and others has been related to the popularity of instrumental music in Edinburgh, London and regional centres such as Norwich. In all cases, but especially that of Twining, this has given their explorations of musical aesthetics and of the differences between specific instruments a recognisable foundation. Therefore, when the application of that aesthetics is applied to poetics, whether in Twining himself or in more 'literary' writers, it has still remained possible to see that what is at issue is a serious analysis of language and of meaning. That analysis, and its inclusion within the practice of poetry, is continuous with the philosophies of language developed, in particular, by George Campbell and Dugald Stewart.

The new theories of meaning and of language recognise its uncertainties and put them to work. The idea of structure, of context, of figurative processes, all move away from the tyranny of the word or of the name. Such ideas specify the relationship in language between the text and the reader as paramount. It takes two to talk. More than anywhere else it is here, concentrated upon the dynamics of listening and of active response, that ideas of music prove useful. As developments from ideas of music, we find in both linguistics and poetics an emphasis upon the power of suggestion, upon varying the figures of a discourse, upon the imaginative process of the reader/listener. This 'imperfection' or uncertainty of language becomes, therefore, its value: it shows how the mind can work. These elements are nowhere more evident than in Wordsworth's poetic practice.

Music appears, in writers as different as James Usher and Adam Smith, to be the most abstract of the arts. Its appeal to Coleridge also is often in terms of its ideality. However, the practical experience of instrumental music, which I have emphasised as a part of our history of this period, did not let these writers forget the materiality of sound, the grain of the music. Nor did it let them forget the specifically temporal structure of music.

Coleridge, following from Adam Smith's essay on imitation with which he was familiar, makes use of the idea of structured temporality to define the complex and dynamic unity of a work of art.[11] More important, in his view, he emphasises also the materiality of sound. This element is a part of his strategy of freeing language from the 'despotism of the eye'. For if the sign of music is an empty one, it is also a material one. Furthermore, the materiality of music, being addressed to the sensual ear and not to the abstracted eye, decisively contrasts it with notions of a picture-language and with notions of etymology from Condillac to Horne Tooke. For Coleridge, therefore, poetry can remain one of the highest activities of human life because pleasure in the music or material sound of words makes possible a relative freedom and liveliness of mind.

It has become, since Jacques Derrida's *Of Grammatology*, an accepted idiom in theories of literature to value writing and to devalue speech. Writing is thought of as the play of difference and of the material sign. However, it is clear that the materiality, diversity and uncertainty of language can also be thought of in terms of its sound. So it is with Coleridge: 'The delight in richness and sweetness of sound, even to a faulty excess'; 'the sense of musical delight'.

It is reasonable to put the question: why did this conflict between picture-theories and music-theories occur in late eighteenth-century and early nineteenth-century ideas of language? It has been a purpose of this book to indicate the complex inter-relationships – of epistemology, of a history of the theory and practice of music, of poetics, of concepts of writing and of representation – that affect ideas of language in this period. The sense of the 'empty sign', and its application in theories both of music and of language, is clearly open to many alternative levels or models of explanation. One could locate an explanation in the mere popularity of instrumental music itself, or in the new subjectivist psychology of experience, or in the reaction against Lockean ideas of signs and in the new analysis of language as a formal structure. If one pursues a more comprehensive model of explanation one might conjecture (and such a conjecture is at least a pleasing one) that in the early years of the eighteenth century the invention, within the state's finances, of the national debt placed at the centre of social life a determining and ultimate 'empty sign'. One might argue that the invention and persistence of the national debt – by successive governments and for purposes of war – caused not only the indignation of Alexander Pope and of Jonathan Swift, who so vehemently opposed this 'Blest paper credit!', but more indirectly determined a new poetic which from Collins to Coleridge opposed the substantial relationship of signifier and signified which Swift and Pope had defended.

It has not been within the scope of this book to justify or to deny such a conjecture, but more moderately to correlate evidence about the change itself. Other models of explanation might well be the object of another book. It is, however, reasonable to indicate one cause which is well-established among theories of the arts in general during the eighteenth century. The enormous growth in the size of the reading public and of those with access to the arts during this period produced an audience for poetry that was both more varied within itself and also more out of touch with the poet. The first prefaces of Coleridge and of Wordsworth are, as we have seen, dramatic indices of this fact. The growth of that reading public brought with it a relative loss in a precise familiarity with shared classical contexts which had – at least up to Pope and Swift – provided a common language between author, poem and reader. With similar effect that larger audience brings into popular existence in literature the novel, and in painting the water-colour landscape. What these new popular forms have in common is not only their low-brow appreciation or their greater or lesser realism, but their equal requirement that their audience participate in them by attaching to a 'content' a 'meaning' that is not revealed in the work itself.

Wolfgang Iser has emphasised the ways in which from Henry Fielding to Laurence Sterne it is typical of eighteenth-century novelists to provoke the reader to engage in a 'constructive' relation to the text. Fielding insists to his reader that

we shall not indulge thy laziness where nothing but thy own attention is required; for thou art highly mistaken if thou dost imagine that we intended, when we began this great work, to leave thy sagacity nothing to do.

And Sterne gives this pattern a more radical twist:

no author, who understands the just boundaries of decorum and good-breeding, would presume to think all: The truest respect which you can pay to the reader's understanding, is to halve this matter amicably, and leave him something to imagine, in his turn, as well as yourself. For my own part, I am eternally paying him compliments of this kind, and do all that lies in my power to keep his imagination as busy as my own.[12]

We can notice affiliations between that idea of the imaginative novel-reader and the proposals made about the art of water-colour in 1786 by Alexander Cozens. In his *A New Method of Assisting the Invention in Drawing Original Compositions of Landscape* Cozens proposes that one compose a landscape merely by staining a piece of paper or by working with blots. These blots are 'vague and indeterminate' – particularly so if (as he advises) one makes a variety of blots and crumples the paper in order to multiply them – and therefore they enlarge the powers of invention in 'the production of whole compositions new to the performer'. As A. P. Oppé has pointed out, Cozens's method is more radical than the similar method he affects to borrow from Leonardo da Vinci, who had proposed an abstract shape as a point of departure. Cozens insists on what is suggested by the medium itself. It is interesting to observe that Cozens argues that this method is especially suited to a mind that is not well-stocked and has little store of its own acquired ideas.[13] Sir Joshua Reynolds had insisted two years beforehand that, in approaching 'Nature',

an Artist who brings to his work a mind tolerably furnished with the general principles of Art, and a taste formed upon the works of good Artists, in short who knows in what excellence consists, will, with the assistance of Models, which we will likewise suppose he has learnt the art of using, be an over-match for the greatest Painter that ever lived who should be debarred such advantages.[14]

As with the novel and the water-colour landscape, which appear to engage and to satisfy what can only seem to Reynolds inventive but thinly-fed minds, so it might also be with a poetic of the 'empty sign'. A larger and less educated readership could then appear to participate in a common language, in a universal language of humanity, much in the same way as seventy-five years previously Joseph Addison had decided that people with no more than an 'ordinary ear' are competent to do with music.

NOTES

Introduction

1 John Locke, *An Essay Concerning Human Understanding*, edited by Peter H. Nidditch (Oxford, 1975), p. 405 (Book III, Chapter 2, 'Of the Signification of Words'): 'The use then of Words, is to be sensible Marks of *Ideas*; and the *Ideas* they stand for, are their proper and immediate Signification'; see also Book IV, Chapter 21, 'Of the Division of the Sciences', p. 720. Significant studies of this tradition after Locke include Hans Aarsleff, *From Locke to Saussure* (London, 1982); Robert L. Armstrong, 'Locke's "Doctrine of Signs"', *JHI*, 26 (1965), 369–82; S. K. Land, *From Signs to Propositions: The Concept of Form in Eighteenth Century Semantic Theory* (London, 1974); also his 'The Silent Poet: An Aspect of Wordsworth's Semantic Theory', *UTQ*, 42 (1973), 157–69; V. A. Rudowski, 'Theory of Signs in the Eighteenth Century', *JHI*, 35 (1970), 683–90; Jacques Derrida, *Of Grammatology*, translated by G. C. Spivak (Baltimore and London, 1976), pp. 280–95 (Part II, Chapter 4, 'The History and System of Scripts'); Murray Cohen, *Sensible Words: Linguistic Practice in England 1640–1785* (Baltimore and London, 1977).

2 *From Signs to Propositions*, p. 30; and see also p. 186: 'The real question, which a number of writers in the period faced squarely, is what model will explain the meaning of words when the principle of representation will not.' Land also comments that a special problem area for eighteenth-century semantic theory was mathematics. We would add also music. See also Land's 'Lord Monboddo and the Theory of Syntax in the Late Eighteenth Century', *JHI*, 37 (1976), 423–40; and his 'Adam Smith's "Considerations Concerning The First Formation of Languages"', *JHI*, 38 (1977), 677–90.

3 Jean H. Hagstrum, *The Sister Arts: the Tradition of Literary Pictorialism and English Poetry from Dryden to Gray* (Chicago, 1958). Hagstrum later extends this argument to cover subsequent poets, in particular William Blake: 'Blake was saturated with influences from the traditional and contemporary *ut pictura poesis* and . . . his language embodied visual icons, the picture-gallery method of proceeding, and pictorial personification', 'Blake and the Sister-Art Tradition', in *Blake's Visionary Forms Dramatic*, edited by David V. Erdman and John E. Grant (Princeton, New Jersey, 1970), pp. 82–91 (p. 89). See also W. J. Hipple Jr., *The Beautiful, the Sublime, and the Picturesque in Eighteenth Century Aesthetic Theory* (Carbondale, Illinois, 1957); Martin Price, 'The Picturesque Moment', in *From Sensibility to Romanticism: Essays Presented to Frederick A. Pottle*, edited by F. W. Hilles and H. Bloom (New York, 1965), pp. 259–92; John Barrell, *The Dark Side of the Landscape:*

The Rural Poor in English Painting, 1730–1840 (Cambridge, 1980). W. J. Mitchell persuasively disagrees with Hagstrum: 'It is true that all these elements may be found in Blake's poetry, but they are not used in a visual or pictorialist manner, as the eighteenth century understood it . . . Perhaps the simplest test of Blake's anti-pictorialism, however, is the fact that his poems do not refer us visually even to his own illustrations', *Blake's Composite Art: A Study of the Illuminated Poetry* (Princeton, New Jersey, 1978), pp. 22–3.

4 This may seem surprising given M. H. Abrams's assertion that, 'In place of painting, music becomes the art frequently pointed to as having a profound affinity with poetry.' However, Abrams sent the sister-arts down a blind alley by insisting that music was used to assert the values of expressiveness. This insistence has him, for example, completely misunderstand some sentences by Adam Smith on how music is *not* expressive; see *The Mirror and the Lamp: Romantic Theory and the Critical Tradition* (Oxford, 1953), pp. 50, 92.

5 The main research into music in relation to an aesthetics of literature in the eighteenth century includes John Hollander, *The Untuning of the Sky: Ideas of Music in English Poetry, 1500–1700* (Princeton, New Jersey, 1961); see also his *Images of Voice: Music and Sound in Romantic Poetry* (Cambridge, 1970); and his 'Wordsworth and the Music of Sound', in *New Perspectives on Coleridge and Wordsworth: Selected Papers from the English Institute*, edited by Geoffrey Hartman (New York and London, 1972), pp. 41–84; B. H. Fairchild, *Such Holy Song: Music as Idea, Form and Image in the Poetry of William Blake* (Kent, Ohio, 1980); James Malek, *The Arts Compared: An Aspect of Eighteenth Century British Aesthetics* (Detroit, 1974). Malek's book limits itself to the theory, without relation to poetic practice. See also articles by H. M. Schueller in the Bibliography. For additional material see also the Bibliography in *Music and Aesthetics in the Eighteenth and Early-Nineteenth Centuries*, edited by Peter le Huray and James Day (Cambridge, 1981).

6 'Toute Musique qui ne peint rien n'est que du bruit; & sans l'habitude qui dénature tout, elle ne seroit guère plus de plaisir qu'une suite de mots harmonieux & sonores dénués d'ordre et de liaison', *Encyclopédie, ou dictionnaire raisonné des sciences, des arts et des métiers*, 17 vols (Paris, 1751–65), I, xii. (Hereafter, *Encyclopédie*). I use the translation of R. N. Schwab, *Preliminary Discourse to the Encyclopedia of Diderot* (New York, 1963), p. 39. See also A. R. Oliver, *The Encyclopedists as Critics of Music* (New York, 1947).

7 *Encyclopédie*, XV (1755), p. 348.

8 Thomas Twining, *Aristotle's Treatise on Poetry, Translated: with Notes on the Translation, and on the Original; and Two Dissertations, on Poetical, and Musical, Imitation* (London, 1789), p. 49.

9 James Harris, *Philological Inquiries* (London, 1781), p. 197.

10 S. T. Coleridge, *Poems on Various Subjects* (Bristol, 1796), p. v.

11 *The Prose Works of William Wordsworth*, edited by W. J. B. Owen and Jane Worthington Snyser, 3 vols (Oxford, 1974), I, 147. (Hereafter *W Prose*).

12 G. L. Le Coat, 'Comparative Aspects of the Theory of Expression in the

Baroque Age', *18th Century Studies*, 5 (1971–2), 207–23 (p. 210).

For musical emblems see *The Poems of Gray, Collins and Goldsmith*, edited by Roger Lonsdale (London, 1969), Plate 3 and p. 414; Thomas Gray, *Poems* (Dublin, 1768); William Collins, *Odes on Several Descriptive and Allegoric Subjects* (London, 1747); the frontispiece to each volume of *A Collection of Poems by Several Hands*, edited by Robert Dodsley, 3 vols (London, 1748); and (also published by Dodsley) William Shenstone, *The Works in Verse and Prose*, 2 vols (London, 1765).

13 E. H. Gombrich, '*Icones Symbolicae*: Philosophies of Symbolism and their Bearing on Art', in *Symbolic Images: Studies in the Art of the Renaissance*, (London, 1975), pp. 123–95 (pp. 181–2).

14 William Warburton, *The Divine Legation of Moses demonstrated, on the principles of a religious Deist*, 2 vols (London, 1738), II, p. 94 (Book IV); and see also pp. 81–96. For a comparison of Vico and Warburton, in respect of their theories of writing, see Lieselotte Dieckmann, *Hieroglyphics: the History of a Literary Symbol* (St Louis, Missouri, 1970), pp. 124–6.

15 Warburton, p. 86.

16 Warburton, p. 95.

17 Dieckmann, pp. 132–5. See also Land, *From Signs to Propositions*, pp. 62–3, 70–1. It is, of course, Warburton (and not Vico, as Land suggests) who is influential in British eighteenth-century thought: see René Wellek, 'The Supposed Influence of Vico on England and Scotland in the Eighteenth Century', in *Giambattista Vico: an International Symposium*, edited by G. Tagliacozzo and H. White (Baltimore, 1969), pp. 215–23.

18 *From Signs to Propositions*, p. 91.

19 Dieckmann, p. 134.

20 Dieckmann, p. 133.

21 Dieckmann, p. 135. It is not surprising to find, in Diderot's concept of the image, that music should be so considered. See, for example, the following from Norman Bryson, *Word and Image: French Painting of the Ancien Régime* (Cambridge, 1981), p. 179: For Diderot,

> whereas discourse is distributed in time, mind is simultaneous; it is only when the seriality of discourse has been overcome that a communication of the contents of consciousness from one being to another can occur. This can be achieved only by means of a picture, an image, evoked in the hearer's imagination by the hallucinatory power of speech, that "subtle hieroglyphic which rules over a whole description", and which enables the hearer to visualise the scene of a description within his mind and to bypass the inherent obstructions of language.

To this we should add the observations of Michael Fried about the consequences of Diderot's aesthetic for the 'spectator' of the art-work:

> a painting, it was insisted, had to attract the beholder, to stop him in front of itself, and to hold him there in a perfect trance of involvement. At the same time . . . it was only by negating the beholder's presence that this could be achieved: only by

establishing the fiction of his absence or nonexistence could his actual placement before and enthrallment by the painting be secured.

See his 'Towards a Supreme Fiction: Genre and Beholder in the Art Criticism of Diderot and his Contemporaries', *NLH*, 6 (1975), 543–85 (p. 581). See also his *Absorption and Theatricality: Painting and Beholder in the Age of Diderot* (Berkeley and London, 1980).

22 *Essai sur l'origine des langues* (Paris, 1764). I use the translation in *On the Origin of Language: Jean-Jacques Rousseau, Essay on the Origin of Languages; Johann Gottfried Herder, Essay on the Origin of Language*, translated by J. H. Moran and A. Gode (New York, 1966). For evidence of the writing of the sections on music preceding that of the sections on language see Moran and Gode, p. 80.

23 Cited in Paul de Man, *Blindness and Insight: Essays in the Rhetoric of Contemporary Criticism* (Oxford, 1971), p. 126.

24 *Encyclopédie*, XV (1755), p. 348. The remark is attributed to Fontenelle, but is untraceable. See *The New Grove Dictionary of Music and Musicians*, edited by Stanley Sadie, 20 vols (London, 1980), XVII, p. 481. (Hereafter Grove, 1980.)

25 *Blindness and Insight*, pp. 127–8.

26 *Blindness and Insight*, pp. 131–2. Here, also de Man argues that Rousseau opposes the pictorialism of eighteenth-century aesthetics, such as we have seen in Fried's version of Diderot. Instead, for Rousseau, 'the misleading synchronism of the visual perception which creates a false illusion of presence has to be replaced by a succession of discontinuous moments that create the fiction of a repetitive temporality'. See also de Man's quoting, to similar purpose, a letter from Rousseau to Malesherbes: 'I found an unexplainable void that nothing could have filled; a longing of the heart towards another kind of fulfillment of which I could not conceive but of which I nevertheless felt the attraction', *Blindness and Insight*, p. 18.

27 *A Dictionary of Music. Translated from the French of Mons. J. J. Rousseau. By William Waring*, (London, n.d. [1770]), pp. 198–9 (Article: 'Imitation').

28 *W Prose*, I. p. 161.

29 *W Prose*, I, p. 162.

30 *W Prose*, I, p. 138.

31 *ibid.*

32 In evidence against de Man one must cite the article, 'Sonate', from the *Dictionnaire*: 'pour plaire constamment, & prévenir l'ennui, elle doit s'élever au rang des Arts d'imitation', a remark not noticed by de Man, but a part of the ambiguity of Rousseau's concept of music and its limits. Waring's translation runs as follows:

> to please constantly, and prevent languor, it ought to be raised to the rank of imitative arts; . . . To know what all this fracas of sonata's would mean, with which we are loaded, we must do as the ignorant painter, who was obliged to write under his figures, 'This is a tree.' 'This is a man.' 'And this is a horse.'

A Dictionary of Music ('Sonata'). Rousseau leaves finally the impression simply of inconsistency:

> In fact Rousseau was by no means as blind to the value of both harmony and instrumental music as he is often made out to be: this is evident enough from his later admiration for Gluck; less well known perhaps is the following passage from a letter which he wrote to D'Alembert in 1754, just one year before the *Lettre sur la musique française*: 'The symphony itself has learned to speak without the help of words, and often the feelings that come from the orchestra are no less lively than those that come from the mouths of the actors!
>
> Le Huray and Day, pp. 90–1.

33 *Blindness and Insight*, pp. 18–19.

34 James Usher, *An Introduction to the Theory of the Human Mind* (London, 1771), p. 80.

35 Michel-Paul Guy de Chabanon, *Observations sur la musique et principalement sur la metaphysique de l'art*, Réimpression des éditions de Paris, 1779 et 1764 (Genève, 1969), p. 23.

36 Adam Smith, 'Of the Nature of that Imitation which takes place in what are called the Imitative Arts', in *Essays on Philosophical Subjects* (London, 1795), p. 172. This posthumous volume includes Dugald Stewart's account of Smith's life and writings.

37 *W Prose*, I, p. 142.

38 *The Notebooks of Samuel Taylor Coleridge*, edited by Kathleen Coburn (New York, Princeton, N.J. and London, 1957–), II, April 1804, 2035. (Hereafter *CN*.)

39 *CN*, I, 787 (August–September 1800).

40 *From Signs to Propositions*, p. 116.

41 Erasmus Darwin, *The Temple of Nature; or, The Origin of Society* (London, 1803), pp. 114–15: 'Nouns are the names of the ideas of things . . . Verbs are also in reality names of our ideas of things . . .' And see *The Botanic Garden* (London, 1791), p. vii: 'The Egyptians were possessed of many discoveries in philosophy and chemistry before the invention of letters; these were then expressed in hieroglyphic paintings of men and animals; which after the discovery of the alphabet were described and animated by the poets, and became the first deities of Egypt and afterwards of Greece and Rome.' See also Coleridge to R. Southey, 29 July 1802: 'Of course, Darwin & Wordsworth having given each a defence of *their* mode of Poetry, & a disquisition on the nature & essence of Poetry in general, I shall necessarily be led rather deeper', *The Collected Letters of Samuel Taylor Coleridge*, edited by E. L. Griggs, 6 vols (Oxford 1956–71), II, p. 830 (29 July 1802). (Hereafter *CL*.)

42 *From Signs to Propositions*, p. 103.

43 George Campbell, *The Philosophy of Rhetoric*, 2 vols (London, 1776), II, pp. 100–1.

44 I. A. Richards, *The Philosophy of Rhetoric* (New York, 1936), pp. 3, 38.

45 It is useful to notice the relation between Darwin's poetics cited above and

Leibnitz's view of the Chinese written character: 'if we could discover the key to Chinese characters, we would find something that would aid the analysis of thoughts'; see Hans Aarsleff, 'The Study and Use of Etymology in Leibnitz', in *From Locke to Saussure*, pp. 84–100 (p. 90).

46 Dugald Stewart, *Collected Works*, edited by Sir William Hamilton, 10 vols plus 1 supplementary vol (Edinburgh, 1854), V, 154–5. (Hereafter Stewart.)

47 Stewart, V, p. 125; Stewart attributes this concept chiefly to Diderot's version of Locke: '"Every idea must necessarily, when brought to its state of ultimate decomposition, resolve itself into a *sensible* representation or picture . . . Hence an important rule in philosophy, – That every expression which cannot find an external and a sensible object to which it can thus establish its affinity, is destitute of signification".' Also it is the measure by which he estimates his own revision of Thomas Reid; see Stewart, V, p. 154.

48 Paul Ricoeur, *The Rule of Metaphor*, translated by R. Czerny (London, 1978), p. 45.

49 Ricoeur, p. 102.

50 Ricoeur, pp. 78–83. Notice Ricoeur's emphasis on Richards's concept of 'The Interinanimation of Words' (*The Philosophy of Rhetoric*, pp. 47–66), which is itself borrowed from Coleridge.

51 Ricoeur, p. 43.

52 Angus Fletcher, *Allegory: The Theory of a Symbolic Mode* (New York, 1964), p. 13.

53 Fletcher, pp. 14–15.

54 Fletcher, p. 16.

55 Fletcher, pp. 16–18.

56 'By placing the funeral moment rather than passionate utterance at the beginning of his version of language, Wordsworth establishes the sign of mortality at the origin of language, so that the incarnation of language always seems to involve a gesture not merely towards the feelings which precede language but also towards the disembodied state of immortality which no longer has need of language', Frances Ferguson, *Language as Counterspirit* (New Haven, Conn. and London, 1977), p. 33. Paul de Man, 'The Rhetoric of Temporality', in *Interpretation: Theory and Practice*, edited by C. S. Singleton (Baltimore, 1969), pp. 173–209 (p. 179). See also G. Hartman, 'Wordsworth, Inscriptions, and Romantic Nature Poetry', in *From Sensibility to Romanticism*, pp. 389–413. A popular version of the unifying function of the Romantic symbol, which these writers argue against, is P. W. K. Stone, *The Art of Poetry 1750–1820: Theories of Poetic Composition and Style in the late Neo-Classic and early Romantic Periods* (London, 1967). See also W. K. Wimsatt Jr., 'The Structure of Romantic Nature Imagery', in *The Age of Johnson: Essays Presented to Chauncey Brewster Tinker*, edited by F. W. Hilles (New Haven, Conn. and London 1949), pp. 291–303; M. H. Abrams, 'Structure and Style in the Greater Romantic Lyric', in *From Sensibility to Romanticism*, pp. 527–60; Earl R. Wasserman, *The Subtler Language: Critical Readings of Neoclassic and Romantic Poems* (Baltimore, 1959), Chapter 1.

57 De Man, 'The Rhetoric of Temporality', pp. 190–1.

58 Ferguson, p. 194.

59 Jonathan Culler, *In Pursuit of Signs* (London, 1981), p. 162.
60 De Man, 'The Rhetoric of Temporality', pp. 177–8.
61 *W Prose* II, p. 84 ('Essays upon Epitaphs, III').
62 Donald Davidson, 'What Metaphors Mean', *Critical Inquiry*, 5 (1978), 32–47 (p. 32).
63 Davidson, p. 32.
64 *W Prose* I, p. 120.
65 *The Complete Poetical Works of Samuel Taylor Coleridge*, edited by E. H. Coleridge, 2 vols (London, 1912), I, p. 298. (Hereafter *CPW*.) William Wordsworth, *The Prelude, 1798–1799*, edited by Stephen Parrish (New York and Sussex, 1977), p. 43. (Hereafter *Prelude* (1977).) For 'Abora' see John Livingston Lowes, *The Road to Xanadu*, revised edition (London, 1930), pp. 341–3. For 'Was it for this . . . ?' see the *Times Literary Supplement*, April to September, 1975, pp. 428, 627, 779, 840, 1094.
66 Hollander, *The Untuning of the Sky*, pp. 380–8. See also G. L. Finney, *Musical Backgrounds for English Literature: 1580–1650* (New Brunswick, 1961); Leo Spitzer, 'Classical and Christian Ideas of World Harmony', Part 1, *Traditio*, 2 (1944), 409–64; Part 2, *Traditio*, 3 (1945), 307–64. But see also Bertrand H. Bronson's counterview: 'whichever way we turn, while we trace the cultural topography of eighteenth century England – its ideological or artistic hills and vales and water-courses – we are within sound of music', 'Some Aspects of Music and Literature', in *Facets of the Enlightenment* (Los Angeles, 1968), pp. 91–118 (p. 91).
67 Hollander, *Images of Voice*, p. 7.
68 Rose R. Subotnik, 'The Cultural Message of Musical Semiology: Some Thoughts on Music, Language, and Criticism since the Enlightenment', *Critical Inquiry*, 4 (1978), 741–68 (p. 747).
69 Stanley Sadie, 'Concert Life in Eighteenth Century England', *PRMA*, 85 (1958–9), 17–30 (p. 17). See also Grove, 1980, XI, pp. 177–95.
70 C. L. Cudworth, 'The English Symphonists of the Eighteenth Century', *PRMA*, 78 (1951–2), 31–51 (p. 36).
71 Cudworth, p. 37. See also E. D. Mackerness, *A Social History of English Music* (London and Toronto, 1964), pp. 116–25. For an example of opposition to the new symphonic music see William Jackson, *Observations on the Present State of Music* (London, 1791). In a hostile review of this, in the *Monthly Review* (October 1791), pp. 196–202, Dr Burney, attacking Jackson's conservatism, singles out the academics as those most anti-pathetic to Haydn; see H. C. Robbins Landon, *Haydn: Chronicle and Works*, 5 vols (London, 1976–80), III (*Haydn in England, 1791–95*), pp. 100–4; and see Haydn's letter of 13 October 1791: 'There is no doubt that many people in London are also envious of me, and I know almost all of them. Most of them are Italians. But they cannot harm me, for my credit with the common people has been firmly established for a long time. Apart from the professors, I am respected and loved by everyone', *Haydn: Chronicle and Works*, III, p. 105.
72 My emphasis here, given the interests of the thesis, is on the popularity of certain kinds of instrumental music. For theatrical and opera music see

especially Roger Riske, *English Theatre Music in the Eighteenth Century* (London, 1973); and also F. C. Petty, *Italian Opera in London, 1760–1800* (Ann Arbor, Michigan, 1980).

73 *Haydn: Chronicle and Works*, III, pp. 126–8.

74 Grove, 1980, XI, pp. 177–95. *Haydn: Chronicle and Works*, III, p. 305.

75 Mackerness, p. 105. Grove, 1980, XI, p. 177. David Johnson, *Music and Society in Lowland Scotland in the Eighteenth Century* (London, 1972), p. 52

76 Haydn's benefit concert of 16 May 1791 brought him £350. For evidence of Haydn's pleasure in his independence see his letter of 1791 from London to Maria Anna von Genzinger: 'Oh, my dear gracious lady! how sweet this bit of freedom really is! I had a kind Prince, but sometimes I was forced to be dependent on base souls. I often sighed for release, and now I have it in some measure. I appreciate the good side of all this, too, though my mind is burdened with far more work. The realization I am no bond-servant makes ample amends for all my toils', *The Collected Correspondence and London Notebooks of Joseph Haydn*, edited by H. C. Robbins Landon (London, 1959), p. 118.

77 *Haydn: Chronicle and Works*, III, p. 297.

78 Waring, for example, translates Rousseau's *Dictionnaire* article, 'Symphonie', as follows: 'At present, the word symphony is applied to all instrumental music, as well for pieces which are destined only for instruments, as Sonata's and Concerto's, as for those, where the instruments are found mixed with the voice, as in our Opera's, and in several sorts of music', *A Dictionary of Music* ('symphony'). See also Cudworth, p. 38.

79 H. C. Robbins Landon, *The Symphonies of Joseph Haydn* (London, 1955), p. 552.

80 *Haydn: Chronicle and Works*, III, p. 234.

81 *Haydn: Chronicle and Works*, III, p. 103.

82 It is indicative of how extraordinarily close to Burney's attitudes this reviewer is that, in the review of Haydn's benefit concert of 4 May 1795, he echoes a figure from Burney's *Verses on the Arrival of Haydn in England*: 'And those who pouring water on their leaves, / By a more humble and less dangerous theft, / Extracted all the spirit that was left'. See *Haydn: Chronicle and Works*, III, p. 33; and see note 85 below.

83 *Haydn: Chronicle and Works*, III, pp. 234–6.

84 *Haydn: Chronicle and Works*, III, p. 241.

85 *Haydn: Chronicle and Works*, III, p. 308. The gentleman was probably Burney: see note 82 above.

86 *Haydn: Chronicle and Works*, III, pp. 242, 245.

87 *The Works of William Collins*, edited by Richard Wendorf and Charles Ryskamp (Oxford, 1979), pp. 85–9 (hereafter Collins).

88 British Library, Additional MS 39,929, fo. 317. And see Chapter 3, note 7 below.

89 Grove, 1980, XI, p. 182.

90 *ibid.*

91 See Chapter 2, pp. 75–6 below.

92 *CN*, III, 4313 (April–May 1816).

93 *Haydn: Chronicle and Works*, III, pp. 114, 234, 272–3. See also Grove, 1980, XVII, pp. 253–5; and Fiske, pp. 441–86 (Chapter 13: 'Shield in the Ascendant, 1782–1788').

94 Johnson, p. 42. See Donald W. MacArdle, 'Beethoven and George Thomson', *Music and Letters*, 37 (1956), 27–49.

95 Kelly studied at Mannheim under Stamitz, and his influence, along with that of C. F. Abel and J. C. Bach, extended to numerous minor symphonists, Yates, Hook, Collett, Norris. See Cudworth, pp. 36–8.

96 Johnson, p. 13.

97 James Beattie, *An Essay on Poetry and Music as they affect the Mind* (Edinburgh, 1776). For Smith see note 36, above.

98 David Johnson, commenting that 'It is curious that Robertson regards Kelly's Mannheim style as a Scottish national characteristic', fails to notice that such an opinion has its curious consistency within Robertson's aesthetic. See Johnson, p. 76.

99 Cudworth, p. 37.

1 William Collins

1 Geoffrey Hartman, *The Fate of Reading* (Chicago and London, 1975), p. 138. Hartman here develops his earlier argument about 'Romanticism and the Genius Loci', in *The Disciplines of Criticism*, edited by P. Demetz and others (New Haven, Connecticut, 1968), pp. 289–314. Hartman refers both to W. K. Wimsatt, 'The Structure of Romantic Nature Imagery', and to Martin Price, *To the Palace of Wisdom* (Carbondale, Illinois, 1964).

2 Hagstrum, *The Sister Arts*, pp. xxi, xxii, 318.

3 *The Sister Arts*, pp. xxi, 140, and Chapters 5 and 10 *passim*.

4 See Hagstrum, 'Blake and the Sister-Art Tradition', pp. 82–91.

5 *The Collected Works of Oliver Goldsmith*, edited by Arthur Friedman, 5 vols (Oxford, 1966), I, p. 31 (hereafter Goldsmith).

6 Goldsmith, I, p. 32.

7 James Harris, *Three Treatises. The First Concerning Art. The Second Concerning Music, Painting and Poetry. The Third Concerning Happiness* (London, 1744), p. 96.

8 *Three Treatises*, p. 99.

9 Edmund Burke, *A Philosophical Enquiry into the Origin of our Ideas of the Sublime and Beautiful* (London, 1757). I use the edition of J. T. Boulton (London, 1958), p. 163.

10 David Hartley, *Observations Upon Man, his Frame, his Duty and his Expectations* (London, 1749), p. 277.

11 Burke, pp. 163, 166–7.

12 Hartley, p. 233; and see Burke, p. 165.

13 Hartley, pp. 233–4.

14 Alan Lessem, 'Imitation and Expression: Opposing French and British Views on Music in the 18th Century', *Journal of the American Musicological Society*, 27 (1974), 325–30.

15 See Heinrich Wölflinn, *Renaissance and Baroque*, translated by K. Simon (London, 1964), p. 38; Schueller, '"Imitation" and "Expression" in British

Music Criticism in the Eighteenth Century', p. 546; Manfred Bukofzer, *Music in the Baroque Era* (New York, 1947), pp. 5–8, 388; Brewster Rogerson, 'The Art of Painting the Passions', *JHI*, 14 (1953), 68–94.

16 Schueller, *ibid.*

17 Bronson, p. 108.

18 William G. Waite, 'Bernard Lamy, Rhetorician of the Passions', *Studies in Eighteenth Century Music in tribute to Karl Geiringer*, edited by H. C. Robbins Landon, in collaboration with R.E. Chapman (London, 1970), p. 392.

19 Bronson, p. 99. During the seventeenth century the principles underlying this concept of music had been extended, however consistently, to painting by Nicolas Poussin; see Edward Lockspieser, *Music and Painting: A Study in Comparative Ideas from Turner to Schoenberg* (London, 1973), pp. 145–8 (Appendix B: 'Poussin and the Modes').

20 'Musick, Architecture and Painting, as well as Poetry and Oratory, are to deduce their Laws and Rules from the general Sense and Taste of Mankind, and not from the Principles of those Arts themselves; or in other words, the Taste is not to conform to the Art, but the Art to the Taste. Music is not design'd to please only Chromatick Ears, but all that are capable of distinguishing harsh from disagreeable Notes', Joseph Addison, *The Spectator*, edited by D. F. Bond, 5 vols (Oxford, 1965), I, p. 123 (No. 29, Tuesday, 3 April 1711). (Hereafter *The Spectator.*)

21 Bronson, p. 111; Bronson cites Manfred Bukofzer, 'Allegory in Baroque Music', *JWCI*, 3 (1939–40), 1–21.

22 John Gregory, *A Comparative View of the State and Faculties of Man with those of the Animal World*, 4th edition (London, 1767), pp. 145, 154, 156–7; the first edition had appeared in 1765.

23 Gregory, pp. 110 15, 137, 154.

24 Charles Avison, *An Essay on Musical Expression* (London, 1752); and see Schueller, 'Correspondences between Music and the Sister Arts', p. 346.

25 William Hayes, *Remarks on Mr Avison's Essay on Musical Expression* (London, 1753), p. 69.

26 Lawrence Lipking, *The Ordering of the Arts in Eighteenth Century England* (New Jersey, 1970), p. 219.

27 Lipking, p. 214; and Oliver, *The Encyclopedists as Critics of Music*, p. 63.

28 Avison, *Essay on Musical Expression*, pp. 2, 3, 75; and also his *A Reply to the Author of Remarks on the Essay on Musical Expression* (London, 1753), p. 4.

29 *The Spectator*, II, p. 506 (No. 258, Wednesday, 26 December 1711); this is found in a letter over the names Thomas Clayton, Nicolino Haym and Charles Dieupart.

30 Avison, *A Reply to the Author*, p. 33.

31 *The Spectator*, III, p. 559 (No. 416, Friday, 27 June 1712).

32 John Dryden, *Alexander's Feast; or, the Power of Musique. An Ode in Honour of St. Cecilia's Day* (London, 1697).

33 Collins, pp. 49–53; for a commentary on Collins's poems to be set to music, and on 'The Passions' in particular, see Richard Wendorf, *William Collins and Eighteenth Century Poetry* (Minneapolis, 1981), pp. 135–65.

34 See also *The Spectator*, IV, p. 585 (No. 580, Friday, 13 August 1714): 'There

is nothing which more ravishes and transports the Soul than Harmony.'
35 John Lampe, *The Art of Musick* (London, 1740), p. 7; Benjamin Stillingfleet, *Principles and Powers of Harmony* (London, 1771), p. 153; William Turner, *A Philosophical Essay on Musick*, (London, n.d. [*c.* 1750]); *Critical Review*, 10 (1760), p. 249.
36 William Shenstone, 'Elegy vi', *The Works in Verse and Prose*, 2 vols (London, 1765), I, pp. 39–40, 62–6.
37 Daniel Webb, *Observations on the Correspondence between Poetry and Music* (London, 1769), pp. 35, 53. (Hereafter Webb.) A German translation of the *Observations* was published at Leipzig in 1771.
38 Webb, pp. 1–2, 11.
39 Locke, *An Essay Concerning Human Understanding*, p. 395.
40 Locke, p. 226.
41 David Hume, *A Treatise of Human Nature* (London, 1739), p. 2, fn. 1.
42 Hume, *ibid.*, and also pp. 1, 194.
43 Hume, pp. 9–10.
44 Hume, p. 10.
45 *Three Treatises*, p. 102.
46 *Three Treatises*, p. 98.
47 *ibid.*
48 Webb, p. 55.
49 Webb, p. 58.
50 Webb, pp. 45–6.
51 Webb, pp. 66, 78–9, 83, 136–7. Notice also Webb's comments on Rousseau's theory of musical imitation, to which he objects on the basis that music is movement and cannot 'paint' visible objects: 'These observations lead us to the necessary distinction of the image from its effect; of its beauty as a visible object from its energy as a source of pathetic emotions. Thus we draw the line between painting and music', Webb, p. 195.
52 Webb, p. 78.
53 Webb, p. 153.
54 Webb, pp. 150, 153.
55 *Three Treatises*, p. 34.
56 *The Sister Arts*, p. 281.
57 Collins, pp. 76–7.
58 *CPW*, I, p. 101: 'the mute still air / Is Music slumbering on her instrument'. John Keats, *The Poems*, edited by M. Allott (London, 1970), p. 529: 'Called him soft names in many a mùsed rhyme, / To take into the air my quiet breath'. James Thomson, *Poetical Works*, edited by J. L. Robertson (Oxford, 1908), p. 432: 'Ethereal race, inhabitants of air, / Who hymn your God amid the secret grove, / Ye unseen beings, to my harp repair'.
59 Collins, p. 44.
60 *ibid.*
61 *The Pleasures of Imagination. A Poem in Three Books* (London, 1744), pp. 15–16 (Book I, ll. 109–25).
62 E. von Erhardt-Siebord, 'Some Inventions of the Pre-Romantic Period and their Influence upon Literature', *Englische Studien*, 66 (1931–2), 347–63 (p. 347).

63 Von Erhardt-Siebord, pp. 354–5. Algarotti's comments on Gray's poems are found in a letter 'Al Gugliemo Taylor How' (1762) in *The Poems of Thomas Gray*, edited by Rev. T. Mitford (London, 1814), pp. 77–80.

64 *The Poetical Works of Christopher Smart*, edited by Karina Williamson (Oxford, 1980), I, p. 76 (*Jubilate Agno*). The editor notices only Newton in the note on 'ocular harmony'.

65 See Marjorie H. Nicolson, *Newton Demands the Muse* (Princeton, New Jersey, 1966), p. 86.

66 Nicolson, p. 35.

67 Robert Smith, *Harmonics, or the Philosophy of Musical Sounds* (Cambridge, 1749); as quoted Stewart, V, pp. 146–7.

68 *Jubilate Agno*, pp. 84–5.

69 As published in *The Gleaner*, edited by Nathan Drake (London, 1820), pp. 452–3.

70 *CPW*, I, p. 100. And see M. H. Abrams, 'Coleridge's "A Light in Sound": Science, Metascience, and Poetic Imagination', *Proceedings of the American Philosophical Society*, 116 (1972), 458–77.

71 William Porterfield, M.D., *A Treatise on the Eye, the Manner and Phaenomena of Vision*, 2 vols (Edinburgh, 1759), II, pp. 353, 355.

72 See Arthur Sherbo, *Christopher Smart: Scholar of the University* (Michigan, 1967), p. 161 and *passim*, and Hartman, *The Fate of Reading*, p. 78.

73 *The Collected Poems of Christopher Smart*, edited by Norman Callan, 2 vols (London, 1949), II, p. 812 (*Hymns and Spiritual Songs*).

74 *Jubilate Agno*, p. 85.

75 Abraham Tucker, *The Light of Nature Pursued*, 6th edition, 2 vols (London, 1842), I, pp. 16–17; the first edition appeared in 1768.

76 Tucker, I, p. 78.

77 Richard Price, *A Review of the Principal Questions and Difficulties in Morals* (London, 1758); I use the edition by D. Daiches Raphael (Oxford, 1948), p. 33.

78 Joseph Priestley cites Price, above, in *An Examination of Dr. Reid's Inquiry into the Human Mind on the Principles of Common Sense, Dr. Beattie's Essay on the Nature and Immutability of Truth, and Dr. Oswald's Appeal to Common Sense in Behalf of Religion* (London, 1774), p. 325. And see Darwin, *The Temple of Nature*, p. 194 (canto III, ll. 136–44):

> The eye's clear glass the transient beams collects;
> Bends to their focal point the rays that swerve,
> And paints the living image on the nerve.
> So in some village-barn, or festive hall
> The spheric lens illumes the whiten'd wall;
> O'er the bright field successive figures fleet,
> And motley shadows dance along the sheet. –
> Symbol of solid forms is colour'd light,
> And the mute language of the touch is sight.

Dugald Stewart finds it absurd that 'the various theories, which have been formed to explain the operations of our senses, have a more immediate reference to that of seeing; and the greater part of the metaphysical language, concerning perception in general, appears evidently, from its etymology, to have been suggested by the phenomena of vision', Stewart, II, p. 92. Coleridge agrees with that diagnosis so far as to argue: 'Hence we are to account for the preference which the divine Plato gives to expressions taken from the objects of the ear, as terms of music and harmony, and in part at least for the numerical symbols in which Pythagoras clothed his philosophy. On this principle I do not object to the extension of the term "image" (or "idea" in Hume's usage) from the re-presentations of the sight to the analogous relicts of the other senses – and if other reasons had not induced me to reject the *Humian* terminology of "impressions" and "ideas", the same concession would have been made to the phrase "audital and tactual *ideas*"', *The Collected Works of Samuel Taylor Coleridge*, edited by Kathleen Coburn and Bart Winer, 16 vols (London and Princeton, N.J., 1969–), XIII (1981), p. 243 (*The Logic*, edited by J. R. de J. Jackson). (Hereafter *CC*.)

79 Gregory, *Comparative View*, p. 185.

80 A. D. McKillop argues that 'The personification of Evening is not a single picture but a series of manifestations', and that Collins makes use of 'imperfect vision', in his 'Collins's *Ode to Evening* – Background and Structure', *Tennessee Studies in Literature*, 5 (1960), 73–83; Elizabeth W. Manwaring had indeed argued that Collins was not at all pictorial, in her *Italian Landscape in Eighteenth Century England* (New York, 1925), p. 112; Hagstrum's contrary claim rests on a limited reading of Collins's drafts and fragments; see also Chapter 1, note 1 above. Richard Wendorf develops the view, in relation to Collins's 'The Manners: an Ode', that 'The argument of Collins's ode is not that the poet has exhausted nature but that – in realizing its elusiveness – he can no longer celebrate it in a traditional way', that is in a 'pictorial' or permanent way. Hence, according to Wendorf, we have Collins's elegy on James Thomson. R. Wendorf, 'Collins's Elusive Nature', *MP*, 76 (1979), 231–9.

81 McKillop, p. 77.

82 *Three Treatises*, pp. 77–8.

83 *Three Treatises*, p. 95.

84 Collins, pp. 68–9; and notice variants to line 21.

85 Northrop Frye, 'Towards Defining an Age of Sensibility', *Eighteenth Century English Literature*, edited by James L. Clifford (New York, 1959), pp. 311–18 (pp. 313–14); first published in *ELH*, 23 (1956), 144–52.

2 William Blake and William Cowper

1 See Chapter 4, pp. 175–6.

2 James Usher, *Clio, or a Discourse on Taste. Addressed to a Young Lady* (London, 1767); *with large additions* (London, 1769); J. Mathews published the two editions of 1803 and 1809. Samuel Holt Monk, *The Sublime: a Study of Critical Theories in 18th Century England* (New York, 1935; Ann Arbor, Michigan, 1960), pp. 142–4.

3 *Introduction to the Theory of the Human Mind*, p. 80 and *passim*.

4 *Clio* (1769), p. 123.

5 *Clio* (1769), pp. 110–11, 116.
6 *Clio* (1769), pp. 129–32.
7 See Francis X. J. Coleman, *The Aesthetic Thought of the French Enlightenment* (Pittsburgh and London, 1971), p. 39.
8 *Clio* (1767), pp. 75–6; *Clio* (1769), p. 190.
9 *Clio* (1769), p. 190.
10 *Clio* (1767), pp. 26–7, 41–2.
11 John Baillie, *An Essay on the Sublime* (London, 1747), pp. 7, 38–9, and section 5 *passim*.
12 *Clio* (1767), p. 52.
13 *Clio* (1767), pp. 52–4.
14 *Clio* (1767), p. 55; *Clio* (1769), pp. 149–56.
15 *Introduction to the theory of the Human Mind*, pp. 80–1.
16 *Rameaus Neffe* (Leipzig, 1805); it seems that Schiller had provided Goethe with a MS copy.
17 See Chapter 3, p. 97. The footnote in question is in *Aristotle's Treatise on Poetry, Translated*, p. 49.
18 *Clio* (1767), pp. 19–21; *Introduction to the Theory of the Human Mind*, p. 82.
19 *Clio* (1769), pp. 240–1.
20 See A. D. McKillop, *The Background to Thomson's 'Liberty'* (Houston, 1951).
21 J. G. von Herder, *Outlines of a Philosophy of the History of Man* (1784–91), translated by Charles Churchill (London, 1800), pp. 193–4 (Book 8, Chapter 2):

> but Nature has conferred another beneficent gift on our species, in leaving to such of it's members as are least stored with ideas the first germe of superiour sense, exhilarating music. Before the child can speak, he is capable of song, or at least of being affected by musical tones; and among the most uncultivated nations music is the first of the fine arts, by which the mind is moved. The pictures, which Nature exhibits to the eye, are so variable, changeable and extensive, that imitative taste must long grope about, and seek the striking in wild and monstrous productions, ere it learns justness of proportion. But music, however rude and simple, speaks to every human heart; and this, with the dance, constitutes Nature's general festival throughout the Earth. Pity it is, that most travellers, from too refined a taste, conceal from us these infantile tones of foreign nations. Useless as these are to the musician, they are instructive to the investigator of man.

See R. T. Clarke, *Herder: his Life and Thought* (Berkeley and Los Angeles, 1955), pp. 308–47, for an explication of Herder's philosophy of history. For Herder's theory of the arts as forms of expression, both individual and social, see Isaiah Berlin, *Vico and Herder: Two Studies in the History of Ideas* (London, 1976).
22 Thomas Robertson, *An Inquiry into the Fine Arts* (London, 1784), p. 445.
23 E. Anderson, *Harmonious Madness: A Study of Musical Metaphors in the*

Poetry of Coleridge, Shelley and Keats (Salzburg, 1975); Sue E. Coffmann, *Music of Finer Tone: Musical Imagery of the Major Romantic Poets* (Salzburg, 1979); H. G. Schenk, *The Mind of the European Romantics: An Essay in Cultural History* (London, 1966), p. 232: 'For the Romantics, who, in general, preferred to live as it were in the past or the future, music constituted the sphere in which the present could best be experienced in a kind of enchanting dream.'

24 Lessem, 'Imitation and Expression', pp. 326–7; Maria Rika Maniates, '"Sonate, Que Me Veux-Tu?": The Enigma of French Musical Aesthetics in the 18th Century", *Current Musicology*, 9 (1969), 117–40 (p. 136): 'Many are the attempts to solve the specific enigma posed by Fontenelle. However, the impasse created by the interlocking concepts of passion, nature, imitation, and musical significance in effect prevents any satisfactory answer. Having arrived at the crossroads, the French aestheticians lose their way.'

25 *Observations sur la musique*, Chapter 1.

26 Charles Batteux, *Les Beaux-Arts réduits à un même principe* (Paris, 1746). For an account of Batteux's fortunes during the eighteenth century see Le Huray and Day, pp. 40–1.

27 *Encyclopédie*, I (1751), p. xii.

28 *Encyclopédie*, VI (1756), p. 315.

29 *Encyclopédie*, XII (1765), pp. 823–4.

30 E. E. Lowinsky, 'Taste, Style, and Ideology in Eighteenth-Century Music', in *Aspects of the Eighteenth Century*, edited by E. R. Wasserman (Baltimore and London, 1965), pp. 163–205 (p. 165).

31 Lowinsky, pp. 170–5.

32 *On the Origin of Language*, p. 13.

33 *On the Origin of Language*, pp. 15, 74.

34 *On the Origin of Language*, pp. 50–68.

35 *A Dictionary of Music*, p. 198.

36 *A Dictionary of Music*, p. 455.

37 See Oliver, *The Encyclopedists as Critics of Music*, pp. 63, 71–3, for an attack by Chastellux on Rousseau in the article 'Idéal'; and for Diderot's sensitivity to instrumental music as evidenced in his articles on instruments ('Basson', 'Viole') and on 'Instrumentation'.

38 See Marmontel's article, 'Arts Libéraux': 'la nature seroit le guide, mais non pas le modele de la Musique. Tous les sons & tous les accords sont dans la nature sans doute; mais *l'art* est de les réunir ... La musique ressemble donc d'un côté à la Poésie, laquelle embellit la Nature en l'imitant, & de l'autre, à l'Architecture, qui ne consulte que le plaisir du sens qu'elle doit affecter', *Supplément à l'encyclopédie ou dictionnaire raisonné des sciences, des arts et des métiers*, 4 vols (Amsterdam, 1776–7), I (1776), p. 586. (Hereafter *Supplément.*) For identification of the relevant authors I use John Lough, *The Contributors to the Encyclopédie* (London, 1973).

39 François Jean de Chastellux, *Essai sur l'union de la poésie et de la musique* (La Haye, 1765), pp. 46–7.

40 *Observations sur la musique*, p. 46.

41 *Observations sur la musique*, p. 103.

42 *Observations sur la musique*, pp. 133–4.

43 *Observations sur la musique*, pp. 92, 168.
44 *Observations sur la musique*, p. 97.
45 *Observations sur la musique*, p. 171.
46 *Observations sur la musique*, pp. 145–6.
47 *Observations sur la musique*, p. 149.
48 *Observations sur la musique*, pp. 53–63 (Chapter 7): Chabanon here states his disagreement with Rousseau's argument that music is an imitation of speech.
49 Michel-Paul Guy de Chabanon, *De la Musique Considerée en elle-même et dans ses rapports avec la parole, les langues, la poésie et le théâtre*, Réimpression de l'édition de Paris, 1785 (Genève, 1969), pp. 38–64 (Chapter 2); and notice p. 45: 'Ainsi, tandis que l'instinct de l'homme le porte à rendre les premiers essais de la parole imitatifs, il ne fait entrer aucune intention d'imiter dans les premiers essais du chant.'
50 *De la Musique*, pp. 79–101 (Chapter 8).
51 *Observations sur la musique*, pp. 68, 75.
52 *Observations sur la musique*, p. 23.
53 *Observations sur la musique*, p. 28.
54 *De la Musique*, p. 12; and see especially the insertion of new material added to that of 1779 after Chapter 8.
55 *De la Musique*, pp. 99–101.
56 *De la Musique*, p. 101.
57 *The Poems of William Blake*, edited by W. H. Stevenson, text by David Erdman (London, 1971), pp. 8–9.
58 For equivalences between allegory and irony see Fletcher, *Allegory*, pp. 2, 230: allegory 'destroys the normal expectation we have about language, that our words "mean what they say" . . . Pushed to an extreme, this ironic usage would subvert language itself'; 'we might call ironies "collapsed allegories", or perhaps, "condensed allegories". They show no diminishing, only a confusion, of the semantic and syntactic processes of double or multi-levelled polysemy.'
   See also Daniel Webb: 'Music cannot, of itself specify any particular passion, since the movements of every class must be in accord with all the passions of that class', Webb, p. 10.
59 G. E. Bentley, Jr, *Blake Records* (Oxford, 1969), p. 26. See also p. 457: 'Much about this time, Blake wrote many other songs, to which he also composed tunes. These he would occasionally sing to his friends; and though, according to his confession, he was entirely unacquainted with the science of music, his ear was so good, that his tunes were sometimes most singularly beautiful, and were noted down by musical professors.'
60 *Blake Records*, p. 305.
61 Alexander Gilchrist, *Life of William Blake*, 2 vols (London, 1863); I use the Scholar Press edition (London, 1973), p. 405.
62 *Blake Records*, p. 482.
63 See Mitchell, *Blake's Composite Art*, p. 5: Mitchell argues against Roland Barthes' claim that 'the world of signifieds is none other than that of language'. Mitchell insists that 'If Blake teaches us anything about symbolic systems, it is that there is an equally strong tendency for language to fall back into that which cannot be designated, the wordless realm of pure

image and sound, and that this realm may have systematic features independent of language.'

64 Blake, *Poems*, p. 111.

65 Blake, *Poems*, p. 252.

66 'For the emblematists, painting was to be *added to* poetry in order to imitate the larger sum of spatial and temporal reality; for Blake, poetry and painting were to be *multiplied by* one another to give a product larger than the sum of the parts, a reality which might include, but not be limited by, the world of space and time', *Blake's Composite Art*, p. 31.

67 Blake, *Poems*, pp. 628–9.

68 I use the term 'performative' in the simplest sense given to it by J. L. Austin: 'to utter the sentence (in, of course, the appropriate circumstances) is not to *describe* my doing of what I should be said in so uttering to be doing or to state that I am doing it: it is to do it', *How to do things with Words: the William James Lectures delivered at Harvard University in 1955*, edited by J. O. Urmson and M. Sbisà (Oxford, 1975), p. 6.

69 Blake, *Poems*, p. 629.

70 Cowper's 'Adelphi: an account of the Conversion of W. C. Esquire' gives as the first instance of his spiritual life the death of his mother: 'At six years of age I was taken from the nursery and the immediate care of a most indulgent mother and sent to a considerable school in Bedfordshire. Here I had hardships of various kinds to conflict with, which I felt the more sensibly in proportion to the tenderness with which I had been treated at home', *The Letters and Prose Writings of William Cowper*, edited by James King and Charles Ryskamp, 3 vols (Oxford, 1979), I, p. 5. (Hereafter Cowper.) The text of the poem in question can be found in *Cowper: The Poetical Works*, edited by H. S. Milford (Oxford, 1967), pp. 394–6.

71 Michael Riffaterre, *Semiotics of Poetry* (London, 1980), pp. 1–22 (Chapter 1).

72 I use the terms icon and index in the senses adopted by C. S. Peirce; in particular as they are interpreted by Douglas Greenlee: 'The concept of the sign which I have arrived at, then, is the concept of something that is interpreted according to a rule or a convention of interpretation, rather than the concept of something which stands for something else.' An icon signifies by virtue of a convention of resemblance; an index by virtue of a convention of causal contiguity. See Douglas Greenlee, *Peirce's Concept of the Sign* (The Hague and Paris, 1973), pp. 9, 78–80.

The nature of the portrait, for Cowper, as both icon and index, and also some of the tensions which this produces in the poem can be seen in some letters by Cowper shortly after his receipt of the painting. See his letter to Mrs Bodham of 27 February 1790: 'the world could not have furnish'd you with a present so acceptable to me as the picture which you have so kindly sent me. I received it the night before last, and view'd it with a trepidation of nerves and spirits somewhat akin to what I should have felt had the dear Original presented herself to my embraces. I kissed it and hung it where it is the last object that I see at night, and, of course, the first on which I open my eyes in the morning. She died when I had completed my sixth year, yet I remember her well and am an ocular witness of the great fidelity of the

Copy', Cowper, III, p. 349. See also a letter to Mrs King of 12 March 1790: 'I remember her perfectly, find the picture a strong likeness of her, and because her memory has been ever precious to me, have written a poem on the receipt of it. A poem which, one excepted, I had more pleasure in writing than any that I ever wrote. That one was addressed to a lady whom I expect in a few minutes to come down to breakfast, and who has supplied to me the place of my own mother, my own invaluable mother, these six and twenty years. Some sons may be said to have had many fathers, but a plurality of mothers is not common', Cowper, III, pp. 359–60. The other poem in question is, of course, 'The Winter Nosegay'. For the relative unimportance of fathers and their portraits, see Cowper's letter to Lady Hesketh acknowledging her husband's 'approbation of my picture-verses . . . I wrote them, not without tears, therefore I presume it may be that they are felt by others. Should he offer me my father's picture, I shall gladly accept it', Cowper, III, p. 371.

73 Sir Joshua Reynolds, *Discourses on Art*, edited by Robert R. Wark (New Haven and London, 1975), p. 265. (Hereafter Reynolds.)

74 Reynolds, p. 247.

75 Reynolds, pp. 278, 249.

76 Reynolds, p. 253.

77 Reynolds, pp. 257–8.

78 Reynolds, pp. 258–60. For John Gregory see p. 51 above.

79 Reynolds, p. 259. It is of perhaps coincidental interest to notice Gainsborough's unusually enthusiastic attention to music: an excessive amateur, Gainsborough included among his friends William Jackson of Exeter, the Bachs, the Abels and the Linleys. Charles Cudworth has observed that, 'What it all adds up to is that Gainsborough, as he himself admitted, was "mad for music", and especially for instrumental music', 'Gainsborough and Music', *Gainsborough, English Music and the Fitzwilliam* (Cambridge, 1977), pp. 11–16 (p. 14). See also M. I. Wilson, 'Gainsborough, Bath and Music', *Apollo*, 105 (1977), 107–10.

80 *Poetical Works*, p. 312.

81 *Poetical Works*, pp. 219–20.

82 *Poetical Works*, pp. 220–1.

83 *Prelude* (1977), p. 123.

84 *Poetical Works*, p. 414. It is worth noting the contradiction that appears elsewhere in Cowper's view of music: it has been commented that with music Cowper 'remained on the threshold because he could not yield himself to its greater manifestations'; he had contempt for the Handel commemoration of 1784, and approved of John Newton's sermon against it; 'music without words – and I suppose one may say, consequently, without devotion', he writes to Newton in denunciation of clergy who enjoy Sunday music. Music, Cowper writes, 'destroys spiritual discernment', but he writes also (to John Johnson in 1790) that 'You may treat us too, if you please, with a little music, for I seldom hear any, and delight much in it'; see Sydney Grew and Eva Mary Grew, 'William Cowper: His Acceptance and Rejection of Music', *Music and Letters*, 13 (1932), 31–41 (pp. 31, 37–8).

3 William Wordsworth

1 See *Recreations and Studies of a Country Clergyman of the Eighteenth Century: Being selections from the correspondence of the Rev. Thomas Twining, M.A.* (London, 1882); and *Selections from Papers of the Twining Family: a sequel to the Recreations and Studies*, edited by Richard Twining (London, 1887). Notice, for example, Twining to his brother, 27 August 1786: 'Oh, I have a very mean idea of the concert spiritual. Indeed, no man must go from England to France to hear music. I hope, however, you will see one serious opera, for I believe it is quite unlike what is to be seen and heard anywhere else. If the French do not prize Diderot, *tant pis pour eux* . . .', *Recreations and Studies*, p. 138. These editions perform the familiar censorship of nineteenth-century nephews; a fuller, although still censored, correspondence appears below from BL Add MSS 39,929, 39,930, 39,936.

2 See Roger Lonsdale, *Dr. Charles Burney: A Literary Biography* (Oxford, 1965), pp. 134–88 (Chapter 4: 'The First Volume of the *History of Music*, 1773–1776'). See letters from Burney to Twining, 28 April 1773 and 30 August 1773, agreeing with Twining's suggestions that his *A General History of Music, from the Earliest Ages to the Present Period*, 4 vols (London, 1776–89), I (1776) confine its 'narrative to Circumstances merely historical'. Twining had written to Burney indicating how it 'always makes you sick to hear People talking about the *Invention* of music'. Both agree to despise Sir John Hawkins's antiquarianism. After publication of Burney's first volume Twining further advises Burney to amend the early sections so that there will be 'not so many Apollos'; for the second volume Twining reminded Burney that 'a *history* of *Music*, and a *history* of *Poetry* are distinct Things', and that he looked forward to the later volumes 'when you get to the times of *real* music', BL Add MS 39,929: fos. 54, 59–63, 225, 246 (letters to Burney, 17 September 1776, 20 March 1780, 4 December 1780).

3 'I don't know anything – any musical thing – that would delight me so much as to meet him [i.e. Haydn] in a snug quartett party, and hear his manner of playing his own music', *Recreations and Studies*, p. 147 (letter to Burney, 4 May 1791); Burney and Twining had been enthusing about Haydn in their letters since at least 1783: on 5 July of that year Twining wrote to Burney that he would be taking some quartets of Haydn to friends for their musical weekend to make 'them acquainted with that delightful fellow . . . For variety, and endless resources, I know no composer like him', BL Add MS 39,929, fos. 317–18.

4 Twining was at Cambridge from 1755–63. See also Charles Cudworth, 'Thomas Gray and Music', *Musical Times*, 112 (1971), 646–8.

5 BL Add MS 39,929, fos. 253, 257, 327 (letters to Burney, 12 October 1780, 4 May 1781, 3 February 1784).

6 Letter to Daniel Twining, 22 February 1765: 'L'encyclopedie is the joint undertaking of some of the cleverest French writers now living; but not *near* compleated. I long to have it, but cannot afford to buy it, & have *no opportunity* of *stealing it*'; letter to Burney, 16 June 1777, recounting the arrival from Paris of prints of Diderot and D'Alembert for his study; letter to Burney, 19 December 1778, on principles of 'liberal' criticism; letter to Burney, 12 February 1781: 'I am reading one of the best metaphysician

books I ever read, Condillac's Essai sur l'Origin . . .'; letter to Richard Twining, 10 November 1788, praises the French version he has received of Lessing's *Dramaturgie* as 'excellent, original, philosophical, criticism', BL Add MS 39,929, fos. 35, 137, 188, 236–7, 253, 384; *Aristotle's Treatise on Poetry, Translated*, p. xviii.

7 *Recreations and Studies*, p. 106 (letter to Burney, 8 December 1781); BL Add MS 39,929, fo. 287.

8 *Dr. Charles Burney*, pp. 134–88; A. Bosker, *Literary Criticism in the Age of Johnson*, 2nd edition (Djakarta, 1954), pp. 276–8; Malek (Chapter 4); Rudowski, pp. 683–90; Spitzer (Part 2), p. 316. E. E. Lowinsky attributes the collapse in the concept of world harmony to Rousseau, and to the *Dictionnaire* (so admired and argued against by Twining) in particular: 'No longer is polyphony a metaphysical cypher, it is merely an art appealing to the senses. In Rousseau's view of music all echoes of a harmony of the universe are dead. Only the listener is alive', 'Taste, Style, and Ideology', p. 192.

9 Thomas Twining, *A Sermon, preached . . . at Colchester, May 17, 1790*; BL Add MS 39,930, fos. 25–39 (letters of 16 April, 12 June, 7 July 1790).

10 *A Sermon*, pp. 12–13 and *passim*.

11 BL Add MS 39,929, fos. 77, 258 (letter to his brother, 10 May 1781; and see letter to Burney, 7 March 1776).

12 The deconstructive ironies of Hume's conclusion are well known: 'the *Christian Religion* not only was at first attended with miracles, but even at this day cannot be believed by any reasonable person without one. Mere reason is insufficient to convince us of its veracity: and whoever is moved by *Faith* to assent to it, is conscious of a continued miracle in his own person, which subverts all the principles of his understanding, and gives him a determination to believe what is most contrary to custom and experience', David Hume, *Essays: Moral, Political and Literary* (Oxford, 1963), pp. 517–44 (p. 544).

13 BL Add MS 39,929, fo. 10 (letter to Daniel Twining, 27 February 1763).

14 Brewster Rogerson, '*Ut Musica Poesis*: The Parallel of Music and Poetry in Eighteenth Century Criticism' (unpublished dissertation, Princeton University, 1945), p. 105.

15 *Aristotle's Treatise on Poetry, Translated*, p. xvi.

16 BL Add MS 39,929, fo. 195 and *passim* (letter to Burney, 12 March 1779), about Palestrina's music with 'that sort of solemn wildness, that melancholy harmony and modulation that characterizes it'; accounts of C. P. E. Bach, of Haydn's 'comedy', of Pachierotti's singing.

17 BL Add MS 39,929, fo. 246 (letter to Burney, 4 December 1780).

18 *Recreations and Studies*, p. 133 (letter to Burney, 27 March 1786).

19 *Recreations and Studies*, pp. 25–6 (letter to Burney, 4 April 1774).

20 BL Add MS 39,929, fo. 255 (letter to Burney, 4 May 1781).

21 Robert Smith, *Harmonics, or the Philosophy of Musical Sounds* (Cambridge, 1749), p. ix: 'a person of no ear at all for music may soon learn to tune an organ according to any proposed temperament of the scale; and to any desired degree of exactness, far beyond what the finest ear unassisted by theory can possibly attain to'.

22 Charles Clagget, *A Discourse on Musick to be delivered at Mr. Clagget's Attic*

Concert, at the King's Arms, Cornhill, October 31, 1793, not only displays evidence of his perfected pianoforte, but also produces a letter from Josephus Hadyn (*sic*) congratulating Clagget. Clagget argues that his instrument will be always reliable irrespective of climatic or other changes.

23 See J. Murray Barbour, *Tuning and Temperament: A Historical Survey* (New York, 1972).

24 BL Add MS 39,929, fo. 51 (letter to Jenner, 12 June 1769). For the inadequacies of Smith's adding 'extra pipes and strings' to organs and harpsichords, see Murray Barbour, pp. 40–2.

25 BL Add MS 39,929, fo. 51.

26 BL Add MS 39,929, fo. 323 (letter to Burney, 5 July 1783).

27 BL Add MS 39,929, fos. 123–4 (letter to Burney, 24 January 1777).

28 BL Add MS 39,929, fo. 122.

29 *Observations sur la musique*, p. 210.

30 Jean le Rond D'Alembert, *Élémens de musique théorique et pratique, suivant les principes de M. Rameau* (Paris, 1752), p. 48.

31 BL Add MS 39,929, fo. 48 (letter to Jenner, 20 February 1769).

32 Sir John Hawkins, *A General History of the Science and Practice of Music*, 5 vols (London, 1776).

33 BL Add MS 39,929, fos. 60–3 (letter to Twining, 30 August 1773).

34 BL Add MS 39,929, fo. 63.

35 BL Add MS 39,936, fo. 46 (Twining's notes on letters to Burney, April 1773 to 22 July 1773). The allusion to Plato refers to John 'Estimate' Brown, *A Dissertation on the Rise, Union, and Power, the Progressions, Separations, and Corruptions, of Poetry and Music* (London, 1763).

36 BL Add MS 39,929, fo. 140 (letter to Burney, 30 August 1777).

37 *Aristotle's Treatise on Poetry, Translated*, p. 46.

38 *Aristotle's Treatise on Poetry, Translated*, p. 49.

39 *ibid.*

40 Archibald Alison, *Essays on the Nature and Principles of Taste* (Edinburgh, 1790), p. 115.

41 Alison, p. 202; notice how Twining distinguishes 'association' from 'imitation', because, if this is not done, anything may imitate any other; *Aristotle's Treatise on Poetry, Translated*, pp. 44–5. It is useful to contrast Alison's few comments on instrumental music with those of Twining:

> A song or an Air leads us always to think of the Sentiment, and seldom disposes us to think of any thing else. An Overture or a Concerto disposes us to think of the Composer. It is a work in which much invention, much judgment and much taste may be displayed; and it may have therefore to those who are capable of judging of it, all that pleasing effect upon the mind which the composition of an excellent Poem or Oration has upon the minds of those who are judges of such works.
>
> Alison, p. 193.

42 Alexander Gerard, *An Essay on Taste*, third edition, revised (Edinburgh, 1780), p. 27.

43 Gerard, pp. 58–60.

44 Alison, p. 208; sounds here are taken in contrast to colours.
45 Gerard, pp. 275–84 (Appendix), especially p. 283.
46 *Essays on Philosophical Subjects*, p. 173.
47 Adam Smith, *A Dissertation on the Origin of Languages* (Tubingen, 1970),
    p. 512; for the date of this text and its first appearance under the title,
    'Considerations concerning the first Formation of Languages' (1761), see
    Aarsleff, *From Locke to Saussure*, pp. 148, 200. See also Christopher J. Berry,
    'Adam Smith's *Considerations* on Language', *JHI*, 35 (1974), 130–8.
48 *Dissertation*, p. 507.
49 *Dissertation*, p. 517.
50 *Dissertation*, p. 538.
51 *Essays*, pp. 226–7.
52 *Essays*, p. 233.
53 *Essays*, pp. 145–6.
54 Dora and Erwin Panofsky, *Pandora's Box: The Changing Aspects of a
    Mythical Symbol* (London, 1956), pp. 90–102; Robert Rosenblum, *Trans-
    formations in Late Eighteenth Century Art*, third edition (Princeton, New
    Jersey, 1974), pp. 146–191 ('Towards the *Tabula Rasa*'). For Towne see
    Joseph Burke, *English Art: 1714–1800* (Oxford, 1974), pp. 398–400.
55 *Essays*, p. 145.
56 *Essays*, p. 172.
57 *Essays*, pp. 173–4.
58 *Essays*, p. 164.
59 *Aristotle's Treatise on Poetry, Translated*, p. 61.
60 *Aristotle's Treatise on Poetry, Translated*, p. 18, and cf. p. 104, above.
61 *Poems on Various Subjects*, p. v. See also Alison's comment that musical
    'compositions are not read in private, but are publicly recited. There is
    therefore the additional circumstance of the performance to be attended to;
    a circumstance of no mean consequence, and of which every man will
    acknowledge the importance, who recollects the different effects the same
    composition has produced on him, when performed by different people',
    Alison, pp. 193–4.
62 *Poems on Various Subjects*, p. vii.
63 *Poems on Various Subjects*, pp. viii–ix:

> Surely it would be candid not merely to ask whether the Poem
> pleases ourselves, but to consider whether or no there may not
> be others to whom it is well-calculated to give an innocent
> pleasure. With what anxiety every fashionable author avoids
> the word *I!* – now he transforms himself into a third person, –
> 'the present writer' – now multiplies himself and swells into
> '*we*' – and all this is the watchfulness of guilt. Conscious that
> this said *I* is perpetually intruding on his mind and that it
> monopolizes his heart, he is prudishly solicitous that it may
> not escape his lips.

64 Samuel Taylor Coleridge, *Poems . . . to which are now added Poems by Charles
    Lamb, and Charles Lloyd* (London, 1797), p. xvii ('Preface to the Second

Edition'): 'My poems have been rightly charged with a profusion of double-epithets, and a general turgidness.' This replies to the reviewer for the *Analytical Review*; see Derek Roper, *Reviewing Before the Edinburgh, 1788–1802* (London, 1978), pp. 89–90.

65 *Poems* (1797), p. xvi.

66 'A poem that abounds in allusions, like the Bard of Gray, or one that impersonates high and abstract truths, like Collins's Ode on the poetical character; claims not to be popular – but should be acquitted of obscurity. The deficiency is in the Reader', *Poems* (1797), p. xviii.

67 See Rachel Trickett, *The Honest Muse* (Oxford, 1969); and Paul Fussell, *The Rhetorical World of Augustan Humanism* (Oxford, 1965).

68 Further editions appeared in 1816 and 1823.

69 George Berkeley, *The Principles of Human Knowledge* (Dublin, 1710), p. 27 (Introduction No. 18).

70 *ibid.*

71 *ibid.*

72 Berkeley, p. 30 (No. 20).

73 *ibid.*

74 Berkeley, p. 35 (No. 22).

75 Berkeley, pp. 93–4 (Part 1, Nos. 51, 52). Campbell's scrupulous re-reading of Berkeley goes beyond David Hume's argument which defends the autonomy of reason in the face of language and nonsense:

> I believe every one, who examines the situation of his mind in reasoning, will agree with me, that we do not annex distinct and compleat ideas to every term we make use of, and that in talking of *government, church, negotiation, conquest*, we seldom spread out in our minds all the simple ideas, of which these complex ones are compos'd. 'Tis however observable, that notwithstanding this imperfection we may avoid talking nonsense on these subjects, and may perceive any repugnance among the ideas, as well as if we had a full comprehension of them.   *A Treatise of Human Nature*, p. 23.

76 Campbell, II, p. 92.

77 Campbell, II, pp. 102–3.

78 Campbell, II, pp. 92, 96.

79 Campbell, II, pp. 99–101.

80 Campbell, II, p. 111.

81 Campbell, II, pp. 104, 112.

82 Campbell, II, p. 104.

83 See above, Introduction, note 1.

84 Campbell, II, p. 108.

85 Stewart, II, pp. 202, 205.

86 Volume II appeared in 1814, and Volume III in 1827.

87 Stewart, II, p. 92.

88 *A Treatise of Human Nature*, 'Appendix', pp. 623–39 (p. 634).

89 Stewart, II, pp. 141–3. See also Hartley:

> The Doctrine of Sounds does also furnish us with an Answer to one of the principal and most obvious Difficulties attending

the Supposition, that all Sensation, Thought, and Motion, is performed by Vibrations in the medullary Substance. For it may be objected that such a number of different Vibrations, as seems to be required in certain Cases, can scarce exist together in the medullary Substance. Thus it is not uncommon for a Person to receive a Series of Sensations, carry on a Train of Thought, and perform a Course of external Actions, which have little connexion with each other, at the same time. Now to this we may answer, That Vibrations as different from each other do, in fact, exist together in common Air, in such a manner as to appear distinctly. Thus a Person may listen to what part he pleases in a Concert of Music, and Masters in the Art can listen to more than one.

Observations Upon Man, p. 232.

Gerard also develops this point by describing music in terms of memory and anticipation: 'sense, memory, and imagination . . . conjunctively employed, in exhibiting to the interior organ a succession of sounds, which, properly disposed, especially in music, fill us with exquisite delight', Gerard, pp. 58–9. See also Stewart's student, Dr Thomas Brown, who also prefers the sense of hearing as an analogy for all forms of perception: 'In this the great circumstance distinguishing musical feeling, is to be found, that the feeling arises *not from the separate impressions*, but from their *succession* or *co-existence*', *Lectures on the Philosophy of the Human Mind, by the late Thomas Brown, M.D.*, 4 vols (Edinburgh, 1820), I, p. 264. Brown delivered these lectures in 1808–9; see Richard Olson, *Scottish Philosophy and British Physics, 1750–1880: a Study in the Foundations of the Victorian Scientific Style* (Princeton, New Jersey, 1975), p. 125n.

90 Stewart, II, p. 439.
91 Stewart, II, pp. 439–40.
92 Stewart, II, pp. 441–?
93 Stewart, II, pp. 438–9.
94 Stewart, V, p. 286.
95 Stewart, V, pp. 286–7. This contrasts with 'the ubiquity (if I may be allowed the phrase) of the Poet's eye' (p. 287).
96 Stewart, II, p. 467.
97 Stewart, II, pp. 181–2.
98 See *From Signs to Propositions*, pp. 110–24. Land's discussion of Stewart, though of great value, is restricted by his failure to explore the connections in particular between Campbell and Stewart.
99 Stewart, III, p. 98.
100 Stewart, X, p. lvii.
101 Joseph-Marie de Gérando, *Des Signes et de l'art de penser dans leurs rapports mutuels*, 4 vols (Paris, 1800) (Ann. VIII), I, p. i ('Avertissement'). Johann David Michaelis had been first in this tradition with his 1759 prize essay, *A Dissertation on the Influence of Opinions on Language and of Language on Opinions, which gained the Prussian Royal Academy's Prize on that Subject . . . Together with an Enquiry into the Advantages and Practicability of an Universal Learned Language* (London, 1769). Michaelis argues that language

is an 'immense heap of truths and errors' and 'may do hurt several ways'. However, he does not approve the projects for a universal, algebraic language which had been urged from Descartes, through Wilkins, to Leibnitz and Condillac. Given that 'language is a democracy where use or custom is decided by the majority', a universal character would throw up 'a partition between them and the sciences, as the hieroglyphics among the Egyptians. No middle class is left between the scholar and the rude plebeian.' As an alternative, and in a spirit close to that of Campbell and Stewart, he urges readers to 'Credit no proposition purely because the etymology implies it or seems to imply it', and writers to 'Vary your expressions . . . when error is become the universal opinion, a new expression, at first looked upon only as a beautiful figure, has restored truth . . . Thus it is very probable, that for all the erroneous expressions the poetic still furnishes an antidote. Not that the poets have discovered truth; but, in the quest of new similitudes, they have hit on it without knowing it', pp. 2–3, 40, 73, 86. See also *Encyclopaedia of Philosophy*, edited by Paul Edwards, 8 vols (New York, 1967), VII, pp. 358–406 (Norman Kretzmann, 'History of Semantics'); and also Sergio Moravia, *Il pensiero degli idéologues: scienza e filosofia in Francia, 1780–1815* (Firenze, 1974).

102 De Gérando, I, p. xxxiv.
103 De Gérando, I, p. xxii.
104 De Gérando, II, p. 251.
105 De Gérando, II, p. 322.
106 De Gérando, II, pp. 294–5.
107 De Gérando, II, p. 316.
108 De Gérando, II, p. 317.
109 De Gérando, II, pp. 371–2.
110 Samuel Taylor Coleridge, *The Philosophical Lectures*, edited by Kathleen Coburn (London, 1949), p. 168. (Hereafter *PL*.)
111 De Gérando, II, pp. 369–70.
112 Stewart, III, pp. 94–5.
113 Stewart, V, p. 171.
114 Stewart, V, p. 125.
115 Stewart, V, pp. 146–8.
116 Stewart, III, p. 108; V, p. 174.
117 Stewart, V, p. 153.
118 Brown, II, pp. 336–7.
119 Brown, II, p. 339.
120 Brown, II, pp. 226–8.
121 Stewart, V, p. 174.
122 Stewart, V, p. 166.
123 Stewart, V, p. 174.
124 Thomas Brown M.D., *Poems*, 2 vols (Edinburgh, 1804), II, p. 187.
125 *W Prose*, III, p. 82.
126 *W Prose*, II, p. 98.
127 *W Prose*, I, p. 120.
128 *W Prose*, I, pp. 131–2.
129 *W Prose*, I, p. 161.

130 *W Prose*, I, p. 139.
131 *W Prose*, I, pp. 138, 147.
132 *W Prose*, I, pp. 129, 138, 149.
133 *Prelude* (1977), p. 59.
134 Stewart, II, p. 141.
134 *Prelude* (1977), pp. 50–2.
136 Stewart, V, p. 287.
137 De Gérando, p. 370. One member of the 'common sense' school, John Gregory, had noticed as early as 1765 that Blair's idea of the sublime might be so developed. He quotes Blair on *Ossian*: 'The main secret of being sublime, is to say great things in few and plain words . . . The mind rises and swells'; 'The application of these ingenious observations to Music,' comments Gregory, 'is too obvious to need any illustration', *A Comparative View*, p. 137.
138 William Wordsworth, *The Prelude, or Growth of a Poet's Mind*, edited by Ernest De Selincourt, second edition, revised by H. Darbishire (Oxford, 1959), p. 211. (Hereafter *Prelude* (1959).)
139 *The Poetical Works of William Wordsworth*, edited by Ernest De Selincourt, 5 vols (Oxford, 1940–9), V, p. 343. Immediately after these lines we read:

> The clouds are standing still in the mid heavens;
> A perfect quietness is in the air;
> The ear hears not; and yet, I know not how,
> More than the other senses does it hold
> A manifest communion with the heart.

140 *Prelude* (1959), p. 22.
141 *Poetical Works*, V, p. 346; *Prelude* (1977), p. 148.

In his essay on 'Wordsworth, Language, and Romanticism', Hans Aarsleff correctly, refutes the consensus which had settled around M. H. Abrams's view that Wordsworth's ideas about language dismiss British and French philosophy in favour of a German poetics which in the late eighteenth century 'achieved currency throughout western Europe'. Aarsleff traces a history of ideas about language from Locke to Condillac to the *Encyclopédie* to the *idéologues* in the person of Destutt de Tracy, and concludes that, while Wordsworth rejected the eighteenth-century tradition, he did so in the terms of that tradition. However the eighteenth century had already interrogated itself, and Aarsleff finds Condillac to be 'the central figure who brought about the change that lies behind the romantic aesthetic and the role it assigned to language'; *From Locke to Saussure*, pp. 372–81 (p. 373).

However, the parallels he draws between Condillac and Wordsworth are disappointing and vague: 'For both Condillac and Wordsworth language is the central problem of literary theory and poetic art' (p. 378). This is true of almost any eighteenth-century philosopher or poet. Aarsleff mistakes Condillac's primitive equation of poetry and music, largely repeated in Rousseau's *Essai*, as the main tradition in ideas about poetics. In that tradition, of course, music is related to primitive figurative language. We have seen Wordsworth reject that concept of language, but Aarsleff does not notice him doing so. The idea of music and the 'empty sign' relates to developments in theories of instrumental music. Aarsleff is unaware of these. But it is these ideas, as they interact with ideas about language from Campbell to Twining to Smith to Stewart and de Gérando (*not* Destutt de Tracy), which provide the range of a linguistics for Wordsworth's poetics. For de Gérando's rejection of Condillac, see de Gérando, I, pp. xx–xxii. For Stewart's rejection of Condillac, see Stewart, V, pp. 433–4, under the heading *Etymological Metaphysics*: 'Mr Locke himself prepared the way for Mr Tooke's researches, by the following observation, of which, however, I do not recollect that any notice has been taken in the *Diversions of Purley*. "It may also lead us a little towards the original of all our notions and knowledge, if we remark how great a dependence our words have on common sensible ideas; and how those which are made use of to stand for actions and notions quite removed from sense, have their rise from thence, and from obvious sensible ideas are transferred to more abstruse signification, and made to stand for ideas that come not under the cognizance of our senses, viz., to imagine, apprehend, comprehend, adhere, conceive, instil, disgust, disturbance, tranquillity, &c., are all words taken from the operations of sensible things, and applied to certain modes of thinking. Spirit, in its primary signification is breath: Angel, a messenger; *and I doubt not, but if we could trace them to their sources, we should find, in all languages, the names which stand for things, that fall not under our senses, to have had their first rise from sensible ideas"* . . . Condillac, in his *Essai sur l'Origine des Connoissances Humaines*, has given his sanction to this conclusion of Locke (Seconde Partie, sect. i, chap. x).' Stewart also finds fault with Condillac's principle that 'L'art de raissoner se réduit à une langue bien faite', and comments that 'One of the first persons, as far as I know, who objected to the vagueness and incorrectness of this proposition, was M. Degerando', Stewart, III, p. 101. For Stewart and for de Gérando, Condillac's fundamental misconception is that the mind could rest easy with truth 'par un moyen aussi simple que la réforme des langues'. Condillac's assumption falls in precisely with the intentions of a rationalism which runs from Locke to Horne Tooke and Erasmus Darwin.

4   Samuel Taylor Coleridge

1 See, for example, Richard Coleire, *The Antiquity and Usefulness of Instrumental Musick in the Service of God* (London, 1738), p. 7, in which other acts of devotion are thought to acknowledge our wants and miseries, but music is properly exalted; George Horne, *The Antiquity, Use, and Excellence of Church Music* (Oxford, 1784), p. 14, in which the Handel commemoration at Westminster Abbey is said to have 'furnished the best idea we shall ever obtain on earth of what is passing in heaven'. See also Jonas Hanway, *Thoughts on the Use and Advantage of Music, and other amusements . . . In nine letters, In answer to a letter relating to modern musical entertainments* (London, 1765), p. 58, in which it is affirmed that, 'Tho' it is in the power of harmony to rouze the languid soul, and warm it with a heavenly flame, there must be a proper temper to receive the impression.'

See also Richard Eastcott, *Sketches of the Origin, Progress and Effects of Music* (London, 1793), pp. 158, 197–8, 225, in which he asserts that modern music is instrumental music, that '*In Germany*, the people are all *musicians*', and that

> Of all the enjoyments of sense (says an eminent divine [i.e. Jonas Hanway]) music is the least sensual, its effects if rightly improved, terminate not in the bare pleasure of amusement, but seem peculiarly adapted to minds susceptible of religious impressions; its charms being calculated to imagine, a just idea of him, who formed the heart, to a relish of such delights; who endowed us with capacities, to proclaim his praises and taught us how to raise our souls to the rapture of angels.

See also William L. Bowles, *A Word on Cathedral-Oratorios* (London, 1830).

2 *PL*, p. 168. See also F. W. J. von Schelling, 'Concerning the Relation of the Plastic Arts to Nature, 1807', translated by M. Bullock, in Herbert Read, *The True Voice of Feeling* (London, 1957), pp. 321–64. J. C. Friedrich von Schiller, *On the Aesthetic Education of Man*, edited and translated by E. M. Wilkinson and L. A. Willoughby (Oxford, 1967), p. 7. *CL*, I, p. 209 (5 May 1796). G. W. F. Hegel, *Aesthetics: Lectures on Fine Art*, translated by T. M. Knox, 2 vols (Oxford, 1975), II, pp. 959–61.

3 *Biographia Literaria; or, Biographical Sketches of my Literary Life and Opinions*, edited by James Engell and W. Jackson Bate, 2 vols (Princeton, N.J. and London, 1983), II, p. 18n. (Hereafter *BL* (*CC*).) See also *CL*, III, p. 504 (9 June 1814); and J. H. Muirhead, *Coleridge as Philosopher* (New York and London, 1930), p. 281, citing 'On the Divine Ideas', Huntington Library MS (Cambridge University Library, Microfilm 357), fos. 32–5.

4 *PL*, p. 168.

5 'In its' [*sic*] narrower meaning, the Understanding is used for the faculty, by which we form distinct *notions* of Things and *immediate*, positive judgements (ex. gr. Gold *is* a Body) in distinction from Reason or the faculty by which we form necessary conclusions, or *mediate* Judgements', *The Friend*, edited by Barbara E. Rooke, 2 vols (Princeton, N.J. and London, 1969), II, p. 77n. (Hereafter *The Friend* (*CC*).)

6 Immanuel Kant, *The Critique of Judgement*, translated by James C. Meredith (Oxford, 1952), pp. 184–9. Kant makes a threefold classification of the arts: (1) the art of speech; (2) formative art; (3) art of the play of sensations, in descending order of seriousness and value (*ibid.*, p. 184).

7 Kant, pp. 189–94.

8 Schelling's *Philosophie der Kunst*, although written between 1802 and 1805, was published for the first time posthumously in his *Sämmtliche Werke* (Stuttgart und Augsburg, 1859). See in particular V, pp. 488–501; and see also Bernard Bosanquet, *A History of Aesthetics* (London, 1904), pp. 252, 367–8.

9 Schiller, pp. 155, 265.

10 Arthur Schopenhauer, *The World as Will and Representation*, translated by E. F. J. Payne, 2 vols (New York, 1969), I, p. 256.

11 *The World as Will and Representation*, I, pp. 257, 264.

12 For Schopenhauer's education see Bryan Magee, *The Philosophy of Schopenhauer* (Oxford, 1983), pp. 4–6. On the status and background of Schopenhauer's ideas about music see the *Times Literary Supplement*, January–February, 1975, pp. 11, 84, 226.

13 *The Complete Works of William Hazlitt*, edited by P. P. Howe, 20 vols (London and Toronto, 1930), XI, pp. 11, 16 (*The Spirit of the Age*). (Hereafter Hazlitt.)

14 *CL*, I, pp. 465–6 (February 1799).

15 A. G. Baumgarten christened his new 'science' *Aesthetica* in 1750. See J. Isaacs, 'Coleridge's Critical Terminology', in *Essays and Studies by Members of the English Association*, 21 (1936), 86–104: Isaacs quotes Coleridge's own note on his use of 'aesthetic': 'that coincidence of form, feeling, and intellect, that something, which confirming the inner and the outward senses, becomes a new sense in itself, to be tried by laws of its own, and acknowledging the laws of the understanding so far only as not to contradict them'. The *NED* gives 1803 as the first use of 'aesthetic' in its Kantian sense of 'conditions of sensuous perception'.

16 For an opposite view see Roy Park, 'Ut Pictura Poesis: the Nineteenth Century Aftermath', *JAAC*, 28 (1969), 155–64. The materials brought forward in this book, in particular about Coleridge, call into question Park's conclusion that painting, 'in spite of the decline of *ut pictura poesis*, remained the dominant and most potent analogy in the critical vocabulary of the Romantic period' (p. 164).

17 See J. A. Appleyard, *Coleridge's Philosophy of Literature: the Development of a Concept of Poetry, 1791–1819* (Cambridge, Mass., 1965), pp. 245–9.

18 *CL*, II, p. 1066 (17 February 1804); *Inquiring Spirit: A New Presentation of Coleridge from his Published and Unpublished Writings*, edited by K. Coburn (London, 1951), p. 211; Coburn is wrong to suggest that Coleridge's interest in John Callcott's concert in 1808 was personal and not musical; see *CL*, III, pp. 45–6 (14 January 1808), and Coleridge's lending some music to Callcott, *CN*, III, 4106 (1811); *CL*, I, pp. 615–16 (29 July 1800).

19 Wordsworth's revision of archaic terminology appears never to be complete: in a letter to Dorothy from Italy he describes a peasant playing a harpsichord; in the first edition of *Descriptive Sketches* this becomes a hermit with his 'aged lyre'; in the second edition a 'rude viol' is in his hand; Mary Moorman has updated this image further, and it is now a 'primitive violin'. See *The Letters of William and Dorothy Wordsworth: The Early Years*, edited by E. de Selincourt, revised by C. L. Shaver (Oxford, 1967), p. 36; *Poetical Works*, I, pp. 52–3 (*Descriptive Sketches*, 1793, ll. 168–75; 1849, ll. 145–53); Mary Moorman, *William Wordsworth: A Biography*, 2 vols (Oxford, 1957), I, p. 143. See also Hollander, *Images of Voice*, p. 7, and his 'Wordsworth and the Music of Sound', p. 77.

20 *Henry Crabb Robinson on Books and their Writers*, edited by E. J. Morley, 3 vols (London, 1938), I, p. 293 (5 April 1823). See also Lucy E. Watson, *Coleridge at Highgate* (London, 1925), p. 95.

21 See *The Works in Prose and Verse of Charles and Mary Lamb*, edited by T. Hutchinson (London, n.d. [1908]), I, pp. 518–23 ('A Chapter on Ears').

22 Hazlitt, V, pp. 296–8 ('The Oratorios', 1816).

23 *Specimens of the Table Talk of the late Samuel Taylor Coleridge*, 2 vols (London, 1835), II, p. 220. (Hereafter *TT*.)

24 *TT*, II, pp. 219–20; and see I, p. 214–15: 'I have the intensest delight in music, and can detect good from bad. Naldi, a good fellow, remarked to me once at a concert, that I did not seem much interested with a piece of Rossini's which had just been performed. I said, it sounded to me like nonsense verses. But I could scarcely contain myself when a thing of Beethoven's followed.' For Coleridge on Cimarosa, see *The Friend* (*CC*), I, pp. 129–30; *BL* (*CC*), I, p. 118; *Coleridge's Shakespearean Criticism*, edited by T. M. Raysor, 2 vols (London, 1930), II, p. 77. (Hereafter *SC*.)

25 *CN*, III, 4313 (April 1816). For De Quincey, for whom the state of dream and the aesthetics of music appear to be one and the same, see *De Quincey's Collected Writings*, edited by David Masson, 14 vols (London, 1897), III, p. 270 (*Confessions of an Opium-Eater*): 'Too soon I became aware that to the deep voluptuous enjoyment of music absolute *passiveness* in the hearer is indispensable.'

26 *CL*, I, pp. 50–1 (7 February 1793); I, p. 79 (7 April 1794).

27 *CL*, I, p. 52 (7 February 1793).

28 *CL*, I, p. 31 (14 February 1792); *CL*, II, p. 789 (24 February 1802); *Inquiring Spirit*, p. 214.

29 William Crotch, *Substance of several Courses of Lectures on Music, read in the University of Oxford and in the Metropolis* (London, 1831). These lectures were given in 1800–4 and 1820; see Grove, 1980, V, pp. 64–7.

30 See especially *Quarterly Musical Magazine and Review*, edited by R. M. Bacon (London, 1818–).

31 *The Friend* (*CC*), II, p. 18. See also Coleridge's argument that 'All the fine arts are different species of poetry. The same spirit speaks to the mind through different senses by manifestations of itself, appropriate to each', *Biographia Literaria*, edited by John Shawcross, 2 vols (Oxford, 1907), II, pp. 220–1 ('On the Principles of Genial Criticism Concerning the Fine Arts'). (Hereafter *BL* (Shawcross).)

32 *CL*, III, p. 30 (9 September 1807).

33 *CPW*, I, p. 236; *CL*, I, pp. 318–19: the relevant sonnet by Bowles is entitled 'Music':

> O Harmony! thou tenderest nurse of pain,
> If that thy note's sweet magic e'er can heal
> Griefs which the patient spirit oft may feel,
> Oh! let me listen to thy songs again;
> Till memory her fairest tints shall bring;
> Hope wake with brighter eye, and listening seem
> With smiles to think on some delightful dream,
> That waved o'er the charmed sense its gladsome wing!
> For when thou leadest all thy soothing strains
> More smooth along, the silent passions meet
> In one suspended transport, sad and sweet;
> And nought but sorrow's softest touch remains;
> That, when the transitory charm is o'er,
> Just wakes a tear, and then is felt no more.

See *The Poetical Works of William Lisle Bowles*, edited by G. Gilfillan, 2 vols (Edinburgh, 1855), I, p. 22.

34 *CPW*, I, pp. 324–5.

35 *A Word on Cathedral-Oratorios*, p. 27.

36 *Remarks on Psalm Playing. By a Professor of the Organ* (London, 1830), p. 9.

37 Eastcott, pp. 197–8; for full quotation see note 1 above.

38 Alison, p. 151.

39 Thomas Robertson, *An Inquiry into the Fine Arts*, (London, 1784). Laurence Lipking asserts that the *Inquiry*, 'The most pretentious combination of aesthetics with scholarly history . . . expired after only one volume (on music) had been completed', *The Ordering of the Arts in Eighteenth Century England* (Princeton, N.J., 1970), p. 474.

40 Robertson, p. 11.

41 Robertson, pp. 5, 6, 449–50. According to Robertson 'poetry is not strictly an imitative art', p. 8. It is interesting to question whether Twining had read the *Inquiry*: in 1785 Burney asked him if he had seen a copy; the material accompanying the translation of Aristotle was reported by Twining to be complete in 1783; but it was not published until 1789; see BL Add MS 39,929, fo. 361 (letter to Burney, 18 September 1785).

42 Sir William Jones, *Poems consisting chiefly of Translations from the Asiatick Languages. To which are added Two Essays, I. On the Poetry of the Eastern Nations. II. On the Arts, commonly called Imitative* (Oxford, 1772), p. 202: Jones adds, 'It shall be my endeavour in this paper to prove, that, though *poetry* and *musick* have, certainly, a power of *imitating* the manners of men, and several objects in nature, yet, that their greatest effect is not produced by *imitation*, but by a very different principle; which must be sought for in the deepest recesses of the human mind.'

43 See, for example, Robertson on the dignity of the arts being in proportion to their anti-mimetic practice; and see Robertson on Tartini; Robertson, pp. 449–50.

44 Robertson, pp. 20–1.

45 Robertson, pp. 445–6. See also Robertson's precocious admiration for Haydn, his novelty, fertility, and surprise; Robertson, p. 433.

46 Johnson, p. 76.

47 James Beattie, *An Essay on Poetry and Truth as they affect the Mind* (Edinburgh, 1776), quoted in Le Huray and Day, p. 154.

48 Robertson, p. 447.

49 *TT*, II, p. 220.

50 *CN*, III, 4021 (1810).

51 *CN*, III, 4022 (1810).

52 *CN*, III 4397 (March 1818). Notice also that Coleridge here, in his notes on Schelling, adds music to Schelling's list of the arts.

53 See Chapter 4, pp. 151, 165.

54 Read, pp. 339–40.

55 *CN*, III, 4503 (March 1819).

56 *The Friend* (*CC*), I, p. 464. And see *Anima Poetae: from the unpublished Note-Books of Samuel Taylor Coleridge*, edited by E. H. Coleridge (London, 1895), pp. 200–1: 'Q. What is music? A. Poetry in its grand sense!'

57 *The Friend* (*CC*), I, pp. 464–5.
58 Roman Jakobson, 'Musicologie et linguistique', in *Questions de poétique* (Paris, 1973), pp. 102–4. Robertson notices this difference also in his comments on Chinese musicians who have 'given different names to the same Note, according to the different Instruments on which it is sounded: metal, stone, silk, bambou-reed, gourd, baked earth, skin of animals, wood; without whose eight different Sounds they do not hold music to be complete', Robertson, p. 274.
59 J. Elliott, *Philosophical Observations on the Senses of Vision and Hearing; to which are added, a treatise On Harmonic Sounds, and an essay On Combustion and Animal Heat* (London, 1780), pp. 43, 50–1.
60 Elliott, pp. 17–18, 60–1.
61 Consider the following excerpts from Coleridge's notebooks: 'Analogy always implies a difference in kind & not merely in degree. There is an analogy between dimness, numbers, & a certain state of the sense of Hearing . . . for which we have no name'; 'deep Sky is of all visual impressions the nearest akin to a Feeling / . . . it is the melting away and entire union of Feeling & Sight'; 'All mind must think by some *symbols* . . . yet this ingenerates a *want, pothon,* desiderium, for vividness of Symbol: which something that is *without,* that has the property of *Outness* (a word which Berkly [*sic*] preferred to "Externality") can alone fully gratify'; 'Definites, be they Sounds or Images . . . must be . . . *out* of us', and this contrasts with the sense of touch; 'In the holy eloquent Solitude of when the very stars that twinkle seem to be a *voice* that suits the Dream, a voice of a Dream, a voice soundless and yet for the *Ear* not the *Eye* of the Soul'; *CN*, II, 2319 (December 1804); *CN*, III, 3325 (May 1808), 3700 (February 1810), 4058 (March–April 1811). This emphasis on the creative indistinctness of hearing, as opposed in particular to seeing, remains in Coleridge's thought up to his final dictations to J. H. Green: Coleridge is speaking of the 'sensuous imagination' which we must 'keep at rest, silent', and which 'is a difficulty which arises out of our nature, and while that nature remains, must remain with it . . . nay, will be active, as while the ear is deeply listening to some sweet harmony from an unknown distance, the eye will gaze thitherward, even though it should have been ascertained that it was the music of the air, such as travellers are said to have heard in Ceylon and Sumatra produced by currents and counter-currents, the glancing fingers of electric fire in the highest atmosphere', 'On the Divine Ideas', fo. 35.
62 *CN*, II, 2035 (April 1804).
63 *Poetical Works*, I, p. 2.
64 *CL*, I, p. 511 (19 May 1799); and see pp. 615–16 (29 July 1800).
65 *CL*, I, pp. 465–6 (February 1799). See also *Anima Poetae*, p. 149: 'The confusion of metaphor with reality . . . feeds by its many mouths the sea of blood.'
66 'But all History seems to favor the persuasion, I entertain, that in every age the speculative Philosophy in general acceptance, the metaphysical opinions that happen to be predominant, will influence the *Theology* of that age'; to this Coleridge adds a marginal note: 'Not only the Theology; but

also the Fine Arts. The Greek (Christian) School of Painting before Giotto – the very Allegory of the rigid Outlines & Abstract Surfaces of then reigning Pseudo-Aristotelean Metaphysics – With Giotto, Dante, Petrarch, Platonism revived in the Noblest Minds, and reigned till after the death of Raphael, Michael Angelo, Correggio, Titian &c – . Then arose the *Eclectic* Philosophy and with it the *Academic* School of Caracci &c – After this the Mechanic Philosophy usurped the Metaphysical Throne – & we had inveterate Likenesses, and Statues with Marble *Periwigs* or full Buckle – . – Sir Joshua Reynolds was *platonized* by his Tutor – & the evidences are scattered thro' his Lectures – and embodied in his Paintings – as far as the necessitas crumenaria of sophisticating Grace & Beauty by *Fashion* permitted', *Lay Sermons*, edited by R. J. White (Princeton, N.J. and London, 1972), pp. 103–4 (*The Statesman's Manual*). (Hereafter *Lay Sermons* (*CC*).)

67 *CN*, III, 4397 (March 1818), 4498 (March 1819); Kathleen Coburn argues here that Coleridge's notes from Schelling indicate that his aesthetic is closest to that of Schiller. Her evidence is persuasive, but the centrally important difference in Schiller's and Coleridge's hierarchies of the arts must not go unnoticed. See also *Coleridge's Miscellaneous Criticism*, edited by T. M. Raysor (London and Cambridge, Mass., 1936), pp. 6–8, 12–13. (Hereafter *MC*.)

68 '. . . there is a natural affinity between Despotism and modern Philosophy', *Essays on his Times*, edited by David V. Erdman, 3 vols (Princeton, N.J. and London, 1978), II, p. 81 (1809). (Hereafter *Essays* (*CC*).) See also 'On the Divine Ideas', p. 17; *Coleridge on Logic and Learning*, edited by Alice D. Snyder (New Haven and London, 1929), p. 76; *PL*, pp. 92–3, 268, 342–3. For the extremes being alike, see *TT*, I, p. 35 (30 April 1823). See also *CN*, III, 4397 (March 1818): '*Art* (I use the word collectively for Music, Painting, Statuary and Architecture) is the Mediatress, the reconciliator of Man and Nature.' For Coleridge's judgement that Schelling's philosophy was 'neither more nor less than pantheism' see Thomas McFarland, *Coleridge and the Pantheist Tradition* (Oxford, 1969), pp. 104–5.

69 *Lay Sermons* (*CC*), pp. 103–4.

70 *ibid.*

71 *Lay Sermons* (*CC*), pp. 100–2; and see Coleridge's comment on 'a passage that deserves a mediation beyond the ministry of words, even the words of Plato himself, though in them, or no where, are to be heard the sweet sounds, that issued from the Head of Memnon at the touch of Light', p. 98.

72 *PL*, pp. 166–7.

73 *PL*, p. 168. See also *MC*, pp. 9–10.

74 *PL*, p. 166.

75 *BL* (*CC*), I, pp. 116–18. And see Coleridge's marginalia to Kant in Kathleen M. Wheeler, *The Creative Mind in Coleridge's Poetry* (London, 1981), p. 82: 'The mind does not resemble an Eolian Harp, nor even a barrel-organ turned by a stream of water, conceive as many tunes mechanized in it as you like – but rather, as far as Objects are concerned, a violin, or other instrument of few strings yet vast compass, played on by a musician of Genius. The Breeze that blows across the Eolian Harp, the streams that

turned the handle of the Barrel-Organ, might be called ein mannigfaltiges, a mere sylva incondita, but who would call the muscles and purpose of Linley a confused Manifold?' See also *CL*, IV, pp. 750–1 (4 July 1807). For the use of the harp image for the unity in perception of subject and object, see *Logic*, edited by J. R. de J. Jackson (Princeton, N.J. and London, 1981), pp. 38, 142. (Hereafter *Logic* (*CC*).)

76 *CPW*, I, pp. 362–3.

77 *PL*, pp. 168–9.

78 Edwin H. Zeydel, *Ludwig Tieck and England* (Princeton, N. J., 1931), p. 94, quotes Coleridge recording on 16 January 1819 that he has 'the little volume edited by Tieck of his friend's composition'; see W. H. Wackenroder, *Confessions and Fantasies*, translated by M. H. Schubert (University Park and London, 1971), pp. 178–9 ('The Marvels of the Musical Art'). Coleridge's difference from Wackenroder is clear when we contrast Wackenroder's use of the figure of the 'flowing stream' to describe instrumental music and its 'formless essence' with Coleridge's rejection of the 'formless stream' image in note 75 above; see Bellamy Hosler, *Changing Aesthetic Views of Instrumental Music in 18th-Century Germany* (Ann Arbor, Michigan, 1981), p. 203.

79 *CL*, II, p. 713 (24 March 1801); *PL*, pp. 287–8; *Logic* (*CC*), p. 242.

80 *CN*, II, 2356 (December 1804). The phrases used here are culled from Herder's *Kalligone*; see Hosler, p. 207.

81 Wheeler has described how, in practice, through some of Coleridge's poetry 'the meaning of the words [is] flooded into oblivion by the power of their music', *The Creative Mind*, pp. 73–4, 91.

82 *BL* (*CC*), II, p. 20; *CN*, III, 4115 (October–November 1811).

83 *Coleridge on Logic and Learning*, p. 164.

84 *CL*, I, p. 625 (22 September 1800).

85 *MC*, pp. 389–90 (conversation with H. C. Robinson).

86 *CN*, III, 3762 (April–June 1810).

87 *ibid.*

88 *CL*, I, p. 625 (22 September 1800).

89 *CL*, I, p. 656 (17 December 1800).

90 *BL* (*CC*), II, p. 20.

91 'Milton is not a picturesque, but a musical poet'; he is 'the most musical of all poets'; for Coleridge, Milton is an instance of the specifically *poematic*, that is of 'poetry independent of the thoughts and the images', *MC*, pp. 165, 181. Raysor refers to Schiller, *Essays* (London, 1967), p. 303 ('On Naive and Sentimental Poetry'); Coleridge uses Schiller's categories but not his evaluation of particular poets. See also *TT*, II, p. 83.

92 '... the same judgment is observable in every scene, still preparing, still inviting, and still gratifying, like a finished piece of music', *SC*, II, p. 178.

93 I. A. Richards, *Coleridge on Imagination* (London, 1934), pp. 112–21.

94 *CN*, II, 2999 (February 1807).

95 'On the Divine Ideas', fo. 35.

96 *The Friend* (*CC*) I, p. 20; *CN*, I, fo. 383 (January–May 1799).

97 *Coleridge on Logic and Learning*, pp. 36–7, 138; *Logic* (*CC*), p. 282; and see *PL*, pp. 173–4.

98 *Coleridge on Imagination*, p. 122.

99 *CN*, III, 4337 (January 1817).

100 *MC*, p. 218; *PL*, pp. 190–1.

101 *PL*, p. 352.

102 *BL (CC)*, I, p. 38.

103 *CN*, III, 4334 (January 1817).

104 *PL*, p. 290; *CN*, II, 2599 (May–August 1805).

105 *Logic (CC)*, pp. 242–3.

106 *CL*, I, p. 252 (7 November 1796); *Aids to Reflection*, second edition (London, 1831), pp. 70–1.

107 *PL*, p. 111: the short-hand transcription of the lectures gives 'chiaro-logical', although the term clearly intended is 'curiologic', as used by Warburton (note 109 below).

108 Gilbert Wakefield, 'On the *Origin* of *Alphabetical Characters*', *Memoirs of the Literary and Philosophical Society of Manchester*, II (1785), pp. 280–95 (pp. 289, 292–3).

109 Warburton, II, pp. 80, 95, 96–156.

110 Warburton, II, p. 97.

111 *The Friend (CC)*, I, p. 106.

112 *Logic (CC)*, p. 243; *PL*, pp. 190, 281.

113 *PL*, pp. 111–12.

114 *PL*, pp. 90–3; *Essays*, II, p. 81.

115 *PL*, p. 343.

116 *PL*, p. 190.

117 *PL*, pp. 200–1; *CN*, I, p. 787 (August 1800); *CN*, III, 3611 (1809).

118 *The Friend (CC)*, II, p. 193.

119 *CN*, III, 4181 (November 1817).

120 *Of Grammatology*, pp. 10–15. See also I. J. Gelb, *A Study of Writing: The Foundations of Grammatology* (London, 1952), p. 10: 'the conclusion that speech forms the background of all human intercommunication seems a fallacy'. See *CN*, III, 4397 (1818): 'The primary Art is *writing* . . . the *translation*, as it were, of Man into Nature – the use of the visible in place of the Audible. The (so called) Music of savage Tribes as little deserves the name of Art . . .'

121 *CN*, III, 4350 (April 1817).

122 *MC*, pp. 173–4.

123 Muirhead, pp. 204–5.

124 Stewart, II, pp. 141–3.

125 Jean-Jacques Champollion, *Lettre à M. Dacier relative à l'alphabet des hiéroglyphes phonétiques* (Paris, 1822).

126 *CL*, II, p. 1066 (17 February 1804).

127 *CL*, II, p. 1110 (28 March 1804).

128 'He spoke of Lessing's *Laocoon* as very unequal and in its parts contradictory, his examples destroying his theory', *MC*, p. 395.

129 *CL*, I, p. 513 (17 May 1799); *CN*, III, 3700 (February 1810); *CN*, II, 2454 (February 1805).

130 *CN*, II, 2599 (May–August 1805).

131 *CN*, II, 2831 (April–May 1806).

132 CN, II, 2797 (February–March 1806).
133 CN, II, 2831 (April–May 1806). See also Carl Woodring, 'What Coleridge Thought of Pictures', in *Images of Romanticism*, edited by Karl Kroeber and William Walling (New Haven, Conn. and London, 1978), pp. 91–106; and also James Heffernan, 'The English Romantic Perception of Color', in *Images of Romanticism*, pp. 133–48.
134 S. T. Coleridge, 'On the Principles of Genial Criticism Concerning the Fine Arts', *Felix Farley's Bristol Journal* (August–September, 1814), in *BL* (Shawcross), II, pp. 219–46 (p. 220).
135 'It seems evident then, first, that beauty is harmony, and subsists only in composition', *BL* (Shawcross), p. 233.
136 William T. Whitley, *Art in England 1800–1820* (Cambridge, 1928), pp. 235–6.
137 Quoted by Hugh Honour, *Romanticism* (London, 1979), p. 120.
138 *Inquiring Spirit*, pp. 214–15.
139 CN, II, p. 2828 (March–April 1806); E. K. Waterhouse, *Painting in Britain 1530–1790* (London, 1953), p. 194.
140 *Images of Romanticism*, p. 103.
141 *Images of Romanticism*, p. 104.
142 *The Friend* (CC), I, p. 464.
143 SC, I, p. 131; II, p. 174.
144 SC, II, p. 178.
145 SC, II, p. 170; and see I, p. 224.
146 Quoted in Robertson, p. 254.
147 Robertson, pp. 240–5.
148 CN, II, 2224 (October 1804).
149 BL (CC), II, p. 20; for 'multëity in unity' as the 'most general definition of beauty', see *BL* (Shawcross), II, p. 232.
150 *Lay Sermons* (CC), p. 9.
151 *The Friend* (CC), I, p. 130.
152 BL (CC), II, pp. 26–7.
153 MC, pp. 181, 186.
154 MC, pp. 159–63.
155 TT, II, p. 83.
156 MC, pp. 337–9.
157 TT, II, p. 214.
158 Joshua Steele, *An Essay Towards Establishing the Melody and Measure of Speech* (London, 1775). Steele makes this point explicit in the second edition (1779); see the Scholar Press facsimile (London, 1969), p. 236. The context of Steele's work is explained in Murray Cohen, *Sensible Words: Linguistic Practice in England, 1640–1785* (Baltimore and London, 1977), pp. 115–20.
159 See, for example, Steele's disagreement with Monboddo's view that the number of syllables is essential to the rhythm of verse; also Steele applies musical scansion to Milton's verse, as Coleridge will; Steele, pp. 77, 108, 158–62, and see John Walker, *The Melody of Speaking Delineated; or, Elocution taught like Music, by visible signs, Adapted to the Tones, Inflexions, and Variations of voice in Reading and Speaking; with Directions for Modulation, and expressing the Passions* (London, 1787), p. 8: 'verse,

properly pronounced, is sometimes, not only figuratively, but literally a song'.

160 *The Quarterly Review*, 52 (1834), 8.

161 *SC*, II, p. 112. See also Coleridge's marginalia to Selden's *Table Talk*: 'verse is in itself a music, and the natural symbol of that union of Passion with Thought and Pleasure, which constitutes the *Essence* of all *Poetry*, as contradistinguished from Science, and distinguished from History, civil or natural'; cited in Paul Hamilton, *Coleridge's Poetics* (Oxford, 1983), p. 153.

Conclusion

1 Hazlitt, XII, p. 336.

2 Hazlitt, XII, p. 337.

3 Hazlitt, VIII, p. 170. It is ironic that Hazlitt should select Poussin, given Poussin's interest in developing painting according to an aesthetics of music; see Lockspieser, pp. 145–8.

4 *Observations sur la musique*, p. 23. For Abrams's argument about music see *The Mirror and the Lamp*, pp. 50–1, 91–3.

5 See Introduction, note 31 above.

6 *Poetical Works*, II, p. 513 (Note to 'The Thorn').

7 Hazlitt, V, pp. 12, 297.

8 Charles Maturin, *Melmoth the Wanderer: A Tale*, edited by Alethea Hayter (Harmondsworth, 1977), pp. 464–5.

9 See J. W. Oliver, *The Life of William Beckford* (London, 1932), p. 89.

10 Ann Radcliffe, *The Mysteries of Udolpho*, edited by Bonamy Dobrée (Oxford, 1966), p. 9.

11 *Images of Romanticism*, pp. 95–6, fn. 10.

12 See Wolfgang Iser, *The Implied Reader: Patterns of Communication in Prose Fiction from Bunyan to Beckett* (Baltimore and London, 1974), p. 31.

13 Alexander Cozens, *A New Method of Assisting the Invention in Drawing Original Compositions of Landscape* (London, n.d. [1786]), reprinted as an Appendix to A. P. Oppé, *Alexander and John Robert Cozens* (London, 1952), pp. 165–87. See Oppé, pp. 167, 170–1, 177, 180.

14 Reynolds, p. 224.

SELECT BIBLIOGRAPHY

Primary material

Addison, Joseph, *The Spectator*, edited by D. F. Bond, 5 vols (Oxford, 1965)

Aikin, John, *Essays on Song-Writing; with a Collection of such English Songs as are most Eminent for Poetical Merit* (London, 1772)

Akenside, Mark, *The Pleasures of Imagination. A Poem in Three Books* (London, 1744)

Algarotti, Francesco, *An Essay on the Opera* (London, 1767)

Alison, Archibald, *Essays on the Nature and Principles of Taste* (Edinburgh, 1790)

Anonymous, *Remarks on Psalm Playing. By a Professor of the Organ* (London, 1830)

  An Account of the Institution and Progress of the Academy of Ancient Music with a Comparative View of the Music of the Past and Present Times (London, 1770)

  Essays on Song-Writing: with a Collection of such English Songs as are most eminent for Poetical Merit (London, n.d.)

  Melody – the Soul of Music (Glasgow, 1798)

  An Explanation of the Ocular Harpsichord Upon Shew to the Public (London, 1757); with Postscript by Robert Smith (London, 1762)

  A Miscellany of Lyric Poems; the greatest part written for and performed in the Academy of Music (London, 1740)

  The Progress of Music, an Ode, occasioned by the grand Celebration at the Abbey (London, 1787)

  An Essay on Sacred Harmony (London, 1753)

  Polite Arts, or a Dissertation on Poetry, Painting, Music, Architecture and Eloquence (London, 1749)

  'Chabanon on Music', *Monthly Review*, 73 (1785), 490–6

Apthorp, East, *Discourses on Prophecy* (Warburton Lectures, 1785), 2 vols (London, 1786)

Armstrong, John, *The Art of Preserving Health* (London, 1744)

Astle, Thomas, *The Origin and Progress of Writing, as well hieroglyphic as elementary* (London, 1784)

Avison, Charles, *An Essay on Musical Expression* (London, 1752)

  A Reply to the Author of Remarks on the Essay on Musical Expression (London, 1753)

Baillie, John, *An Essay on the Sublime* (London, 1747)

Barrington, Daines, *Miscellanies* (London, 1781)

Batteux, Charles, *Les Beaux-Arts réduits à un même principe* (Paris, 1746)

Bayly, Anselm, *The Alliance of Musick, Poetry, and Oratory* (London, 1789)

Beattie, James, *An Essay on Poetry and Music as they affect the Mind* (Edinburgh, 1776)

Beckford, William, *Dreams, Waking Thoughts, and Incidents; in a series of Letters from various parts of Europe* (London, 1783)
   Vathek, edited by Roger Lonsdale (Oxford, 1970)
Bedford, A., *The Great Abuse of Music* (London, 1711)
Bemetzrieder, A., *Music Made Easy to Every Capacity, in a series of dialogues*, translated by Giffard Bernard, with Preface and Conclusion by Diderot (London, 1778)
Berkeley, George, *The Principles of Human Knowledge* (Dublin, 1710)
   The Works of George Berkeley, Bishop of Cloyne, edited by A. A. Luce and T. E. Jessop, 9 vols (London, 1948–57)
Blackwell, Thomas, *Enquiry into the Life and Writings of Homer* (London, 1735)
Blair, Hugh, *Lectures on Rhetoric and Belles Lettres*, 2 vols (London, 1783)
Blake, William, *The Poems*, edited by W. H. Stevenson, text by David Erdman (London, 1971)
Bowles, William Lisle, *The Poetical Works*, edited by G. Gilfillan, 2 vols (Edinburgh, 1855)
   A Word on Cathedral-Oratorios (London, 1830)
[Brocklesby, R.], *Reflections on Antient and Modern Musick, with the Application to the Cure of Diseases* (London, 1749)
Brown, John, *Letters on the Italian Opera: addressed to the Hon. Lord Monboddo*, second edition (London, 1791)
Brown, John, 'Estimate', *A Dissertation on the Rise, Union, and Power, the Progression, Separations, and Corruptions, of Poetry and Music* (London, 1763)
   Remarks on Some Observations on Dr. Brown's Dissertation on Poetry and Musick (London, 1764)
   et al., *The Lyric Muse Revived in Europe, or a Critical Display of the Opera in All its Revolutions* (London, 1768)
Brown, M.D., Thomas, *Poems*, 2 vols (Edinburgh, 1804)
   Lectures on the Philosophy of the Human Mind, by the late Thomas Brown, M.D., 4 vols (Edinburgh, 1820)
Bruce, Michael, *Poems on Several Occasions* (London, 1770)
Burgh, A., *Anecdotes of Music, Historical and Biographical* (London, 1814)
Burke, Edmund, *A Philosophical Enquiry into the Origin of our Ideas of The Sublime and Beautiful* (London, 1757)
Burnett, James, Lord Monboddo, *Of the Origin and Progress of Language*, 6 vols (Edinburgh, 1773–92)
Burney, Charles, *A General History of Music, from the Earliest Ages to the Present Period*, 4 vols (London, 1776–89)
   An Account of the Musical Performances in Westminster-abbey, and the Pantheon (London, 1785)
   Verses on the Arrival in England of the Great Musician Haydn (London, 1791)
Burns, Robert, *Poems*, edited by James Kinsley, 3 vols (Oxford, 1968)
Busby, Thomas, *Concert Room and Orchestra Anecdotes of Music and Musicians Ancient and Modern*, 3 vols (London, 1825)
Campbell, George, *The Philosophy of Rhetoric*, 2 vols (London, 1776)
Castel, Louis-B., *Optiques des couleurs* (Paris, 1740)
   Esprits, saillies et singularités (Amsterdam, 1763)
Chabanon, Michel-Paul Guy de, *Observations sur la musique et principalement sur*

la metaphysique de l'art, Réimpression des éditions de Paris, 1779 et 1764 (Geneva, 1969)

De la Musique considerée en elle-même et dans ses rapports avec la parole, les langues, la poésie et le théâtre, Réimpression de l'édition de Paris, 1785 (Geneva, 1969)

Sur le Sort de la poésie en ce siècle philosophe, Réimpression de l'édition de Paris, 1764 (Geneva, 1970)

Chalmers, Alexander, *The Works of the English Poets* (London, 1810)

Champollion, *Lettre à M. Dacier relative à l'alphabet des hiéroglyphes phonétiques* (Paris, 1822)

Chapman, James, *The Music, or Melody and Rhythms, of Language* (Edinburgh, 1818)

Chastellux, François Jean de, *Essai sur l'union de la poésie et de la musique* (La Haye, 1765)

Clagget, Charles, *A Discourse on Musick to be delivered at Mr. Clagget's Attic Concert, at the King's Arms, Cornhill, October 31, 1793* (London, n.d.)

Coleire, Richard, *The Antiquity and Usefulness of Instrumental Musick in the Service of God* (London, 1738)

Coleridge, Samuel T., *The Collected Works*, edited by Kathleen Coburn and Bart Winer, 16 vols (London and Princeton, N.J., 1969–)

Biographia Literaria; or, Biographical Sketches of my Literary Life and Opinions, edited by James Engell and W. Jackson Bate, 2 vols (Princeton, N.J. and London, 1983)

Essays on his Times, edited by David V. Erdman, 3 vols (Princeton, N.J. and London, 1978)

The Friend, edited by Barbara E. Rooke, 2 vols (Princeton, N.J. and London, 1969)

Lay Sermons, edited by R. J. White (Princeton, N.J. and London, 1972)

Logic, edited by J. R. de J. Jackson (Princeton, N.J. and London, 1981)

Anima Poetae: from the unpublished Note-Books of Samuel Taylor Coleridge, edited by E. H. Coleridge (London, 1895)

Biographia Literaria, edited by John Shawcross, 2 vols (Oxford, 1907)

Coleridge on Logic and Learning, edited by Alice D. Snyder (New Haven and London, 1929)

Coleridge's Miscellaneous Criticism, edited by T. M. Raysor (London and Cambridge, Mass., 1936)

Coleridge's Shakespearean Criticism, edited by T. M. Raysor, 2 vols (London, 1930)

The Collected Letters of Samuel Taylor Coleridge, edited by E. L. Griggs, 6 vols (Oxford, 1956–71)

The Complete Poetical Works of Samuel Taylor Coleridge, edited by E. H. Coleridge, 2 vols (London, 1912)

Inquiring Spirit: A New Presentation of Coleridge from his Published and Unpublished Writings, edited by Kathleen Coburn (London, 1951)

The Notebooks of Samuel Taylor Coleridge, edited by Kathleen Coburn (New York, Princeton, N.J. and London, 1957–)

'On the Divine Ideas', Huntington Library MS (Cambridge University Library, Microfilm 357)

The Philosophical Lectures, edited by Kathleen Coburn (London, 1949)

Poems on Various Subjects (Bristol, 1796)

Poems . . . to which are now added Poems by Charles Lamb, and Charles Lloyd (London, 1797)

Specimens of the Table Talk of the late Samuel Taylor Coleridge, 2 vols (London, 1835)

Collier, J., *Essays on Several Moral Subjects* (London, 1697)

Collins, William, *Odes on Several Descriptive and Allegoric Subjects* (London, 1747)

The Works, edited by Richard Wendorf and Charles Ryskamp (Oxford, 1979)

Condillac, Étienne Bonnot de, *Oeuvres complètes*, 16 vols (Paris, 1822)

An Essay on the Origin of Human Knowledge, translated by Thomas Nugent (London, 1756)

Cowden Clarke, Charles and Mary, *Recollections of Writers* (London, 1878)

Cowper, William, *The Poetical Works*, edited by H. S. Milford, fourth edition revised (London, 1971)

The Letters and Prose Writings, edited by James King and Charles Ryskamp, 3 vols (Oxford, 1979)

Cozens, Alexander, *A New Method of Assisting the Invention in Drawing Original Compositions of Landscape* (London, n.d. [1786])

Crotch, William, *Substance of several Courses of Lectures on Music, read in the University of Oxford and in the Metropolis* (London, 1831)

D'Alembert, J. le R., *Élémens de musique théorique et pratique, suivant les principes de M. Rameau* (Paris, 1752)

Mélanges de littérature, 5 vols (Amsterdam, 1759–73)

Darwin, Erasmus, *The Botanic Garden* (London, 1791)

The Temple of Nature; or, The Origin of Society (London, 1803)

De Gérando, Joseph-Marie, *Des Signes et de l'Art de penser dans leurs rapports mutuels*, 4 vols (Paris, 1800) (Ann. VIII)

De Quincey, Thomas, *Collected Writings*, edited by David Masson, 14 vols (London, 1897)

Descartes, René, *Musicae Compendium*, translated (London, 1653)

Diderot, Denis, ed., *Encyclopédie, ou dictionnaire raisonné des sciences, des arts et des métiers*, 17 vols (Paris, 1751–65)

Supplément à l'encyclopédie ou dictionnaire raisonné des sciences, des arts et des métiers, 4 vols (Amsterdam, 1776–7)

Rameau's Nephew and D'Alembert's Dream, translated by L. W. Tancock (Harmondsworth, 1966)

Dodsley, Robert, ed., *A Collection of Poems by several hands*, 3 vols (London, 1748)

Donaldson, J., *Elements of Beauty. Also Reflections on the Harmony of Sensibility and Reason* (Edinburgh, 1780)

Drake, Nathan, ed., *The Gleaner* (London, 1811)

Drummond, William, *Academical Questions* (London, 1805)

Dryden, John, *Alexander's Feast; or, the Power of Musique. An Ode in Honour of St. Cecilia's Day* (London, 1697)

Dubos, Jean Baptiste, *Réflexions Critiques sur la poésie et la peinture*, 2 vols (Paris, 1719)

Critical Reflections on Poetry, Painting and Music, translated by Thomas Nugent, enlarged edition, 3 vols (London, 1748)

Duff, William, *Essay on Original Genius* (London, 1767)

Eastcott, Richard, *Sketches of the Origin, Progress and Effects of Music* (London, 1793)

Elliott, J., *Philosophical Observations on the Senses of Vision and Hearing; to which are added, a treatise On Harmonic Sounds, and an essay On Combustion and Animal Heat* (London, 1780)

Ferguson, Adam, *An Essay on the History of Civil Society* (Edinburgh, 1767)

Gardiner, William, *The Music of Nature; or, An Attempt to Prove that what is Passionate and Pleasing in the Art of Singing, Speaking, and Performing upon Musical Instruments, is Derived from the Sounds of the Animated World. With Curious and Interesting Illustrations* (London and Leicester, 1832)

Gerard, Alexander, *An Essay on Taste*, third edition, revised (Edinburgh, 1780)

Goldsmith, Oliver, *The Collected Works*, edited by Arthur Friedman, 5 vols (Oxford, 1966)

Gray, Thomas, *Poems* (Dublin, 1768)

The Poems of Thomas Gray, edited by Rev. T. Mitford (London, 1814)

Correspondence, edited by Paget Toynbee and Leonard Whibley, 3 vols (Oxford, 1935)

Green, Thomas, *The Diary of a Lover of Literature* (London, 1803)

Gregory, John, *A Comparative View of the State and Faculties of Man with those of the Animal World*, fourth edition (London, 1767)

[Hanway, Jonas], *Thoughts on the Use and Advantage of Music, and other amusements . . . In nine letters, In answer to a letter relating to modern musical entertaintments* (London, 1765)

Harper, John, *The Nature and Efficacy of Musick to prepare the Mind for good Impressions: a Sermon* (London, 1730)

Harris, James, *Philological Inquiries* (London, 1781)

Three Treatises. The First Concerning Art. The Second Concerning Music, Painting and Poetry. The Third Concerning Happiness (London, 1744)

Hartley, David, *Observations Upon Man, his Frame, his Duty and his Expectations* (London, 1749)

Hawkins, Sir John, *A General History of the Science and Practice of Music*, 5 vols (London, 1776)

Haydn, Joseph, *The Collected Correspondence and London Notebooks*, edited by H. C. Robbins Landon (London, 1959)

Hayes, William, *Remarks on Mr Avison's Essay on Musical Expression* (London, 1753)

Hayley, William, *The Triumph of Music; A Poem: in six cantos* (Chichester, 1804)

Hazlitt, William, *The Complete Works*, edited by P. P. Howe, 20 vols (London and Toronto, 1930)

Hegel, G. W. F., *Aesthetics: Lectures on Fine Art*, translated by T. M. Knox, 2 vols (Oxford, 1975)

Herder, J. G., *Outlines of a Philosophy of the History of Man*, translated by Charles Churchill (London, 1800)

'Essay on the Origin of Language', in *On the Origin of Language: Jean Jacques Rousseau, Essay on the Origin of Languages; Johann Gottfried Herder, Essay on the Origin of Language*, translated by J. H. Moran and A. Gode (New York, 1966)

Home, Henry, Lord Kames, *Elements of Criticism*, third edition with additions and improvements (Edinburgh, 1765)

Horne, George, *The Antiquity, Use, and Excellence of Church Music* (Oxford, 1784)

Hume, David, *A Treatise of Human Nature* (London, 1739)

  Essays: Moral, Political and Literary (Oxford, 1963)

Hutcheson, Francis, *An Inquiry into the Original of Our Ideas of Beauty and Virtue, in Two Treatises: I. Concerning Beauty, Order, Harmony Design; II. Concerning Moral Good and Evil* (London, 1725)

Jackson, William, *Observations on the Present State of Music* (London, 1791)

Jacob, Hildebrand, *Works* (London, 1735)

  Of the Sister Arts (London, 1734)

Jenner, Charles, *Poems* (Cambridge, 1763)

  The Placid Man, second edition, 2 vols (London, 1773)

Johnson, Samuel, *Dictionary, with a Grammar and History of the English Language* (London, 1755)

  Works, 11 vols (Oxford, 1825)

Jones, Sir William, *Poems consisting chiefly of Translations from the Asiatick Languages. To which are added Two Essays, I. On the Poetry of the Eastern Nations. II. On the Arts, commonly called Imitative* (Oxford, 1772)

  Institutes of Hindu Law: or, the Ordinances of Menu (Calcutta and London, 1796)

Jones, Rev. William, *A Treatise on the Art of Music* (Colchester, 1784)

Kant, Immanuel, *The Critique of Judgement*, translated by James C. Meredith (Oxford, 1952)

Keats, John, *The Poems*, edited by M. Allott (London, 1970)

  The Letters of John Keats 1814–1821, edited by H. E. Rollins, 2 vols (Cambridge, Mass., 1958)

Lamb, Charles and Mary, *The Works in Prose and Verse*, edited by T. Hutchinson (London, n.d. [1908])

Lampe, John, *The Art of Musick* (London, 1740)

Locke, John, *An Essay Concerning Human Understanding*, edited by Peter H. Nidditch (Oxford, 1975)

Longinus, *A Treatise on the Sublime*, translated by Leonard Welsted (London, 1712)

Lowth, Robert, *Lectures on the Sacred Poetry of the Hebrews* (London, 1753)

Malcolm, A., *A Treatise of Musick, Speculative, Practical and Historical* (Edinburgh, 1721)

Marsh, John, 'A Comparison between the Ancient and Modern Styles of Music', *Music and Letters*, 36 (1955), 155–64

Mason, John, *An Essay on the Power of Numbers and the Principles of Harmony in Poetical Compositions* (London, 1749)

  An Essay on the Power and Harmony of Prosaic Numbers (London, 1749)

Maturin, Charles, *Melmoth the Wanderer: A Tale*, edited by Alethea Hayter (Harmondsworth, 1977)

Michaelis, Johann David, *A Dissertation on the Influence of Opinions on Language and of Language on Opinions, which gained the Prussion Royal Academy's Prize on that Subject . . . Together with an Enquiry into the Advantages and Practicability of an Universal Learned Language* (London, 1769)

Morell, T., *The Use and Importance of Music in the Sacrifice of Thanksgiving. A Sermon . . . Sep. 3, 1746* (London, 1747)

Morellet, André, *De l'expression en musique* (Paris, 1771)

Mount Edgcumbe, Richard, *Musical Reminiscences* (London, 1834)

Nares, James, *Treatise on Singing* (London, 1770)

Newton, John, *The Natural, moral, and divine influences of Musick. A sermon* (Gloucester, 1748)

Norris, John, *A Collection of Miscellanies*, sixth edition (London, 1717)

Parke, W. T., *Musical Memoirs, comprising an account of the general state of music in England from 1784–1830*, 2 vols (London, 1830)

Percy, Thomas, *Reliques of Ancient English Poetry*, 3 vols (London, 1765)

Plato, *The Collected Dialogues*, edited by E. Hamilton and H. Cairns (Princeton, N.J., 1961)

Pope, Alexander, *The Poems*, edited by John Butt (London, 1963)

Porterfield, M.D., William, *A Treatise on the Eye, the Manner and Phaenomena of Vision*, 2 vols (Edinburgh, 1759)

Price, Richard, *A Review of the Principal Questions and Difficulties in Morals* (London, 1758)

Price, Uvedale, *An Essay on the Picturesque, As Compared with the Sublime and Beautiful* (London, 1794)

Priestley, Joseph, *An Examination of Dr. Reid's Inquiry into the Human Mind on the Principles of Common Sense, Dr. Beattie's Essay on the Nature and Immutability of Truth, and Dr. Oswald's Appeal to Common Sense in Behalf of Religion* (London, 1774)

Quarterly Musical Magazine and Review, edited by R. M. Bacon (London, 1818–)

Radcliffe, Ann, *The Mysteries of Udolpho*, edited by Bonamy Dobrée (Oxford, 1966)

Rameau, J. P., *Traité de l'harmonie* (Paris, 1722)
    A Treatise of Musick (London, 1752)

Rawlins, John, *The Power of Musick, and the particular Influence of Church-Musick: A Sermon . . . 1773* (Oxford, n.d.)

Reid, Thomas, *Works*, edited by Sir William Hamilton (Edinburgh, 1846)

Reynolds, Sir Joshua, *Discourses on Art*, edited by Robert R. Wark (New Haven and London, 1975)

Robertson, Thomas, *An Inquiry into the Fine Arts* (London, 1784)

Robinson, H. C., *Henry Crabb Robinson on Books and their Writers*, edited by E. J. Morley, 3 vols (London, 1938)

Rousseau, Jean-Jacques, *Essai sur l'origine des langues* (Paris, 1764)
    'Essay on the Origin of Languages which treats of Melody and Musical Imitation', in *On the Origin of Language: Jean-Jacques Rousseau, Essay on the Origin of Languages; Johann Gottfried Herder, Essay on the Origin of Language*, translated by J.H. Moran and A. Gode (New York, 1966)
    Dictionnaire de musique (Geneva, 1767)
    A Dictionary of Music. Translated from the French of Mons. J.J. Rousseau. By William Waring (London, n.d. [1770])
    Oeuvres Complètes, 4 vols (Paris, 1856)

Schelling, F. W. J. von, 'Concerning the Relation of the Plastic Arts to Nature, 1807', translated by M. Bullock, in Herbert Read, *The True Voice of Feeling* (London, 1957)

Sämmtliche Werke, 5 vols (Stuttgart und Augsburg, 1859)

System of Transcendental Idealism (1800), translated by P. Heath (Charlottesville, 1978)

Schiller, J. C. F. von, *On the Aesthetic Education of Man*, edited and translated by E. M. Wilkinson and L. A. Willoughby (Oxford, 1967)

    Essays Aesthetical and Philosophical (London, 1846)

Schlegel, Friedrich von, *The Aesthetic and Miscellaneous Works*, translated by E. J. Millington (London, 1849)

Schopenhauer, Arthur, *The World as Will and Representation*, translated by E. F. J. Payne, 2 vols (New York, 1969)

Shaftesbury, Anthony Ashley Cooper, 3rd Earl, *Characteristicks of Men, Manners, Opinions and Times* (London, 1711)

Shenstone, William, *The Works in Verse and Prose*, 2 vols (London, 1765)

Smart, Christopher, *The Poetical Works of Christopher Smart*, edited by Karina Williamson (Oxford, 1980–)

    The Collected Poems of Christopher Smart, edited by Norman Callan, 2 vols (London, 1949)

Smith, Adam, *Essays on Philosophical Subjects* (London, 1795)

    Works, edited by Dugald Stewart, 5 vols (Edinburgh, 1811–12)

    A Dissertation on the Origin of Languages (Tubingen, 1970)

Smith, Robert, *Harmonics, or the Philosophy of Musical Sounds* (Cambridge, 1749)

Steele, Joshua, *An Essay Towards Establishing the Melody and Measure of Speech* (London, 1775)

['Stendhal'], *The Life of Haydn, The life of Mozart, with Observations on Metastasio, and on the Present State of Music in France and Italy. Translated from the French of L.A.C. Bombet. With Notes by the Author of the Sacred Melodies* (London, 1817)

    Lives of Haydn, Mozart and Metastasio (1814), translated by R. N. Coe (London, 1972)

Stewart, Dugald, *Collected Works*, edited by Sir William Hamilton, 10 vols plus 1 supplementary vol (Edinburgh, 1854)

Stiles, Francis, *An Explanation of the Modes or Tones in the Antient Greek Music* (London, 1761)

Stillingfleet, Benjamin, *Principles and Powers of Harmony* (London, 1771)

Temple, William, *Miscellanea* (London, 1696)

Thomson, James, *Poetical Works*, edited by J. L. Robertson (Oxford, 1908)

    Letters and Documents, edited by A. D. McKillop (Lawrence, Kansas, 1958)

Thornton, Bonnell, *An Ode on Saint Cecilia's Day, Adapted to the Ancient British Musick* (London, 1749)

Thorowgood, Henry, *A description of the aeolian-harp, or harp of Aeolus* (London, n.d. [c. 1754])

Tooke, John Horne, 'Επεα πτερόεντα, *or the Diversions of Purley*, 2 vols (London, 1786, 1798)

Traherne, Thomas, *Centuries, Poems and Thanksgivings*, edited by H. M. Margoliouth, 2 vols (Oxford, 1958)

Trydell, J., *Two Essays on the Theory and Practice of Music* (Dublin, 1766)

Tucker, Abraham, *The Light of Nature Pursued*, sixth edition, 2 vols (London, 1842)

Twining, Richard, ed., *Recreations and Studies of a Country Clergyman of the Eighteenth Century: Being selections from the correspondence of the Rev. Thomas Twining, M.A.* (London, 1882)

Selections from Papers of the Twining Family: a sequel to the Recreations and Studies (London, 1887)

Twining, Thomas, *Aristotle's Treatise on Poetry, Translated: with Notes on the Translation, and on the Original; and Two Dissertations, on Poetical, and Musical, Imitation* (London, 1789)

A Sermon, preached . . . at Colchester, May 17, 1790 (Colchester, 1790)

British Library, Additional MSS 39,929, 39,930, 39,936.

Usher, James, *Clio, or a Discourse on Taste. Addressed to a Young Lady* (London, 1767); *with large additions* (London, 1769)

An Introduction to the Theory of the Human Mind (London, 1771)

Vico, Giambattista, *The New Science*, translated by T. G. Bergin, and M. H. Fisch (Ithaca and London, 1970)

Wackenroder, W. H., *Confessions and Fantasies*, translated by M. H. Schubert (University Park and London, 1971)

Wakefield, A. M., ed., *Ruskin on Music* (London, 1894)

Wakefield, Gilbert, 'On the *Origin* of *Alphabetical Characters*', *Memoirs of the Literary and Philosophical Society of Manchester*, II (1785), 280–95

Walker, John, *The Melody of Speaking Delineated; or, Elocution taught like Music, by visible signs, Adapted to the Tones, Inflexions, and Variations of voice in Reading and Speaking; with Directions for Modulation, and expressing the Passions* (London, 1787)

Warburton, William, *The Divine Legation of Moses demonstrated, on the principles of a religious Deist*, 2 vols (London, 1738)

Essai sur les hiéroglyphes des Egyptiens, 2 vols (Paris 1744)

Warton, Joseph, *Essay on the Genius and Writing of Pope* (London, 1756)

Warton, Thomas, *The History of English Poetry*, 3 vols (London, 1774–81)

Webb, Daniel, *Observations on the Correspondence between Poetry and Music* (London, 1769)

Miscellanies (London, 1802)

Webb, F., *Panharmonicon: Designed as an illustration of an engraved plate, in which is attempted to be proved, that the principles of harmony more or less prevail throughout the whole system of nature; but more especially in the human frame: and that where these principles can be applied to works of art, they excite the pleasing and satisfying ideas of proportion and beauty* (London, n.d.)

Welsh, Rev. David, *Account of the Life and Writings of Thomas Brown, M.D., Late Professor of Moral Philosophy in the University of Edinburgh* (Edinburgh, 1825)

Winckelmann, Johann J., *Writings on Art*, selected and edited by David Irwin (London, 1972)

Wordsworth, Christopher, *Social Life at the English Universities in the Eighteenth Century* (Cambridge, 1874)

Wordsworth, Dorothy, *The Journals*, edited by Mary Moorman (Oxford, 1971)

Wordsworth, William, *The Prose Works*, edited by W. J. B. Owen and Jane Worthington Snyser, 3 vols (Oxford, 1974)

The Poetical Works of William Wordsworth, edited by Ernest de Selincourt, 5 vols (Oxford, 1940–1949)

The Prelude, or Growth of a Poet's Mind, edited by Ernest de Selincourt, second edition revised by H. Darbishire (Oxford, 1959)

The Prelude, 1798–1799, edited by Stephen Parrish (New York and Sussex, 1977)

The Letters of William and Dorothy Wordsworth: The Early Years, edited by Ernest de Selincourt, revised by C. L. Shaver (Oxford, 1967)

Young, Edward, *Conjectures on Original Composition* (London, 1759)

Young, Matthew, *An Enquiry into the principal Phaenomena of Sounds and Musical Strings* (London, 1784)

Secondary material

Aarsleff, Hans, *The Study of Language in England, 1780–1860* (Princeton, N.J., 1967)

From Locke to Saussure (London, 1982)

Abrams, M. H., *The Mirror and the Lamp: Romantic Theory and the Critical Tradition* (Oxford, 1953)

'Coleridge's "A Light in Sound": Science, Metascience, and Poetic Imagination', *Proceedings of the American Philosophical Society*, 116 (1972), 458–77

Ainsworth, E. G., *Poor Collins: His Life and Art and his Influence* (New York, 1937)

Allen, Warren D., *Philosophies of Music History: A Study of General Histories of Music, 1600–1960*, second edition, revised (New York, 1962)

Anderson, E., *Harmonious Madness: A Study of Musical Metaphors in the Poetry of Coleridge, Shelley and Keats* (Salzburg, 1975)

Anderson, H. and Shea, J. S., eds., *Studies in Criticism and Aesthetics 1660–1800: Essays in Honor of Samuel Holt Monk* (Minneapolis, 1967)

Appleyard, J. A., *Coleridge's Philosophy of Literature: the Development of a Concept of Poetry, 1791–1819* (Cambridge, Mass., 1965)

Armstrong, Robert L., 'Locke's "Doctrine of Signs"', *JHI*, 26 (1965), 369–82

Arthos, John, *The Language of Natural Description* (Ann Arbor, Michigan, 1949)

Austin, J. L., *How to do things with Words: The William James Lectures delivered at Harvard University in 1955*, edited by J. O. Urmson and M. Sbisà (Oxford, 1975)

Baldensperger, F., *Sensibilité Musicale et Romantisme* (Paris, 1925)

Barbour, J. Murray, *Tuning and Temperament: A Historical Survey* (New York, 1972)

Barrell, John, *The Dark Side of the Landscape: the Rural Poor in English Painting, 1730–1840* (Cambridge, 1980)

Barricelli, Jean-Pierre, 'Romantic Writers and Music: The Case of Mazzini', *Studies in Romanticism*, 14 (1925), 95–117

Beer, John, ed., *Coleridge's Variety: Bicentenary Studies* (London, 1974)

Bentley, Jr., G. E., *Blake Records* (Oxford, 1969)

Blake Books (Oxford, 1977)

Berlin, Isaiah, *Vico and Herder: Two Studies in the History of Ideas* (London, 1976)

Berry, Christopher J., 'Adam Smith's *Considerations* on Language', *JHI*, 35 (1974), 130–8

Bloom, Harold, ed., *Romanticism and Consciousness: Essays in Criticism* (New York, 1970)

Bosanquet, Bernard, *A History of Aesthetics* (London, 1904)

Bosker, A., *Literary Criticism in the Age of Johnson*, second edition (Djakarta, 1954)

Bronson, Bertrand H., 'Some Aspects of Music and Literature', in *Facets of the Enlightenment* (Los Angeles, 1968), 91–118

Brown, Calvin S., 'The Relation between Music and Literature as a Field of Study', *Comparative Literature*, 22 (1970), 97–107

Tones into Words: Musical Compositions as Subjects of Poetry (Athens, Georgia, 1953)

Brownell, Morris R., *Alexander Pope and the Arts of Georgian England* (Oxford, 1978)

Bryson, Norman, *Word and Image: French Painting of the Ancien Régime* (Cambridge, 1981)

Bukofzer, Manfred, *Music in the Baroque Era* (New York, 1947)

'Allegory in Baroque Music', *JWCI*, 3 (1939–40), 1–21

Burke, Joseph, *English Art: 1714–1800* (Oxford, 1974)

Bury, Francis, *Francis Towne: Lone Star of Water-Colour Painting* (London, 1962)

Butterfield, Herbert, *Man on His Past: The Study of the History of Historical Scholarship* (Cambridge, 1955)

Cobban, A., *Edmund Burke and the Revolt against the Eighteenth Century* (London, 1929)

Coffmann, Sue E., *Music of Finer Tone: Musical Imagery of the Major Romantic Poets* (Salzburg, 1979)

Cohen, Murray, *Sensible Words: Linguistic Practice in England 1640–1785* (Baltimore and London, 1977)

Coleman, Francis X.J., *The Aesthetic Thought of the French Enlightenment* (Pittsburgh and London, 1971)

Crane, Ronald S., ed., *Critics and Criticism; Ancient and Modern* (Chicago, 1952)

Cudworth, Charles, 'The English Symphonists of the Eighteenth Century', *PRMA*, 78 (1951–2), 31–51

'Gainsborough and Music', in *Gainsborough, English Music and the Fitzwilliam* (Cambridge, 1977), 11–16

'Thomas Gray and Music', *Musical Times*, 112 (1971), 646–8

Culler, Jonathan, *In Pursuit of Signs* (London, 1981)

Davidson, Donald, 'What Metaphors Mean', *Critical Inquiry*, 5 (1978), 32–47

Davie, Donald, *Purity of Diction in English Verse* (London, 1952)

Articulate Energy: An Inquiry into the Syntax of English Poetry (London, 1955)

The Language of Science and the Language of Literature, 1700–1740 (London, 1963)

Davies, Cicely, 'Ut Pictura Poesis', *Modern Language Review*, 30 (1935), 159–69

De Man, Paul, *Blindness and Insight: Essays in the Rhetoric of Contemporary Criticism* (Oxford, 1971)

'The Epistemology of Metaphor', *Critical Inquiry*, 5 (1978), 13–30

Demetz, P., et al., eds., *The Disciplines of Criticism* (New Haven, Conn., 1968)

Derrida, Jacques, *Of Grammatology*, translated by G. C. Spivak (Baltimore and London, 1976)

Dieckmann, Lieselotte, *Hieroglyphics: The History of a Literary Symbol* (St Louis, Missouri, 1970)

Draper, J. W., 'Poetry and Music in Eighteenth-Century English Aesthetics', *Englische Studien*, 67 (1932–3), 70–85

    Eighteenth Century English Aesthetics: A Bibliography (New York, 1931, 1968)

Elledge, Scott, ed., *Eighteenth Century Critical Essays*, 2 vols (New York, 1961)

Erdman, David V., and Grant, John E., eds., *Blake's Visionary Forms Dramatic* (Princeton, N.J., 1970)

Erhardt-Siebord, E. von, 'Some Inventions of the Pre-Romantic Period and their Influences upon Literature', *Englische Studien*, 66 (1931–2), 347–63

Fairchild, B. H., *Such Holy Song: Music as Idea, Form and Image in the Poetry of William Blake* (Kent, Ohio, 1980)

Ferguson, Frances, *Language as Counterspirit* (New Haven, Conn. and London, 1977)

Finney, G. L., *Musical Backgrounds for English Literature: 1580–1650* (New Brunswick, 1961)

Fiske, Roger, *English Theatre Music in the Eighteenth Century* (London, 1973)

Fletcher, Angus, *Allegory: The Theory of a Symbolic Mode* (New York, 1964)

Foucault, Michel, *The Order of Things* (London, 1970)

Fried, Michael, 'Towards a Supreme Fiction: Genre and Beholder in the Art Criticism of Diderot and his Contemporaries', *NLH*, 6 (Spring 1975), 543–85

    Absorption and Theatricality: Painting and Beholder in the Age of Diderot (Berkeley and London, 1980)

Frye, Northrop, 'Towards Defining an Age of Sensibility', in *Eighteenth Century English Literature*, edited by James L. Clifford (New York, 1959), 311–18

Fussell, Paul, *The Rhetorical World of Augustan Humanism* (Oxford, 1965)

Gay, Peter, *The Enlightenment: An Interpretation*: I, *The Rise of Modern Paganism*; II, *The Science of Freedom* (London, 1966–9)

Gelb, I. J., *A Study of Writing: The Foundations of Grammatology* (London, 1952)

Gilbert, K. E., and Kuhn, H., *A History of Aesthetics* (New York, 1972)

Gilchrist, Alexander, *Life of William Blake*, 2 vols (London, 1863)

Gleckner, Robert F., 'Most Holy Forms of Thought: Some Observations on Blake and Language', *ELH*, 4 (1974), 555–77

Gombrich, E. H., *Symbolic Images: Studies in the Art of the Renaissance* (London, 1975)

Greenlee, Douglas, *Peirce's Concept of the Sign* (The Hague and Paris, 1973)

Grew, Sydney and Eva Mary, 'William Cowper: His Acceptance and Rejection of Music', *Music and Letters*, 13 (1932), 31–41

Grigson, Geoffrey, *The Harp of Aeolus* (London, 1947)

Hagstrum, Jean H., *The Sister Arts: The Tradition of Literary Pictorialism and English Poetry from Dryden to Gray* (Chicago, 1958)

Hamilton, Paul, *Coleridge's Poetics* (Oxford, 1983)

Harding, Rosamund, *The Pianoforte*, second edition, revised (Surrey, 1978)

Hartman, Geoffrey, *Wordsworth's Poetry, 1787–1814* (New Haven, Conn., 1964)

    The Fate of Reading (Chicago and London, 1975)

Havens, Michael K., 'Coleridge on the Evolution of Language', *Studies in Romanticism*, 20 (1981), 163–83

Heartz, Daniel, 'From Garrick to Gluck: The Reform of Theatre and Opera in the mid-Eighteenth Century', *PRMA*, 94 (1967–8), 111–27

Hilles, F. W., ed., *The Age of Johnson: Essays Presented to Chauncey Brewster Tinker* (New Haven, Conn. and London, 1949)

Hilles, F. W., and Bloom, H., eds., *From Sensibility to Romanticism: Essays Presented to Frederick A. Pottle* (New York, 1965)

Hipple, Jr., W. J., *The Beautiful, the Sublime, and the Picturesque in Eighteenth Century Aesthetic Theory* (Carbondale, Illinois, 1957)

Hollander, John, *The Untuning of the Sky: Ideas of Music in English Poetry, 1500–1700* (Princeton, N.J., 1961)

Images of Voice: Music and Sound in Romantic Poetry (Cambridge, 1970)

'Wordsworth and the Music of Sound', in *New Perspectives on Coleridge and Wordsworth: Selected Papers from the English Institute*, edited by Geoffrey Hartman (New York and London, 1972), 41–84

Honour, Hugh, *Neo-classicism* (London, 1969)

Romanticism (London, 1979)

Hosler, Bellamy, *Changing Aesthetic Views of Instrumental Music in 18th-Century Germany* (Ann Arbor, Michigan, 1981)

Howard, Patricia, *Gluck and the Birth of Modern Opera* (London, 1963)

Husk, W. H., *An Account of the Musical Celebrations on St. Cecilia's Day* (London, 1857)

Hussey, Christopher, *The Picturesque: Studies in a Point of View* (London, 1927)

Isaacs, J., 'Coleridge's Critical Terminology', *Essays and Studies by Members of the English Association*, 21 (1936), 86–104

Iser, Wolfgang, *The Implied Reader: Patterns of Communication in Prose Fiction from Bunyan to Beckett* (Baltimore and London, 1974)

Isherwood, R. M., 'The Third War of the Musical Enlightenment', *Studies in Eighteenth Century Culture*, 4 (1975), 223–45

Jack, Ian, *Keats and the Mirror of Art* (Oxford, 1967)

Jakobson, Roman, *Questions de poétique* (Paris, 1973)

Jensen, H., *Sign, Symbol and Script* (London, 1970)

Johnson, David, *Music and Society in Lowland Scotland in the Eighteenth Century* (London, 1972)

Kastler, J. C., *The Science of Music in Britain, 1714–1830: A Catalogue of Writings, Lectures and Inventions* (New York, 1977)

Ketton-Cremer, R. W., *Thomas Gray: A Biography* (Cambridge, 1955)

Kretzmann, Norman, 'History of Semantics', in *Encyclopedia of Philosophy*, edited by Paul Edwards, 8 vols (New York, 1967), VII, pp. 385–406

Kristeller, P. O., 'The Modern System of the Arts', *JHI*, 13 (1952), 17–46

Kroeber, Karl, and Walling, William, eds., *Images of Romanticism* (New Haven, Conn. and London, 1978)

Kuehner, Paul, *Theories on the Origin and Formation of Language in the Eighteenth Century in France* (Philadelphia, 1944)

Land, S. K., *From Signs to Propositions: The Concept of Form in Eighteenth Century Semantic Theory* (London, 1974)

'The Silent Poet: An Aspect of Wordsworth's Semantic Theory', *UTQ*, 42 (1973), 157–69

'Universalism and Relativism: A Philosophical Problem of Translation in the Eighteenth Century', *JHI*, 35 (1974), 597–610

'Lord Monboddo and the Theory of Syntax in the Late Eighteenth Century', *JHI*, 37 (1976), 423–40

'Adam Smith's "Considerations Concerning The First Formation of Languages"', *JHI*, 38 (1977), 677–90

Landon, H. C. Robbins, *The Symphonies of Joseph Haydn*, (London 1955)
Haydn: Chronicle and Works, 5 vols (London, 1976–80)
and Chapman, R. E., *Studies in Eighteenth Century Music in tribute to Karl Geiringer* (London, 1970)

Le Coat, G. L., 'Comparative Aspects of the Theory of Expression in the Baroque Age', *Eighteenth Century Studies*, 5 (1971–2), 207–23

Le Huray, Peter and Day, James, eds., *Music and Aesthetics in the Eighteenth and Early-Nineteenth Centuries* (Cambridge, 1981)

Leech, G. N., *A Linguistic Guide to English Poetry* (London, 1969)

Leichentritt, Hugo, *Music, History and Ideas* (Cambridge, Mass., 1938)
'Aesthetic Ideas as the Basis of Musical Styles', *JAAC*, 4 (1945), 65–73

Lessem, Alan, 'Imitation and Expression: Opposing French and British Views on Music in the 18th Century', *Journal of the American Musicological Society*, 27 (1974), 325–30

Lipking, Lawrence, *The Ordering of the Arts in Eighteenth Century England* (Princeton, N.J., 1970)

Lockspeiser, Edward, *Music and Painting: A Study in Comparative Ideas from Turner to Schoenberg* (London, 1973)

Loesser, Arthur, *Men, Women and Pianos* (New York, 1954)

Lonsdale, Roger, 'Dr. Burney and the *Monthly Review*', *Review of English Studies*, 14 (1963), 346–58
Dr. Charles Burney: A Literary Biography (Oxford, 1965)
ed., *The Poems of Gray, Collins and Goldsmith* (London, 1969)

Lough, John, *The Contributors to the Encyclopédie* (London, 1973)

Lowinsky, E. E., 'Musical Genius – Evolution and Origins of a Concept', *Musical Quarterly*, 50 (1964), 321–40, 476–95

MacArdle, Donald W., 'Beethoven and George Thomson', *Music and Letters*, 37 (1956), 27–49

Mace, D. T., 'Musical Humanism, the Doctrine of the Rhythmus and the St. Cecilia Odes of Dryden', *JWCI*, 27 (1964), 251–92
'*Ut Pictura Poesis*: Dryden, Poussin and the Parallel of Poetry and Painting in the Seventeenth Century', in *Encounters*, edited by J. D. Hunt (London, 1971)

McFarland, Thomas, *Coleridge and the Pantheist Tradition* (Oxford, 1969)

Mackenzie, Gordon, *Critical Responsiveness: A Study of the Psychological Currents in Later Eighteenth-Century Criticism*, University of California Publications in English, 20 (Berkeley, 1949)

Mackerness, E., *A Social History of English Music* (London and Toronto, 1964)

McKillop, A. D., *The Background to Thomson's 'Liberty'* (Houston, 1951)
'Collins's *Ode to Evening* – Background and Structure', *Tennessee Studies in Literature*, 5 (1960), 73–83

Magee, Bryan, *The Philosophy of Schopenhauer* (Oxford, 1983)

Malek, James, *The Arts Compared: An Aspect of Eighteenth Century British Aesthetics* (Detroit, 1974)

Maniates, Maria Rika, '"Sonate, Que Me Veux-Tu?": The Enigma of French Musical Aesthetics in the 18th Century', *Current Musicology*, 9 (1969), 117–40

Manwaring, Elizabeth W., *Italian Landscape in Eighteenth Century England* (New York, 1925)

Marks, Paul F., 'The Rhetorical Element in Musical *Sturm und Drang*: Christian Gottfried Krause's *Von der musikalischen poesie*', *The Music Review*, 33 (1972), 93–107

'Aesthetics of Music in the Philosophy of *Sturm und Drang*: Gestenberg, Hamann and Herder', *The Music Review*, 35 (1974), 247–59

Marsh, Robert, *Four Dialectical Theories of Poetry: An Aspect of Neoclassical Criticism* (Chicago and London, 1965)

Matthews, Betty, 'The Davies Sisters, J. C. Bach and the Glass Harmonica', *Music and Letters*, 56 (1975), 150–69

Mellers, Wilfred, *Harmonious Meeting: A Study of the Relationship between English Music, Poetry and Theatre, 1600–1900* (London, 1965)

Mitchell, W. J., *Blake's Composite Art: A Study of the Illuminated Poetry* (Princeton, N.J., 1978)

Monk, Samuel Holt, *The Sublime: A Study of Critical Theories in 18th Century England* (New York, 1935; Ann Arbor, Michigan, 1960)

Moorman, Mary, *William Wordsworth: A Biography*, 2 vols (Oxford, 1957)

Moravia, Sergio, *Il pensiero degli idéologues: scienza e filosofia in Francia, 1780–1815* (Firenze, 1974)

Muirhead, J. H., *Coleridge as Philosopher* (New York and London, 1930)

Myers, Robert M., 'Neo-Classical Criticism of the Ode for Music', *PMLA* (1947), 399–421

Newman, Ernest, *Gluck and the Opera: A Study in Musical History* (London, 1895)

Nicolson, Marjorie Hope, *Mountain Gloom and Mountain Glory* (New York, 1959)

Newton Demands the Muse (Princeton, N.J., 1966)

Nurmi, Martin K., *William Blake* (London, 1972)

Oliver, A. R., *The Encyclopedists as Critics of Music* (New York, 1947)

Oliver, J. W., *The Life of William Beckford* (London, 1932)

Olson, Richard, *Scottish Philosophy and British Physics, 1750–1880: A Study in the Foundations of the Victorian Scientific Style* (Princeton, N.J., 1975)

Oppé, Adolf P., *Alexander and John Robert Cozens; with reprint of Alexander Cozens' 'A new method of assisting the invention in drawing original compositions of landscape'* (London, 1952)

Panofsky, Dora and Erwin, *Pandora's Box: The Changing Aspects of a Mythical Symbol* (London, 1956)

Park, Roy, 'Ut Pictura Poesis: The Nineteenth Century Aftermath', *JAAC*, 28 (1969), 155–64

Hazlitt and the Spirit of the Age (Oxford, 1970)

Paul, C. B., 'Music and Ideology: Rameau, Rousseau and 1789', *JHI*, 32 (1971), 395–410

Petty, F. C., *Italian Opera in London, 1760–1800* (Ann Arbor, Michigan, 1980)

Petzholdt, Richard, *Georg Philipp Telemann*, translated by H. Fitzpatrick (London, 1974)

Pevsner, Nikolaus, 'Richard Payne Knight', *Art Bulletin*, 31 (1949), 294–320

Price, Martin, *To the Palace of Wisdom* (Carbondale, Illinois, 1964)

Raynor, Henry, *A Social History of Music* (New York, 1972)
Music in England (London, 1980)

Rennert, J., *William Crotch, 1775–1874, Composer, Artist, Teacher* (Lavenham, 1975)

Richards, I. A., *The Philosophy of Rhetoric* (New York, 1936)
Coleridge on Imagination (London, 1934)

Ricoeur, Paul, *The Rule of Metaphor*, translated by R. Czerny (London, 1978)

Riffaterre, Michael, *Semiotics of Poetry* (London, 1980)

Rogerson, Brewster, 'The Art of Painting the Passions', *JHI*, 14 (1953), 68–94
'*Ut Musica Poesis*: The Parallel of Music and Poetry in Eighteenth Century Criticism' (unpublished dissertation, Princeton University, 1945)

Ronga, Luigi, *The Meeting of Poetry and Music*, translated by E. Gianturo and C. Rosanti (New York, n.d.)

Roper, Derek, *Reviewing Before the Edinburgh, 1788–1802* (London, 1978)

Rosen, Charles, *The Classical Style: Haydn, Mozart, Beethoven*, revised edition (London, 1976)

Rosenblum, Robert, *Transformations in Late Eighteenth Century Art* (Princeton, N.J., 1967)

Ross, Ian S., *Lord Kames and the Scotland of his Day* (Oxford, 1972)

Rudowski, V. A., 'Theory of Signs in the Eighteenth Century', *JHI*, 35 (1970), 683–90

Ryskamp, Charles, *William Cowper of the Inner Temple* (Cambridge, 1959)

Sadie, Stanley, 'Concert Life in Eighteenth Century England', *PRMA*, 85 (1958–9), 17–30
ed., *The New Grove Dictionary of Music and Musicians*, 20 vols (London, 1980)

Schenk, H. G., *The Mind of the European Romantics: An Essay in Cultural History* (London, 1966)

Schueller, H. M., '"Imitation" and "Expression" in British Music Criticism in the Eighteenth Century', *MQ*, 34 (1948), 544–66
'The Use and Decorum of Music as Described in English Literature, 1700–1780', *JHI*, 13 (1952), 73–93
'Correspondences between Music and the Sister Arts, According to Eighteenth Century Aesthetic Theory', *JAAC* 11 (1953), 334–59
'The Quarrel of the Ancients and Moderns', *Music and Letters*, 41 (1960), 313–30
'Immanuel Kant and the Aesthetics of Music', *JAAC*, 14 (1955–6), 218–47
'Schelling's Theory of the Metaphysics of Music', *JAAC*, 15 (1956–7), 461–76
'The Pleasures of Music: Speculation in British Music Criticism, 1750–1800', *JAAC*, 8 (1950), 155–71

Schwab, R. N., editor and translator, *Preliminary Discourse to the Encyclopedia of Diderot* (New York, 1963)

Sewell, Elisabeth, *The Orphic Voice* (London, 1961)

Sherbo, Arthur, *Christopher Smart: Scholar of the University* (Michigan, 1967)

Singleton, C. S., ed., *Interpretation: Theory and Practice* (Baltimore, 1969)

Spacks, Patricia M., *The Poetry of Vision* (Cambridge, Mass., 1967)

Spitzer, Leo, 'Classical and Christian Ideas of World Harmony', Part 1, *Traditio*, 2 (1944), 409–464; Part 2, *Traditio*, 3 (1945), 307–64

Stephen, Leslie, *History of English Thought in the Eighteenth Century*, 2 vols (London, 1876)

Stone, P. W. K., *The Art of Poetry 1750–1820: Theories of Poetic Composition and Style in the late Neo-Classic and early Romantic Periods* (London, 1967)

Strunk, Oliver, *Source Readings in Music History* (London, 1952)

Subotnik, Rose R., 'The Cultural Message of Musical Semiology: Some Thoughts on Music, Language and Criticism since the Enlightenment', *Critical Inquiry*, 4 (1978), 741–68

Trickett, Rachel, *The Honest Muse* (Oxford, 1969)

Tuveson, E. L., *The Imagination as a Means of Grace* (Berkeley, 1960)

Wasserman, Earl R., *The Subtler Language: Critical Readings of Neoclassic and Romantic Poems* (Baltimore, 1959)

'Pope's *Ode for Musick*', *ELH*, 38 (1961), 163–86

ed., *Aspects of the Eighteenth Century* (Baltimore and London, 1965)

Watson, Lucy E., *Coleridge at Highgate* (London, 1925)

Weber, W., 'A propos the Figure of Music in the Frontispiece of the Encyclopédie: Theories of Musical Imitation in d'Alembert, Rousseau and Diderot', *Proceedings of the Twelfth Congress of the International Musicological Society* (Berkeley, 1977)

Wellek, René, *Immanuel Kant in England, 1793–1838* (Princeton, N.J. and London, 1931)

The Rise of English Literary History (Chapel Hill, N.C., 1941)

A History of Modern Criticism: 1750–1950, Vol. I, *The Later Eighteenth Century* (New Haven, Conn., 1955)

'The Supposed Influence of Vico on England and Scotland in the Eighteenth Century', in *Giambattista Vico: An International Symposium*, edited by G. Tagliacozzo and H. White (Baltimore, 1969)

Wendorf, R., 'Collins's Elusive Nature', *MP*, 76 (1979), 231–9

William Collins and Eighteenth-Century Poetry (Minneapolis, 1981)

Wheeler, Kathleen M., *Sources, Processes and Methods in Coleridge's Biographia Literaria* (Cambridge, 1980)

The Creative Mind in Coleridge's Poetry (London, 1981)

Whitley, William T., *Artists and their Friends in England, 1700–1799*, 2 vols (London, 1928)

Art in England, 1800–1820 (Cambridge, 1930)

Wilson, M. I., 'Gainsborough, Bath and Music', *Apollo*, 105 (1977), 107–10

Wimsatt, W. K., ed., *Versification: Major Language Types* (New York, 1972)

Wind, Edgar, 'The Revolution of History Painting', *JWCI*, 2 (1938), 116–27

Wölflinn, Heinrich, *Renaissance and Baroque*, translated by K. Simon (London, 1964)

Wollaston, George H., *The Poet's Symphony: Being a collection of verses, written by some of those who in time past have loved music* (Bristol and London, 1913)

Zeydel, Edwin H., *Ludwig Tieck and England* (Princeton, N.J., 1931)

Zuckerkandl, Victor, *Sound and Symbol: Music and the External World*, translated by W. R. Trask (London, 1956)

INDEX